THE GOD
WHO COMMANDS

Richard J. Mouw

UNIVERSITY OF NOTRE DAME PRESS
NOTRE DAME, INDIANA

Library of Congress Cataloging-in-Publication Data

Mouw, Richard J.
    The God who commands / Richard J. Mouw.
      p. cm.
    Includes bibliographical references.
    ISBN 0-268-01019-6
    1. Christian ethics—Reformed authors. 2. Obe-
dience—Religious aspects—Christianity. 3. Reformed
Church—Doctrines. I. Title.
BJ1251.M67 1990
241'.0442—dc20   89-40385

Manufactured in the United States of America

9-24-90

CONTENTS

ACKNOWLEDGMENTS

I am indebted to several scholars who offered me very helpful critical comments on specific chapters: James Hanink and Gary Mar on chapter 2, James McClendon on chapter 7, and Marianne Meye Thompson on chapter 8. At a 1985 symposium sponsored by the Society of Christian Philosophers, Alasdair MacIntyre gave a thoughtful response to an earlier version of chapter 4; Professor MacIntyre graciously saved me from public embarrassment on that occasion by privately calling my attention to a place where I had seriously misinterpreted something he had said in *After Virtue*.

I owe much to Tracy Scott, my research assistant for two years at Fuller Seminary, for her work in preparing the endnotes, and for other critical tasks she performed in helping me prepare the manuscript for publication. I am also grateful to the staff in the Fuller Seminary Word Processing center for their labors on my behalf.

During my seventeen years as a faculty member at Calvin College I discussed the topics addressed in this book at great length with my Philosophy Department colleagues. I am deeply indebted to them for all that they taught me about these and other matters.

And to Phyllis, my profound thanks for many, many things.

Some of the material in this book draws, with permission, from the following published essays: Chapter 1 is a substantial reworking of "Commands for Grown-ups," *Worldview*, July 1972. Chapter 2 draws on materials from "Biblical Revelation and Medical Decisions," *Journal of Medicine and Philosophy*, vol. 4, no. 4, 1979. Chapter 3 is based on "Individualism and Christian Faith," *Theology Today*, January 1982; and "Reflections on Individualism," *Social Science in Christian Perspective*, ed. Paul Marshall and Robert Vander Vennen (University Press of America, 1988). Chapter 4 is an expansion of "Alasdair MacIntyre on Reformation

Ethics," *Journal of Religious Ethics,* vol. 13, no. 2, Fall 1985. Chapter 7 uses materials from "Ethics and Story: A Review Article," *Reformed Journal,* August 1987; "Just War Doctrine: Some Neglected Basics," *Evangelical Roundtable* (Eastern College, 1987), vol. 3; and "The Spiritual Thrust of the Just War Doctrine," *New Oxford Review,* March 1988. Parts of Chapter 8 first appeared in "Life in the Spirit in an Unjust World," in both *Pneuma: The Journal of the Society for Pentecostal Studies,* vol. 9, no. 2, Fall 1987, and *The Holy Spirit: Renewing and Empowering Presence,* ed. George Vander Velde (Woodlake Books, 1989).

INTRODUCTION

W E WERE PLANNING A CONFERENCE for students from several theological schools in southern California. The conversation had turned to the need for an "ice-breaking event"—some kind of opening exercise that would pull everyone into the spirit of our gathering. Someone suggested that we ask the participants to introduce themselves by identifying their favorite movie. "Why not their favorite novel?" someone else suggested. Then a rabbinical student spoke up: "I've got a better idea. Let's have people identify their favorite commandment!"

I thought this was a very witty suggestion, and I responded appropriately. But I noticed that the only people laughing were the other Jewish representatives and myself.

This should not have surprised me. To find commandment jokes funny one needs to have some degree of familiarity with what we might think of as an imperativist moral culture. And Jews and Calvinists are much more likely to have gained the requisite intimacy with such a culture than, say, Methodists or Lutherans.

Among Roman Catholics, the Jesuits, with their strong emphasis on obedience, have often nurtured their own version of an imperativist culture. This can be clearly seen in the kind of advice Jean-Pierre de Caussade gave to the Nuns of the Visitation, when he served as their spiritual director during the early decades of the eighteenth century. Christians ought to think of themselves "as objects sold and delivered, for God to do with what he likes," the French Jesuit told his cloistered charges. When people see themselves in this light, they become free "to spend their entire existence

1

rejoicing that God is God, surrendering themselves so completely that they are happy to obey his commands whatever they may be and without question."[1]

Unlike many Jews and Calvinists, Pere de Caussade did not insist, though, that the only way to manifest a pattern of surrender to the divine commander was by actually thinking about God's commands on a continual basis. Unrelieved attention to divine imperatives seemed to be, for de Caussade, a special vocation. There are also Christians, he observed, whose obedience to God is displayed in the kind of virtuous living that comes from "obedience to divinely inspired inclinations and intuitions." These people, de Caussade argued, do not "follow the path of surrender any less"; for "just as there are souls whose whole duty is indicated by an external law to which they are bound by God's will to conform, there are others who, in addition, must also obey that inner law engraved on their heart by the Holy Spirit."[2]

This book is about divine command morality, and de Caussade's point is helpful for understanding my project. On one level, an emphasis on divine commands can be thought of as just one of several competing ways of understanding the nature of Christian morality. In this sense, divine command ethics will make much of the need to pay heed, in a very explicit manner, to the dictates of what de Caussade refers to as the "external law." This kind of ethical system will feature constant references to commands and surrender and obedience.

But there is also a broader sense in which a divine command morality is coextensive with all systems of thought that view God as the supreme moral authority. In this more comprehensive sense, virtue ethics and agapism and an emphasis on a divinely implanted sense of justice can all be seen—along with the ethics of "external law"—as diverse proposed strategies for exhibiting a pattern of moral surrender to the divine will.

My main concern in this book is to set forth a case for divine command ethics in the more comprehensive sense. It would not be misleading to characterize my project here as an exercise in moral apologetics. I explore the patterns of God's moral authority, with specific attention to the objections raised by thinkers who are offended by the very idea of surrender to a divine will.

But a proper philosophical response to specific criticisms of Christian beliefs must include, as Marilyn McCord Adams has put it, the kind of "mapping of . . . alternative positions" that will inevitably lead Christian philosophers into the business of "mounting theological theories" regarding, among other topics, the nature of "moral value and the human good."[3] I also engage in this kind of "mapping" in this book, spelling out some implications of a Christian worldview for an understanding of moral well-being.

As I have already noted, Christian morality comes in various textures. We cannot get too far into the mapping out of a conception of moral value and the human good without paying attention to these specific textures. I have chosen to examine in some detail the moral perspective of classical Calvinism, which makes it possible for me to consider an actual theological embodiment of divine command morality.

Personal theological loyalties obviously had something to do with my decision to focus on Calvinism as an ethical style. But there are also good reasons why Calvinist morality provides a helpful context for thinking about a divine command ethic. The important conceptual issues that are at stake in thinking about the appropriateness of human surrender to God's dictates are exhibited in bold relief in the Calvinist scheme.

Some scholars have been arguing of late that the Reformation's understanding of moral selfhood—of which the Calvinist scheme is often treated as paradigmatic—exhibits some of the worst moral traits of modernity: the "individualism" of an emphasis on "naked" moral self; a moral style that features "volitionalism" and "decisionism"; and the inevitable "hierarchism" that comes with an emphasis on surrender and obedience.

One could respond to this line of argument, of course, by trying to show that these traits are not essential to a Calvinist perspective. But since I am convinced that this would be a misguided strategy, I argue a case for a Calvinism that includes something like these allegedly defective characteristics. If thinking highly of "naked" moral individuals who exercise volitions and who make decisions in a universe that is structured by a Creator-creature hierarchy—if this means being branded with the corresponding "isms" mentioned above, then I am willing to submit to the branding.

But not without considerable explanation—and even some significant qualifications. Calvinism, even at its best, does contain some regrettable harshness. I hope that it will be obvious that my narrower theological loyalties are capable of being overwhelmed at crucial points by broader ecumenical impulses.

I pursue the argument of this book through three main stages. In the first three chapters I lay some apologetic groundwork by responding to several secularist objections to divine command theory, as well as by exploring questions of moral justification, and arguing for the importance of the moral individual.

In the next three chapters I take a close look at some actual Calvinist treatments of divine authority and human obedience. After defending the Reformers against some of Alasdair MacIntyre's criticisms of what he views as the Reformation's proto-emotivism, I go on to explore the differences and similarities between the conceptions of moral selfhood portrayed in classical Calvinism and recent existentialism. I then continue my exploration of a Calvinist version of divine command ethics by looking at the early development of Calvinist understandings of God's political authority.

In my examination of Calvinist thought I show how Reformed thinkers have regularly followed a pattern of offering rather harsh theological formulations, which they then quickly "soften" by introducing important modifications: for example, a divine will that seems for all the world to be thoroughly arbitrary turns out to be bound by a commitment to lawful activity and covenantal fidelity.

But these typical modifications, as important as they are, do not completely satisfy my own desire for a "softer" divine command ethic. In the final three chapters, then, I show how a Calvinist perspective can benefit from an openness to some contemporary projects in the Christian community, such as narrativist ethics, the charismatic renewal, and feminist thought. I then conclude with some observations about possible points of contact between a divine command ethic and various secularist explorations of the shape of moral solidarity.

1

COMMANDS FOR GROWN-UPS

In what, then Lord, does true perfection stand?

It stands in a man offering all his heart wholly to God, not seeking himself or his own will, either in great things or in small, in time or in eternity, but abiding always unchanged and always yielding to God equal thanks for things pleasing and displeasing.

THUS THOMAS À KEMPIS.[1] But the sentiments he expresses in these sentences could just as easily come from other Christian writers in other times and places: from, say, Catherine of Siena or John of Damascus or John Knox or Catherine Booth. And those hosts of Christians who agree with Thomas that human beings are at their best when they are surrendering to the will of God in all things can also claim solid biblical support for their conviction. The whole of our human duty, says the writer of Ecclesiastes, can be summarized in these words: "Fear God and keep his commandments" (Ecclesiastes 12:13), an emphasis that is repeated in the Pauline call for human creatures to yield themselves completely to God as ones "who have been brought from death to life" (Romans 6:13).

As Christians have traditionally viewed things, a posture of obedience to God's revealed will is foundational to moral well-being, indeed to human well-being as such. For those who assume such a posture it is unthinkable that people might legitimately struggle with a moral issue for any length of time without asking, "What is it that the Lord requires?" Since there is a God who has provided guidance for the living of human life, obedience to divine directives is essential for human flourishing.

And yet, as Peter Geach has observed: "In modern ethical

treatises we find hardly any mention of God; and the idea that if there really is a God, his commandments might be morally relevant is wont to be dismissed by a short and simple argument."[2] The argument that Geach has in mind is a contemporary appropriation of Plato's well-known discussion in the *Euthyphro*. But it seems clear that such a line of argument, if it is used at all, merely serves as an optional tool to be appealed to when convenient by those who are actually committed to the outlook that John Courtney Murray called "postulatory atheism";[3] often the moral irrelevance of divine directives is simply accepted as a postulate of modernity.

Many thinkers today take it for granted that anyone who looks to divine commandments for moral direction fails to understand, in a very basic way, the proper requirements of moral decision making. Indeed, the belief that there is something fundamentally wrong with people who submit to moral directives "imposed" upon them from "above" seems capable of uniting proponents of rather diverse philosophical perspectives: Marxists, Freudians, existentialists, scientific humanists, New Age religionists, and "go-with-the-flow" romanticists.

There are even self-styled Christian thinkers who are willing to join this consensus. For example, Graeme de Graff once offered this candid observation, in the course of developing what he took to be a defense of Christian morality: "There is no room in morality for commands, whether they are the father's, the schoolmaster's, or the priest's. There is still no room for them when they are God's commands."[4]

Anyone who is familiar with recent theological trends will be able to think of various reasons why a contemporary Christian thinker might dismiss the notion that God issues commands that we must obey. Some Christians manage to avoid references to divine commands by denying the view of revelation that was presupposed in the more traditional Christian perspective. Others seem to hold that, whatever revelations might have occurred in the past, the directives recorded in the Bible are not binding for us today.

There are complex issues at stake in such discussions. These sorts of deviations from the tradition concern us here only insofar as they serve as evidence that some Christians share the modern conviction that there is something wrong with basing a morality, to say nothing of a whole way of life, on submission to God's directives. It is this conviction that I am concerned to understand and evaluate in this discussion.

My own commitment, in dealing with issues of religious authority, is to the kind of *sola scriptura* emphasis that was a prominent feature of the Protestant Reformation, and is still dear to the hearts of many conservative Protestants. But I want in no way to imply that a belief in the moral relevance of divine commands is the exclusive property of people who spell out the issues of authority in a strong bibliocentric manner. For example, some Christians—especially some Anglicans and Roman Catholics—understand "natural law" in such a way that when someone makes moral decisions with reference to natural law that person is obeying divine commands. Others hold that submission to the *magisterium* of a specific ecclesiastical body counts as obedience to divine directives. Others assume that individual Christians, even those who are not members of ecclesiastical hierarchies, can receive specific and extrabiblical commands from God, such as "Quit smoking!" or "Get out of New Haven!" Still others hold that the will of God can be discerned by examining our natural inclinations or by heeding the dictates of conscience.

None of these is, strictly speaking, incompatible with a *sola scriptura* emphasis. One could hold, for example, that the Bible itself commands us to conform to natural law, or to submit to the church's teachings, or to consult our consciences. Or one could simply view these alternative sources as necessary supplements to, or glosses on, biblical revelation. The view which I am attempting to elucidate here, while formulated in terms that signal my own *sola scriptura* orientation, is not meant to rule out the propriety of appeals to these other sources. Rather, I am assuming a perspective from which the Bible is viewed as a clarifier of these other modes, as the authoritative source against which deliverances from these other sources must be tested.

I should also make it clear that I will be assuming in this discussion that the Bible offers detailed moral guidance to us. On the view that I mean to be elucidating, the good life must be pursued with serious and sustained attention to the rich message of the Scriptures. This is no trivial matter to mention. There have been Christian ethicists in recent years who contend that there is only one divine commandment that is morally relevant, namely, the command to love God and neighbor. That seemed to be Joseph Fletcher's contention when he described himself, in *Situation Ethics*, as "rejecting all 'revealed' norms but the one command—to love God in the neighbor."[5]

If the command to love is the only biblical command which has normative relevance to moral decision making, then much of the substance of Christian ethics can be established without reference to the Scriptures. But if the Bible does offer other commands and considerations which bear on our decision making, then the task will be one of finding correlations between biblical revelation and moral issues at many different points.

It is interesting, though, that when Fletcher explained his grounds for his mono-imperativism, his arguments were not so much directed against the moral relevance of other divine commands as they were against their "absoluteness." To hold, however, that there is a plurality of divine commands which are morally relevant and binding is not to commit oneself to the view that each of these commands is indefeasible. It may well be that there is only one indefeasible command, the so-called "law of love"—such that in any situation in which the course of action prescribed by the law of love is one's duty, it is one's actual duty, and that only the law of love has this property. But this does not rule out the possibility that there are other divine commandments which prescribe courses of action which are at least one's *prima facie* duties to perform in those situations in which the commands in question are morally relevant.

Not that *all* the commandments which are found in the Bible are morally relevant for us today. As Lewis Smedes puts it, they do not all "tell us what God wants us to do."[6] For example, God commanded Abraham to leave Ur of the Chaldees, and Jonah was told by the Lord to preach in Nineveh; it would be silly to suppose that it is a part of our contemporary Christian duty to obey these commands, or even to think of them as included in our functioning moral repertoire.

I do not mean to promote, then, a fascination with all of those biblical sentences that are in the imperative mood. In fact, my references to "commands" here should be taken as a kind of shorthand that I am using to refer to a somewhat broader pattern of divine address. The Bible is much more than a compendium of imperatives; the sacred writings contain historical narratives, prayers, sagas, songs, parables, letters, complaints, pleadings, visions, and so on. The moral relevance of the divine commandments found in the Scriptures can only be understood by viewing them in their interrelatedness with these other types of writings. The history, songs, predictions, and so on, of the Bible serve to sketch out the character of the biblical God; from this diversity of materials we learn what God's creating and redeeming purposes are, what sorts of persons and actions the Lord approves of, and so on. Divine commands must be evaluated and interpreted in this larger context.

Furthermore, we would actually miss some of the divine imperatives which the Bible transmits to us if we only attended to grammatical imperatives. For example, nowhere in the New Testament is there a literal command to the original followers of Jesus to stop discriminating against the Samaritans. But the New Testament record has Jesus telling stories and engaging in activities which make it very clear that he is directing his disciples to change their attitudes toward Samaritans. Thus it is accurate to say that Jesus "commanded" his disciples to love the Samaritans, even though the words (or their Greek or Aramaic equivalents) "Stop discriminating against Samaritans" never appear in the Bible.

When the writer of Ecclesiastes concludes, then, that our whole duty consists in obeying God's commandments, we must not understand him to be instructing us to attend only to divine utterances which have a specific grammatical form. He is telling us, rather, that we must conform to whatever God requires of us, to all that the Creator instructs us to do—whether that guidance is transmitted through parables, accounts of divine dealings with nations and individuals, or sentences which embody commands.

"Infantile" Obedience?

Why is the posture of obedience to divine directives such an affront to so many contemporary thinkers? Why is it that people want to insist that there can be "no room" (remembering de Graff's words) in morality for commands, even when they are commands that come from God?

Patrick Nowell-Smith put the objection very bluntly in an article he wrote for the *Rationalist Annual* in the early 1960s. The Christian posture, he said, is "infantile"; it possesses the "characteristics of deontology, heteronomy, and realism which are proper and indeed necessary in the development of a child, but not proper to an adult."[7] Unfortunately, Nowell-Smith does not offer much by way of an argument to support this negative assessment of the Christian position. But he does refer us to Piaget's work in the area of moral development—indeed, Nowell-Smith's use of the terms "deontology," "heteronomy," and "realism," is an obvious borrowing from Piaget.

Since Nowell-Smith does not elaborate at length on how he sees the relationship between his own claim that Christian morality is "infantile" and Piaget's studies of moral development, it is necessary to try to reconstruct the argument which he might have in mind. Piaget distinguishes, in his book *The Moral Judgment of the Child*, several stages in the moral development of children. For our present purposes we can refer to two major stages. At an early point in the life of the child, moral decision making follows what Piaget calls a "heteronomous" pattern—which is what Nowell-Smith apparently has in mind when he uses the same term. According to Piaget, this stage is dominated by a "primitive consciousness of duty" during which "duty is nothing more than the acceptance of commands received from without."[8] In the process of maturing, however, this stage is replaced by one of "autonomy," in which the rigid sense of duty gives way to a "morality of goodness." Rather than uncritically accepting externally imposed commands, the autonomous person asks *why* the commands ought to be obeyed; the maturing child begins to reflect on the *point* of the moral rules and practices to which submission is demanded. In short, at the autonomous stage the child begins "to appeal to his reason in order to bring unity into the moral material."[9]

It is not difficult to get some idea of what Nowell-Smith has in mind when he refers to these distinctions formulated by Piaget. Nowell-Smith is suggesting that the Christian believer, in submitting to commands which come from "without" or "above," is very much like the child who unquestioningly obeys the command of a parent. But this "heteronomous" posture is one which ought to be outgrown in a properly maturing human being. Thus, it seems, Christians are victims of an arrested moral development. They are "frozen" at the heteronomous stage of moral growth.

But we must push the argument a little further. If we are going to rely on Piaget's analysis to cast aspersions on Christian posture, then we must ask: What would things have been like if the religious believer had developed properly? Here Piaget's description of a normal transition from the heteronomous stage to the autonomous one is helpful:

> It seems to us an undeniable fact that in the course of the child's mental development, unilateral respect or the respect felt by the small for the great plays an essential part: it is what makes the child accept all the commands transmitted to him by his parents and is thus the great factor of continuity between different generations. But it seems to us no less undeniable . . . that as the child grows in years the nature of his respect changes. In so far as individuals decide questions on an equal footing—no matter whether subjectively or objectively—the pressure they exercise upon each other becomes collateral.[10]

For Piaget, then, the normal transition from heteronomy to autonomy takes place when the child experiences a change of attitude toward the commanding parent: the more the child comes to see the parent as an individual similar to herself—in Piaget's words, when "the respect felt by the small for the great" diminishes, or when the parent is seen as one who decides matters on an "equal footing" to that of the child—the less the child will be inclined toward an unquestioning submission to the commands of the parent. And, to take the case a step further, a person who has never come to view adults as near-equals or equals, someone who always views the commanding adult as separated from herself by the gulf which separates the small from the great—such a person might be thought of as being arrested, or frozen, at the heteronomous stage. She views a specific commander as very different from herself, when in fact she ought to view the commander as possessing relevant similarities, characteristics which permit the commandee to think through her own moral decisions.

Once we state Piaget's case in this way, however—and I have

attempted to stay as close as I can to what I think are Piaget's own intentions—it is difficult to see how it bears directly on Nowell-Smith's charge that obedience to divine commands is an "infantile" posture. At the very least we need some transferral of what Piaget says about the child-parent relationship to the kind of relationship which Christians see as holding between themselves and God.

Suppose we try to make that transferral. We might state the case as follows: a human being is arrested at the heteronomous stage, with respect to the relationship between humans and God, when she fails to come to view God as an equal, or near equal, with respect to moral decision making. In order for Nowell-Smith's account to work, then, he must argue that there should come a time when the Christian begins to see God as someone who operates on an "equal footing" with human beings; the "respect felt by the small for the great" must disappear from the relationship between God and adult humans.

But once we put the matter in this way, it hardly seems worthy of serious consideration. Someone might want to argue, of course, that there simply *is* no deity; this might be one way of supporting the claim that we ought not to think of God as greater than ourselves in the area of moral decision making. Short of that kind of argument, however, it would seem quite unreasonable to expect Christian believers to treat God as an equal when, according to the best accounts of what the deity is like, God is obviously *superior* to any human being.

For any pattern of moral decision making to be considered mature, it should presumably be characterized by a willingness to act in the light of the facts as one views them. And the fact is that Christianity views God as being much greater—infinitely greater—than human beings. On such a view of things, a refusal to recognize God's moral greatness would not only be self-deceptive, it would also be, in its own way, a kind of "infantile" discourtesy.

Let me be very clear about exactly what I am arguing in my response to Nowell-Smith. He appeals to Piaget in order to portray Christian morality as "infantile." I have replied by showing that this is an inaccurate use of Piaget's developmental scheme. Now it may also be the case that there are defects in Piaget's own account of moral development. Certainly Kohlberg and others have taken the study of such things well beyond Piaget in some important respects.[11] Nonetheless, however the assessment of the details of such developmental schemes might go, it seems to me very unlikely that those schemes could cast legitimate doubt on the propriety of adopting an attitude of awe before the divine Sovereign.

"Prehuman" Submission?

We must not assume, though, that we can put this line of criticism completely to rest merely by showing that the appeal to developmental theory is less than convincing. There are thinkers who insist that the posture of obedience is associated with an inadequate moral consciousness, without resting their claims on empirical studies in psychology.

Consider, for example, the way in which Erich Fromm presents the biblical story of Adam's fall into sin:

> Acting against God's orders means freeing himself from coercion, emerging from the unconscious existence of prehuman life to the level of man. Acting against the command of authority, committing a sin, is in its positive human aspect the first act of freedom, that is, the first *human* act. In the myth the sin in its formal aspect is the eating of the tree of knowledge. The act of disobedience as an act of freedom is the beginning of reason.[12]

There is no reference here to the ways in which individual human beings pass through the stages of moral development. Fromm simply characterizes the posture of obedience to the divine will as a state of affairs that is intrinsically bad.

Fromm offers this analysis in a context where he is explaining two options which are open to human beings in their attempts to relate to physical and social reality.[13] The first is the pattern of "submission": this is the "prehuman" pattern wherein individuals submit to some external authority, thereby sacrificing their own individuality. The second pattern is one where the individual engages in a "spontaneous relationship to man and nature" in such a way that individuality is kept intact.

Obedience to divine commands, is, for Fromm, an instance of the first pattern. But it is interesting to note how he describes the second, and for him preferable, pattern: it promotes "the integration and strength of the total personality" and is "subject to the very limits that exist for the growth of the self."[14]

Why couldn't a Christian, when faced with the choice between sacrificing her individuality and seeking the "integration and strength of the total personality," actually choose the second pattern as Fromm describes it? To insist that she could not make that choice is to assume that it is necessary for Christians to embrace the "despotic" model of the God-human relationship which Fromm wants to link to obedience to the divine will.

We must, however, challenge this assumption. There is no reason why Christians cannot agree with Fromm when he advocates that we human beings involve ourselves in the kind of "growth process" that encourages integrated personhood. Having sided with him in this, though, we will also want to underscore Fromm's own insistence that this growth process is "subject to [certain] limits." The rub comes, of course, when we ask: What limits are *proper* to the pattern of human growth? From what *source* do we come to know what these limits are? In what sorts of *activities* does the "total personality" gain its "strength"?

Fromm's case here is very similar to that of Karl Marx, who tells us that "in religion the spontaneous activity of the human imagination, of the human brain and the human heart, operates independently of the individual—that is, operates on him as an alien, divine or diabolical activity"—resulting in "the loss of his self."[15] For Marx any authority relationship seems to be one in which one person "possesses" another, with the result that the commandee becomes the "property" of the commander.

The Christian can respond to this kind of charge by insisting that obedience to divine commands is best understood as another way of engaging in the "spontaneous" patterns of relationship which Fromm cherishes; it is another way of avoiding the "loss of self" which Marx fears. But it should also be admitted that this line of response will not work if we assume some of the views which Christians themselves have offered as explanations of the relationship between God and human beings. For example, consider the explanation offered by Peter Geach:

> I shall be told by [some] philosophers that since I am saying not: It
> is your supreme moral duty to obey God, but simply: It is insane to
> set about defying an Almighty God, my attitude is plain power-

worship. So it is: but it is worship of the Supreme power, and as such is wholly different from, and does not carry with it, a cringing attitude towards earthly powers. An earthly potentate does not compete with God, even unsuccessfully: he may threaten all manner of afflictions, but only from God's hands can any affliction actually come upon us.[16]

Geach's contention here is that we ought to submit to the will of God because God has the power to destroy us if we do not—and that, furthermore, the divine Sovereign will exercise that power. This is a very Hobbesian account of the relationship between God and human creatures. We submit to God's power out of a fear of being destroyed by that power. The appeal here is not so much to a sense of the fittingness of that submission as it is to an awareness of what is in our self-interest.

As stated, this view seems to be similar to what Fromm calls the "prehuman" pattern of "submission." And if that were the only alternative, we might well reject it. It may be in some sense "insane" to defy supreme power, but it does not seem to be *ipso facto* immoral. We are not inclined, for example, to despise someone who resists the will of a perverse human despot, even though he knows with near certainty that he will be killed for his resistance. Such stubbornness may be "insanity," but it is of a rather admirable sort. Taken as a response to Fromm and Marx, then, Geach's defense of the Christian posture does not seem to be adequate.

Indeed, to focus briefly on the Genesis account to which Fromm explicitly refers, it would seem that the despotic model of the relationship between God and humans—which both Fromm and Geach seem to accept—is not the one which the Genesis writer means to present in a favorable light. Rather, despotism is the revisionist view which the serpent—with obvious success—propagates to Eve. Throughout the Scriptures the commandments of God are viewed as the guidelines offered by a loving Creator who desires the well-being of created reality. The serpent in Genesis, however, challenges this assumption. Has God said that disobeying his commands will lead to death? he asks Eve. Well, then, God is deceiving you— "you shall not surely die." Eat from the tree and "you shall be as gods" (Gen. 3:4–5).

This revisionist theology involves what I have called elsewhere "two serpentine falsehoods."[17] First, the decision to eat the fruit was based on a shift from viewing God as a loving Creator to that of a deceptive despot. Second, the subsequent attempt on the part of the first human beings to become their own gods was based on the assumption that they must conform to the despotic model of deity: each human being attempted to become the kind of despotic ruler which the serpent characterized God as being.

If this analysis of the serpent's revisionist theology in the Genesis account is accepted, then we can understand the importance of being very clear about what view of God is being employed when objections are lodged against the Christian posture of obedience to God's commands. If God is a despot, then to say that I belong to God is, as Marx argues, to reduce myself to mere "property." But if God is instead a loving Creator who wants us to experience the divine shalom, then to belong to God is to realize new dimensions of selfhood. And this is what is at stake when the Apostle speaks of "bondage" and "liberty" in a manner that, from the perspective of Fromm's kind of secularism, has things reversed. For on the biblical view a life dedicated to the proving of one's allegedly sovereign mastery over others is a life of fearful bondage, while the ability to obey when that is the proper response, to engage in selfless service when this is required of us, to recognize authority and expertise when that is evident—that is, from a biblical perspective, liberation.

One final observation about Fromm's account. He uses the terms "freedom" and "reason"—matters which he greatly values—as if they refer to features which are the exclusive properties of a humanistic perspective. The Christian ought not to concede this. The loving Creator of the Scriptures desires that human beings freely submit to revealed directives, without coercing them into a grudging obedience. Furthermore, if the Christian's basis for submitting to divine authority is related to the assessment of the credentials of the one who issues authoritative commands, then this too involves a kind of rational evaluation.

BEYOND HETERONOMY

In assessing Nowell-Smith's objection to the Christian moral posture, I allowed his characterization of Christianity as "heteronomous" to stand unchallenged. For apologetic purposes this seems to me to be quite acceptable. If the posture of obedience to divine commands is indeed a heteronomous one, then heteronomy deserves a better reputation than it is often accorded. It might even be necessary to speak of certain heteronomies as mature ones—especially those which view the God-human relationship as a covenantal partnership that is characterized by trust, mutual respect, responsible obedience, and a free acceptance of obligation.

But it is probably wiser to follow the lead of those thinkers who have insisted that neither the heteronomous nor the autonomous is adequate for characterizing a healthy relationship to God. Paul Tillich, as is well known, preferred to think of the Christian pattern as one of "theonomy."[18] The same choice was advocated by the Dutch theologian Herman Bavinck, in the lectures he gave on his tour of North America during the 1908–1909 academic year. The Christian's delight in the Law of the Lord, Bavinck argued, is "the ultimate fulfillment" of the deepest intentions and hopes of "autonomous morality." The autonomous pursuit of

> the true, and the good, and the beautiful . . . can only come to perfection when the absolute good is at the same time the almighty, divine will, which not only prescribes the good in the moral law, but also works it effectually in man himself. The heteronomy of law and the autonomy of man are reconciled only by this theonomy.[19]

Viewed from "inside" the Christian life, it can seem quite inappropriate to describe a Christian's relationship to God simply as one where a human being receives commands from an "external other." In both the Old and New Testaments there is a clear sense of direction toward an "internalization" of the moral life of the believer. The Law at Sinai may have been handed down on tables of stone from the heavens above; but it was not long before those who had received that Law were talking about a word of guidance that was to be written in their own hearts—a sense of inner-directedness that culminates in the New Testament teaching concerning the indwelling of the Holy Spirit. From such a perspective, it may be difficult to identify one's own pattern of obedience as that of submitting to commands which are "handed down" from "above."

Similarly, a purely heteronomous account of Christian morality does not capture the intimacy of relationship between Commander and commandee in the Christian life. The God who commands is the same one who has, in the person of Jesus, entered into a human frame of reference. The Creator became Redeemer, stooping to become like one of us. When God commands, he does so with an intimate knowledge of our condition, having suffered in the same ways that we suffer.

We in turn receive divine guidance as persons who are in the process of internalizing the spirit of Jesus, as temples of the divine Comforter. The intimacy here between God and ourselves is, to be sure, not one of metaphysical merger; rather, it is an interpersonal intimacy—not a unity of undifferentiated being but an increasing merger of purposes in the context of covenantal mutuality. For this kind of relationship "heteronomy" is too formal and lifeless to serve as a proper label in accounting for the facts of the case.

It is very necessary to emphasize all of this lest the arguments offered here be used to endorse heteronomy-as-such. If the defense of obedience to divine commands is formulated in too simple terms, the arguments for obeying God might be extended into arguments for obeying moral "experts" in general.

This suggests that attention must be directed toward the unique status of divine authority. I believe that God possesses the absolute authority to tell us what to do. At the same time I have no desire to expand my case into a more general defense of moral hierarchism. I am convinced that it is on occasion reasonable to submit to commands whose rationale we do not fully grasp, and the relationship between human beings and the God of the Bible satisfies, I am also convinced, the required conditions for such obedience. But I would not want to encourage analogous claims on behalf of obedience to political dictators and religious gurus.

Each case or relationship must be considered on its own merits. Whether a given individual possesses the authority to command our obedience is a matter which must be decided by examining the credentials of the would-be commander. In this regard it is important to note that the God of Scriptures regularly offers credentials for our examination. The God who issues the "Thou shalts" of Exodus 20 is the one who prefaces those directives with the reminder that we have been delivered from the house of bondage. And the one who, in the New Testament, tells us to keep his commandments, does so on the basis of the fact that when we were yet sinners he died for us. The God who commands in the Scriptures is the one who offers the broken chariots of the Egyptians and the nail-scarred hands of the divine Son as a vindication of the right to tell us what to do. This should make us sensitive to the need to examine the credentials of others who claim the authority to be moral commanders.

It is not merely for apologetic purposes, therefore, that we insist that it is possible for Christians to pursue obedience to divine commands in a reasonable fashion. The appeal to reasonableness is also important for the maintenance of a healthy and sensible Christianity. Indeed, such an emphasis, in the final analysis, may have more of a chance of bearing fruit within the Christian community than outside of it. It is not likely that the kind of case I have laid out thus far will convince most unbelievers that obedience to divine commands is a "healthy" way to order one's life. The most we can hope for is that people will see that some of the arguments used against the Christian posture are less than compelling.

A morality based on obedience to divine commands cannot be attacked without also challenging a complex of beliefs with which it is intimately associated. To criticize such a morality on psychological grounds is to enter into a discussion of issues which go far beyond the facts of psychological development. Appeals to "maturity" or "freedom" or "rationality" open up legitimate questions about the larger theoretical frameworks in which those terms can be understood. Ultimately, one is led to issues relating to the human condition, the existence and nature of the deity, and the proper locus of moral authority.

And those questions are very much worth discussing. Even if a Christian thinker should decide that we need not spend much time defending the basic assumptions of our way of viewing things against the present-day cultured despisers of the faith, we would still have much to talk about among ourselves on these basic issues.

I can imagine, for example, Christians who would have strong sympathies with what I have said so far, but who might nonetheless be a bit nervous about pushing too hard on some of these themes. They would have no difficulty admitting that Christianity is characterized by a willingness to conform to God's will for human living, but they would be somewhat uncomfortable with an ethic that places a strong and explicit emphasis on the notion of obeying divine directives.

For one thing, they might worry about the understanding of human agency that such an emphasis could promote. Doesn't a pattern of thinking that refers without embarrassment to a commandee-Commander relationship run the risk of individualism? Isn't there a strong hint here of a naked self standing alone before God? And isn't this a bad thing to promulgate?

What about the picture of God that is strongly suggested by the language I have been using in this chapter? Doesn't it smack, and more than a little, of hierarchism? Isn't the image of a moral Commander—in spite of my efforts in this discussion to "soften" the picture—something that we would do well to abandon? In times when Christians are being asked to recognize the inhumanity that has attended "patriarchy" and the creation of "dependency" relations, would it not be better to formulate the Christian case in very different terms than those which I have been employing?

And what about the "tone" of the moral life as I have been depicting it? Isn't there something quietistic—even compulsively introspective—about a way of life that stresses obedience to God's will? Can't this understanding of the patterns of Christian morality promote—as in some strands of Puritanism—a brooding, sullen spirit of withdrawal?

These are important questions. I sense a special obligation to deal with them, since I have much sympathy for viewpoints and emphases that are sometimes labeled "individualistic," "hierarchical," and "quietistic." In what follows, I will attend to these matters, looking at some key issues relating to individual responsibility, divine authority, and reflective Christian living, as they bear on an ethic of obedience to divine commands.

2

ETHICS AND WORLDVIEW

THE EXPLORATIONS THAT I AM conducting in this book fall within the domain of ethics, but only if the label "ethics" is allowed to roam over a rather broad interdisciplinary territory. My real interests have to do with the general patterns of "the good life," which include the "oughts" that bear on politics, piety, family life, economics, and so on—rather than in "ethics" as a way of slicing out an area of conduct that might stand alongside of these other spheres. I am also interested in the ways in which the broad "oughts" of the good life are related to the even larger Christian vision of what it means to live and move and have our being in a world created by God.

This means that I am not going to worry too much about respecting the borderlines between the domains of philosophy and theology. For one thing, I am not sure exactly where to locate those boundary lines—we Calvinists often seem to be less clear about such matters than others.[1] Furthermore, there is already a widely recognized intersection between philosophy and theology: this is the area of discussion that is referred to as the domain of "philosophical theology." The fact that this common ground between the two disciplines is usually occupied by people who are primarily interested in metaphysical and epistemological issues does not mean that there is no room for discussants who have other questions on their minds. My subject matter here, then, can be thought of as falling under the heading of philosophical moral theology, as informed by those questions that are sometimes associated with the effort to articulate a Christian *worldview.*

Worldview Concerns

Brian Walsh and Richard Middleton have laid out the basic issues associated with worldview concerns in a succinct fashion. They suggest that a person's worldview will address four questions: Who am I? Where am I? What's wrong? What is the remedy?[2] Their list of questions corresponds almost exactly to the four components of a well-formed theory of human nature as set out by Leslie Stevenson in his much-used textbook, *Seven Theories of Human Nature*. Stevenson analyzes various accounts of human nature—Platonistic, Christian, Marxist, Existentialist, etc.—according to their general conceptions of reality, their understandings of what constitutes essential humanness, their diagnoses of what is presently wrong with human beings, and their prescriptions for correcting these defects.[3]

To analyze worldviews, then, is to deal with some crucial areas of investigation that are located at the intersections of these four areas of philosophical and theological thought: general metaphysics, anthropology, hamartiology, and soteriology. These are the areas of concern that I will be keeping in mind as I look at some basic issues bearing on a view of morality that gives a central emphasis to divine commands.

Much that goes on by way of ethical discussion among philosophers and theologians virtually cries out for a more explicit wrestling with worldview type issues. Take the subdiscipline of medical ethics as a case in point. It is not uncommon for writers of books and articles on medical ethics to give the impression that the right sort of medical decisions will be made if only we ensure that medical professional or technical expertise is wedded to an awareness of moral principles or values. If this is allowed to stand as an adequate portrayal of the way things ought to go in medicine, then terms like "values" and "principles" will have to carry considerable freight—which, of course, they often do—and will be misleading labels for designating that body of considerations which must supplement technical skill.

The Christian who wants to understand the full human significance of medical practice will have to look to more than ethics, even to more than theological and philosophical ethics, for help. The contributions of several other philosophical and theological disciplines and subdisciplines are certainly of crucial importance. Only a small sampling of the issues where medicine intersects with various areas of theological and philosophical inquiry would include: metaphysical, epistemological, and anthropological questions concerning the genesis and cessation of human life; dualistic and monistic accounts of human composition, as they touch on basic issues concerning the significance of medical treatments in the careers of human persons; questions about the role of science in human society; issues having to do with the nature, merits, and demerits of human "technique"; analyses of the function of medical institutions in human cultural formation; theological and aesthetic criteria for deciding what counts as "deformity" and "normalcy" in human beings.

The questions often subsumed under the "medical ethics" heading are seldom simply questions of moral rightness and wrongness. They hang on the more general ways in which we view reality. Take the standard textbook case of the woman who has terminal cancer, but whose doctors think it is not in her best interest that she know the facts about her condition. If the patient is a Christian, then certain factors must be taken into account in deciding what is in her best "interest." For one thing, it is in the Christian's interest to be allowed to struggle with the spiritual significance of a specific affliction. Like St. Paul in his struggles with his "thorn in the flesh," the Christian must ask, "Why has God allowed this to happen to me, and what constitutes a faithful response to this development?" In this case, the woman must be allowed to assess the role which this experience of disease plays in her overall career as a human being. And because of what she believes by virtue of her acceptance of a Christian view of things, she will understand her own "career" as extending into the age of the Resurrection. She must go through the struggle of evaluating her own suffering and impending death in the light of the Apostle's declaration: "I consider that the sufferings of this present time are not worth comparing with the glory that is to be revealed to us" (Romans 8:18).

Medical ethics as an area of scholarly and professional inquiry must be tamed—put into its proper place—by the recognition that neither medical nor ethical nor medical ethical discussion is adequate for dealing with the issues which arise in the context of medical decision making. This need is emphasized, with various degrees of clarity, by various groups that operate beyond the pale of medical "orthodoxy": Marxists, critics of the alleged "iatrogenic" nature of much "disease," practitioners of various folk medicines, and religious sects (Jehovah's Witnesses, Christian Scientists) who reject some significant items of contemporary medical orthodoxy. These groups are aware of the crucial role of worldviews in the areas of medical belief and practice. What is true of medical ethics in particular has relevance to our more general understanding of moral reflection. The moral dimension of human life must be put in its proper place by recognizing its connections to a broader agenda of human concerns.

To point to the importance of worldview questions is to highlight the need for a kind of philosophical and theological discussion that looks for connections between, say, ethics and other areas of human concern. This sensitivity is often very much present in the writings of professional philosophers. For example, Alasdair MacIntyre's *After Virtue*, to which I shall be referring often as my discussion proceeds, is a good case in point: MacIntyre's treatment of ethical thinking and practice has an obvious worldview orientation. It can even be plausibly argued that professional philosophy is kept alive by the periodic appearance of important books, such as MacIntyre's, which are aware of the direct relevance of worldview issues, and which pose new questions and concerns for the next phase of intensive professional exploration.

Worldview interests are often very obvious in the professional writings of philosophers who view themselves as departing from the "orthodoxies" of their profession. This is true of Anglo-American philosophers of a Marxist persuasion. It is also true of the work of the members of the Society of Christian Philosophers, who often deem it very important to state explicitly the worldview assumptions that shape their professional work.[4]

Among the theologians, explicit attention to worldview questions is regularly given by people who are convinced of the importance of "narrative" to theological explanation; the call to demonstrate the relationship of beliefs and practices to a larger "story" is often another way of emphasizing the need for worldview explicitness, a matter I will be attending to in detail further on.

My own reason for underscoring the importance of worldview here has to do with the point, made in the previous chapter, regarding the appeal to developmental psychology as a means of criticizing the Christian moral posture. An ethic that features obedience to divine commands cannot simply be dismissed by labeling it as "heteronomous" or "immature." These assessments must themselves be examined in the light of a larger set of beliefs about the kind of universe we live in, the sorts of beings we human persons are, the present condition of our moral equipment, and the proper patterns and goals of human growth. The proper consideration of these matters cannot take place without looking at the way in which obedience to divine commands derives its significance from a certain kind of worldview. And that is my primary concern in this book.

Moral Justification

As a way of showing the relevance of a specific philosophical topic to the larger worldview agenda, I will briefly examine the relationship between the questions of moral justification and an emphasis on the importance of divine commands. I will not provide elaborate details about this relationship because, as I will explain, I do not possess a full-blown theory which provides those details. But it will perhaps be helpful to sketch out some important matters bearing on the relationship.

Let us say that a person has a direct moral justification for a given course of action if that person directly ascertains that the course of action in question, in the light of all relevant and available factual information, satisfies what she takes to be the correct fundamental moral criterion or criteria. Furthermore, let us understand normative theories such as consequentialism, deontology, and virtue accounts as providing different possible understandings of what constitutes the correct moral criterion or criteria. Thus, in one version of consequentialism, a person who is wondering whether to keep a specific promise will ask whether the keeping of that promise will bring about a situation in which there is a greater excess of good over bad consequences than the situation that would result if the promise is not kept. Or a deontologist would ask whether, say, telling Peter that I will give him twenty-five dollars on Wednesday conforms to a rule of practice whose obligatoriness is rationally defensible (or intuitively obvious), and whether in conforming to that rule I would not be violating another rule whose obligatoriness is weightier in that situation.

When a person has gone through the proper moral operations regarding a course of action, with direct reference to fundamental moral criteria, we can say that a person has a *direct* moral justification for what she decides. But there are situations in which persons do not have direct moral justifications—where, for example, sufficient factual information is unavailable, or where there is no time to calculate consequences or to engage in appropriate rational reflection. Nonetheless, in such situations there may be other grounds for making justified moral judgments.

Let us say that a person has an *indirect* moral justification for a course of action under conditions of this sort: the course of action possesses some property distinct from the property of being supportable by fundamental moral criteria, and the person reasonably believes that the possession of this property by a course of action makes it either logically certain or inductively probable that the action has the property of satisfying the correct moral criteria.

Perhaps an analogy will be helpful. Suppose that my car engine's being fixed consists in certain adjustments having been made to the engine. But suppose I do not possess the skills to ascertain whether those adjustments have been made. But if I believe that when my mechanic, Mary, says that the engine is fixed then it is in all likelihood fixed—so that Mary's saying that it is fixed makes it highly probable that it is fixed—then knowing that Mary says so constitutes an indirect justification for the claim that it is fixed. Mary herself, in this case, has a direct justification for that claim.

The following might be a situation in which I have an indirect moral justification for some course of action: I am a consequentialist and have not calculated the consequences of some act, but I know that Jane, whom I believe to be a skilled consequentialist calculator, wants me to perform that act. Or I am a deontologist and have not engaged in proper reflection regarding some course of action, but I know that Jimmy, whose intuitive powers I greatly respect, generally reacts with favor when the course of action is recommended in similar circumstances. In these cases, knowing that Jane or Jimmy approves of a given course of action would count as an indirect justification for my approving of that course of action.

It is important to distinguish between two questions which relate to moral decision making: What *makes* an action right? and How do I *decide* that an action is right? We can decide, of course, that an action is right by directly investigating whether it possesses what we take to be the proper right-making characteristics. But sometimes the two questions receive very different answers. Very often people decide what to do by listening to moral authorities or by looking at moral examples. This is sometimes a dangerous basis for decision making, but not always. Sometimes, as I am suggesting, the appeal to an authority or an example can constitute an indirect justification for a specific decision. In both car repair and morality, the appeal to authority or example must take into account the credentials of the person to whom reference is made.

Right Making or Right Indicating

I am suggesting here that Christians who believe that the good life consists in obeying divine commands have a choice regarding how to spell out the way in which that posture of obedience relates to issues of moral justification. In brief, we can view God's commanding something as either a right-*making* or a right-*indicating* characteristic.

The stronger view, of course, is the one that views God's commanding something as a right-making characteristic. This view has been receiving favorable attention again in recent years. Indeed, very attractive versions of it have been elaborated, especially by Robert Merrihew Adams[5]—although, as James Hanink and Gary Mar have observed, many of these recent "defenses have employed sophisticated metaethical, causal, or 'paradigmatic' versions" of a divine command ethic, of a sort that a "simple believer" might fail to recognize them as supporting a straightforward account of God's will as right making.[6]

It is significant, though, that even Adams concedes, in response to Alasdair MacIntyre's insistence that we must approach obedience to God's will with an understanding of authority grounded in justice, that "[i]t matters what God's attributes are."[7]

And Hanink and Mar develop a version of divine command ethics that employs a helpful distinction between God's "legislative" and "creative" wills; we obey God's legislative demands because we believe that God, in creating us, wants us to "flourish" in the realizing of our happiness by means of "such basic goods as life, knowledge, family, community, play, work, and worship of God."[8]

These accounts do place an important emphasis on the examination of the divine credentials. We obey God because God is just. We serve the Lord because that is the way to attain the "abundant life" for which we were created by a God who wants us to be happy.

These nuances seem to suggest that the will of God is at least being viewed as a right-indicating factor. A morally justified action will certainly be one that promotes justice, or that contributes to human flourishing. And since we believe that God is just, or that God aims at human flourishing, we can at least take God's commands as very reliable indicators that what is being commanded does indeed satisfy the requirements for moral justification.

Is it possible, though, to view God's willing something as nothing more than a right-indicating characteristic? Perhaps. It may not be necessary to insist that knowing that God has commanded something constitutes a direct moral justification for that course of action; one could believe that even God, in commanding a course of action, satisfies certain moral criteria (which are distinct from God's having commanded it). For example, God's commanding marital fidelity may not necessarily be what *makes* marital fidelity right. By holding a loose view of the connection here the Christian believer could open-mindedly consider a number of different theoretical accounts of what constitutes a direct moral justification of a course of action. God might be a consequentialist or a deontologist or a virtue ethicist.

And ordinary Christian piety does seem to leave some conceptual room for this kind of loose view of the connection. Christian believers often say things of this sort: "I don't know why God wants me to do that, or to put up with this hardship, or to cultivate these traits; but I am confident that God knows best." This suggests that what goes into God's "knowing best" is a subject for legitimate theoretical, even metaethical, speculation. We do not have to offer decisive answers to such speculative questions before we can confidently accept God's commands as reliable moral guidelines.

But in the final analysis it does not seem quite right to treat the connection between God's willing something and that something's being morally right in *too* loose a manner. God is, after all, perfect righteousness in the biblical scheme of things. It is difficult to put this matter concisely—but it does seem appropriate to think that in some mysterious sense the right indicating and the right making begin to merge as soon as we pause to reflect upon divine goodness.

A Case in Point: "Christian Hedonism"

The considerations that seem most compelling for *not* linking God's will too closely to any specific account of the right making arise especially when we become nervous about some specific attempt to establish a straightforward link. It will be helpful to consider such an effort.

In his 1986 book, *Desiring God*, John Piper sets forth what he describes in his subtitle as the "Meditations of a Christian Hedonist." While Piper's treatise is not a major philosophical work, it is a rather bold attempt to link Christian ethics with a philosophical theme that is usually thought of as exclusively "secular." Furthermore, Piper manages to focus on some important theological themes in the course of developing his case. And the fact that Piper's arguments have been rather favorably received among Protestant evangelicals—the very Christians who are often most vocal in decrying easy compromises with secular philosophical systems—suggests that his project has some cultural, as well as philosophical and theological, significance.

Piper is very aware of the fact that some Christians might think "that the term *hedonism* carries connotations too worldly to be redeemed"[9] but he believes that the benefits in using the label outweigh the risks. And there can be no doubt, from reading his book, that he is serious about the "Christian" qualifier. Piper obviously intends to place the pursuit of pleasure within a profoundly Christian context.

Strictly speaking, of course, the nineteenth-century British hedonist theorists would find little to object to in Piper's attempt to link strict adherence to divine imperatives with a hedonist account of moral justification. Jeremy Bentham insisted that his hedonistic perspective was intended to explicate "nothing but what the practice of mankind, wheresoever they have a clear view of their own interest, is perfectly conformable to";[10] and he went on to note that one important class of pleasures which human beings pursue is those "pleasures of piety" which

> accompany the belief of a man's being in the acquisition or in possession of the good-will or favour of the Supreme Being: as a fruit of it, of his being in a way of enjoying pleasures to be received by God's special appointment, either in this life, or in a life to come.[11]

And John Stuart Mill made a similar claim on behalf of his own version of utilitarian hedonism:

> We not uncommonly hear the doctrine of utility inveighed against as a *godless* doctrine. If it be necessary to say anything at all against so mere an assumption, we may say that the question depends upon what idea we have formed of the moral character of the Deity. If it be a true belief that God desires, above all things, the happiness of his creatures, and that this was his purpose in their creation, utility is not only not a godless doctrine, but more profoundly religious than any other. If it be meant that utilitarianism does not recognize the revealed will of God as the supreme law of morals, I answer, that a utilitarian who believes in the perfect goodness and wisdom of God, necessarily believes that whatever God has thought fit to reveal on the subject of morals, must fulfill the requirement of utility in a supreme degree.[12]

Piper's account of Christian Hedonism is clearly continuous with this tradition. Piper's differences with Mill have nothing to do with the claims Mill makes in the comments just quoted; rather they relate on a more functional level to Piper's insistence on a very intense devotion to God and to the seriousness with which he treats God's revealed directives. Thus the "five convictions" which Piper offers by way of summarizing the tenets of Christian Hedonism can be seen as filling in the details of the account of moral justification offered by many utilitarian hedonists in the philosophical tradition:

1. The longing to be happy is a universal human experience, and it is good, not sinful.
2. We should never try to deny or resist our longing to be happy, as though it were a bad impulse. Instead we should seek to intensify this longing and nourish it with whatever will provide the deepest and most enduring satisfaction.
3. The deepest and most enduring happiness is found only in God.
4. The happiness we find in God reaches its consummation when it is shared with others in the manifold ways of love.
5. To the extent we try to abandon the pursuit of our own pleasure, we fail to honor God and love people. Or, to put it positively: the pursuit of pleasure is a necessary part of all worship and virtue. That is,

The chief end of man is to glorify God

BY

enjoying him forever.[13]

The notion of "happiness" displayed in these comments of Piper's is obviously a rather complex one. His "hedonism" certainly aims at more than the accumulation of immediate physical pleasure. But this does not distinguish his view from most others who have attempted to give careful expression to a hedonistic perspective. Aristippus may have proposed a rather crude hedonism, but the pursuit of pleasure advocated by the Epicurean school was anything but crude. It aimed, in the formulation offered by Epicurus himself, at "the absence of pain in the body and of trouble in the soul"; and Epicurus explicitly disowned (in spite of the experiences that people today often associate with "epicurean delights") "an unbroken succession of drinking bouts and of revelry . . . sexual love, . . . [and] the enjoyment of fish and other delicacies of a luxurious table," preferring instead a life of "sober reasoning, searching out the grounds of every choice and avoidance, and banishing those beliefs through which the greatest tumults take possession of the soul."[14] Even Bentham, who is often referred to in an offhand manner as one who thought of happiness in "purely quantitative" terms, intended his complex hedonic calculus as a means for lifting the pursuit of pleasure above a preoccupation with vulgar things.

For the Epicureans and Bentham the pursuit of pleasure is certainly a more complicated matter than is often thought of when people consider the nature of hedonistic pursuits. But for John Stuart Mill the complexity takes on such a magnitude that one can legitimately wonder whether Mill is really a hedonist after all. Indeed, if hedonism is thought of as the insistence that the good life aims only at the accumulation of pleasure[15] (or of the greatest excess of pleasure over pain), without attending to the way in which that pleasure is distributed, then Mill was not a hedonist: the fifth chapter of *Utilitarianism* is devoted to a detailed argument that no unjust practice could be genuinely useful in the pursuit of human pleasure. This insistence on Mill's part suggests that his view is actually a kind of "mixed hedonism," in which the pursuit of pleasure is conjoined with a concern for the proper *distribution* of pleasure.

Piper also seems to do quite a bit of "mixing." I say *seems* here because, strictly speaking, he has better reasons than Mill for insisting that his whole case could be formulated in quantitative-consequentialist terms. If, for example, God is capable of infinitely more pleasure than anyone else in the universe, and if God has announced a distinct divine preference for just arrangements, then it would follow that the pursuit of pleasure characterized by justice will in fact maximize the amount of pleasure in the universe. And the same pattern of argument could be employed in support of Piper's insistence that true happiness requires the love of other human beings. In the case of each factor of this sort the observation that God has a preference for the prescribed state of affairs is sufficient to demonstrate its extreme pleasureableness.

The tendency exhibited by many philosophical hedonists to expand their understanding of pleasure to include the items emphasized by other normative theories makes their accounts difficult to assess. And the situation is not improved by the thoroughgoing Christianization of hedonism that Piper attempts. This is not to say that comprehensiveness in a theory is a thing to be avoided. On the contrary, a general theory of moral justification should be expected to show that the important insights of other proposed theories are capable of being absorbed into its own account. But in attempting to demonstrate this capability theorists also run the real risk of stretching their own concepts beyond the point where they are interesting and useful.

Piper seems to do this sort of stretching with the notion of God's "glory." The undeniably biblical teaching that God desires to be glorified, and that human beings are called to promote the divine glory, are spelled out by Piper in hedonistic terms. God desires his own happiness and human beings are created in such a way that their deepest happiness is achieved by promoting God's happiness. And it turns out on this account, as already noted, that any of the moral commodities that we might mention as possible counter-examples to the hedonistic account are in fact crucial ingredients of the happiness at which God and human beings properly aim.

But there are other ways of accounting for these biblical themes, and some of them seem to be at least as plausible as the case made by Piper. We could, for example, explicate the notion of divine glory in deontological terms, arguing that there is a moral ordering of things—say, a *shalom*-ordering—in which peaceful, just, and truthful relationships obtain, and that the full and proper display of this ordered state of affairs constitutes the glory of God. This would be to construe the divine glory in a manner similar to what people mean by "the glory of ancient Rome," where glory is intimately connected to the display of ordered excellence. On this view the happiness which God and human beings experience in the presence of such displays of glory are not the primary "stuff" of the glory, but rather an inevitable by-product of it.

Or one could offer a more "mixed" account in which the glory of the Lord consists in both the display of *shalom*-ordering and the experience of divine delight *in* that display, such that both the experience and the ordering are necessary components of the glory. It may be necessary to add this experiential component in order to account for locutions like "give God the glory," although the "glory"-talk that we find in the Bible and in various systems of piety may not lend itself in every case to translation into any tight interpretative scheme.

It is also possible to unpack the various "glory" locutions in the terms of an ethics of virtue. Here the divine glory might be thought of as consisting in those states of affairs in which various virtues are displayed. On such an account, God's glory is manifested in those situations where divine fidelity or beneficence or justice are actualized, either by God or by human efforts to imitate the divine character. Happiness or pleasure, in this scheme, would be something that attends to, or is merely one component of, such displays of righteous character.

The fact that there do seem to be alternative ways of construing the biblical themes which Piper intends to account for in hedonistic terms means that we must weigh the specific advantages and disadvantages of his account in order to decide its overall worth. And although we may be unable to produce the kinds of arguments that would logically compel him to abandon his Christian Hedonism, there do seem to me to be some good reasons why other Christians should decline to support his project.

THE PILGRIMAGE OF SELFHOOD

One key consideration has to do with the *constancy* of the notion of pleasure in Piper's account. In the five summary comments quoted above he portrays the Christian life as beginning in a desire to attain happiness and as sustained and fulfilled throughout by a "pursuit of pleasure" that we should never "try to abandon": "the pursuit of pleasure is a necessary part of all worship and virtue."

Is it helpful to view the Christian's relationship to God as undergirded at every point by the pursuit of pleasure? Such an account does not seem to capture the sense of the loss-of-self themes in the Scriptures. To construe the Christian life as a continuous pursuit of pleasure fails to address the significant changes that the self undergoes in the pilgrimage of discipleship.

Let me illustrate this by considering a somewhat cruder version of hedonism than Piper's. Suppose I am an adult convert to Christianity and I decide to become a follower of Christ on the basis of this kind of reasoning: I have a rough understanding of what contributes to my own self-interest. I enjoy "peak experiences," and I also feel that I would be fulfilled by power, recognition, and the enjoyment of material goods. The Gospel, as I understand it, promises me that I will "really *be* something" if I am a good Christian: I will be on the winning side in the great battle between good and evil, destined to "reign with Christ for ever and ever"; I can enjoy the confident sense that God loves me in a very special way; and I am attracted to a "name it and claim it" view of Christian prosperity, wherein success and material well-being will come my way if I exercise the proper degree of faith in God's promise of "abundant living." And, with all of that goes the delightful experience of being a Christian, with joy and peace coming my way in ample portions.

There are good reasons to hope that as I proceed on my Christian journey significant changes will take place in the way I look at these self-interested considerations. For one thing, my understanding of what is in my "interest" will change (or at least *ought* to change). The concern to be on the winning side will diminish, and even disappear; the desire to be a "ruler" and to experience material success, and to have pleasurable experiences will not be at the center of my deliberations. My understanding of the appropriate patterns of Christian subjectivity will change. Now my goal is better described in the formulation given by the evangelical hymn-writer, Fannie Crosby: "I shall see in His beauty the King in whose Law I delight." In short, I will have a very different notion of what is in my "interest" than I did in the hour that I first believed.

But the change can be thought of in even more basic terms. My understanding of the "self" that *has* these "interests" will have undergone transformation. Piper might be able to alter the first answer in the Westminster Shorter Catechism—so that glorifying *and* enjoying God becomes glorifying *by* enjoying the deity—to suit his hedonistic purposes, but it is a little more difficult to alter the opening lines of the Heidelberg Catechism: "What is your only comfort in life and death? That I, with body and soul, both in life and death, am not my own but belong unto my faithful Savior Jesus Christ . . ."

To be a Christian is to give oneself over to God for re-making. This transaction is often described in *carte blanche* terms in the expressions of Christian spirituality: as a dying and re-birthing of self, or as a willingness to become clay in the hands of the divine Potter. If there is nonetheless some notion of receiving pleasure for oneself that functions in this piety, it is a very formal one. We may not operate with too clear a notion of what our "pleasure" is, since we must acknowledge God's power and right to alter, even in very radical ways, our conceptions of what gives us pleasure.

The Christian must be willing to say to God, "Make me into the kind of self that you want me to be. Transform, if it pleases you, my understanding of what it is that will bring me happiness." St. John, for example, obviously operates with a very fluid and open-ended notion of what constitutes the eschatological self-fulfillment at which Christians aim:

> Beloved, we are God's children now; it does not yet appear what we shall be, but we know that when he appears we shall be like him, for we shall see him as he is. And every one who thus hopes in him purifies himself as he is pure. (1 John 3:2–3)

The Christian life is thus a process in which we gradually find our earlier understandings of what constitutes selfhood transformed, and even replaced by newer conceptions. Proper self-fulfillment gradually ceases to be understood as "achieving my goals" and more and more becomes a matter of being conformed to the kind of selfhood displayed by God in Jesus Christ.

Is it helpful, then, to posit a constant "pursuit of pleasure" in all of this? Well, it is certainly possible to do so, just as it is possible to construe the whole pilgrimage in terms of a "self-interested" motivation. The question is not whether Christians can consistently stick to terms like "pleasure" and "self-interest" in their characterizations of the journey of faith. Rather the issue is whether it is *helpful* to do so. I am convinced that the changes in the sense of selfhood that occur between the time of a person's conscious embracing of the Christian faith and the eschatological fulfillment of the earthly pilgrimage are so significant that it is not very interesting to view the whole process as undergirded by a pursuit of pleasure or happiness. As C. S. Lewis puts it: "All joy (as distinct from mere pleasure, still more amusement) emphasizes our pilgrim status; always reminds, beckons, awakens desires. Our best havings are wantings."[16]

Not that it is misguided to talk about God's willing our happiness. It is one thing to acknowledge God's genuine interest in our well-being, and another to insist that the attainment of happiness or pleasure is the single motivating and sustaining factor in the Christian life. Piper correctly notes that many Christian writers regularly allude to the divine commitment to human happiness. It is not clear to me, however, that acknowledgments of the importance of human happiness commit one to the sorts of hedonistic formulations that Piper insists on.

Consider an example close at hand, a comment from an article that I have already referred to, by James G. Hanink and Gary R. Mar:

> What God wills for human beings is that they be happy. Their happiness consists in realizing such basic goods as life, knowledge, family, community, play, work, and worship of God. In realizing and participating in such goods, human beings flourish.[17]

Hanink and Mar might be taken, at first glance, to be endorsing hedonism in these comments. But the reason why this might seem initially plausible is that we may have permitted Piper to lure us into his practice of treating "pleasure," "happiness," "joy," and "glory" as virtual synonyms. While I have already suggested why "glory" does not really seem to be susceptible to a hedonistic analysis, there are also good reasons for objecting to the way in which Piper (like Bentham and Mill) moves back and forth so easily between "pleasure" and "happiness." Any genuine version of hedonism will treat pleasure as a "stuff" for which other goods— learning, sexuality, socializing, and even worship—are instruments of attainment. But Hanink and Mar are treating "happiness" in a decidedly non-instrumentalist manner. Happiness is not merely attained *by means of* such things as knowledge, family and worship— it *consists in* the realization of some such "basic goods." The goods which they mention are some of the *constituents* of Christian happiness.

In fact, having mentioned these goods, Hanink and Mar immediately go on to observe that God has given us a certain kind of "nature," and that "God specifically wills and indeed legislates that we fulfill our nature and in so doing achieve happiness."[18] This scenario seems to fit the more "virtue"-oriented picture to which I have already alluded. God wants creation, with its various "natures," to be fulfilled. God wants human beings to "flourish" in such a way that their proper created nature will be on display and, in that state of affairs, human happiness will also be achieved. The human (and more than human) "flourishing" that Hanink and Mar envision here is a condition that seems to reach far beyond anything for which a hedonism can properly account.

Note that I have not quarreled with the suggestion that a person might well embark on the Christian journey with a rather straightforwardly hedonistic set of motives. It is important to distinguish between entry-point considerations and those factors that later nurture and sustain the process into which one has entered. This is certainly an important kind of distinction to acknowledge with regard to such intimate human relationships as marriage and friendship. One might be initially attracted to the person who is to become one's spouse, or one's best friend, for reasons that will seem at later points in the developing relationship to be very crude and superficial. But there is no denying the fact that very rich relationships often have very crude and superficial beginnings.

The same seems to hold for our relationship to God. There is nothing intrinsically wrong, for example, about basing one's initial acceptance of the Gospel on a fear of eternal punishment. The threat of eternal punishment is very real, and it is certainly something to be afraid of. But if a person is, after thirty years of Christian commitment, still obsessed with a fear of divine judgment, something about the relationship of the believer to God has not developed properly.

This is a point, by the way, at which the kind of developmental considerations that were, as we saw in the previous chapter, misused by Nowell-Smith, have a positive contribution to make to our understanding of the Christian life. There is an important distinction to be made between an immature and a mature trust in God. To be sure, the believer's relationship to God will never achieve the "equal basis" that Piaget looks for in the mature child's attitude toward parents. But there are significant differences between an adult acceptance of divine authority and a childish submission.[19]

THE NEED FOR PHILOSOPHICAL TENTATIVENESS

My specific comments here about Piper's account are meant to illustrate a more general point: we ought to be rather tentative in our attempts to link obedience to divine commands to any detailed account of moral justification, even as we refuse to settle for a view that posits *too* loose a connection between God's will and moral rightness. Hanink and Mar offer a helpful observation in this regard. They note that for "the simple believer" the divine will functions in a straightforward way as the central reference point for moral decision making. But when such a person gets exposed to philosophical discussion, this pre-analytic grasp of the basicality of God's moral authority is likely to be shaken. And it is understandable, Hanink and Mar admit,

> that the simple believer can become uneasy about his initial claim that God's will is the fundamental standard of right and wrong. But if the believer remains a simple believer, one suspects that he will not find in modern philosophy much help in seeing just what *is* the standard of right and wrong. Neither the normative theories of intuitionism nor utilitarianism nor social contract thought, at any rate, seem satisfactory. For the believer recognizes that they too often have implications that run counter to what God wills. (Even if God's will is not the *standard* of morality, it remains—any believer contends—that actions that God wills are right and those that are contrary to His will are wrong.)[20]

In this last parenthetical comment Hanink and Mar are emphasizing the right-indicating character of the divine will. But they are also insisting on what we might think of as the *functional centrality* of divine commands in Christian moral decision making. However we construe the logical status of the will of God vis-à-vis questions of moral justification, there can be no doubt that the divine will is crucially significant in the moral life. Again Hanink and Mar:

> the believer should not give up his original insight that God's will is the standard of morality. What the believer must surely pursue, however, is a deeper grasp of just *how* God's will is the standard of right and wrong. The critic, then, actually does the believer a great service in forcing him to articulate this deeper understanding.[21]

The recognition that God's will functions at the very center of the Christian's worldview does not rule out a tentative, open-minded Christian exploration of the basic patterns of moral justification. Indeed the fact that Christians have a reference point—revealed divine directives—against which to test various meta-ethical and normative ethical accounts does not put them in a radically different position in philosophical discussion from the standpoints occupied by their secular partners in philosophical exploration. When Bentham insisted, as we noted earlier, that his consequentialist-hedonist account of moral decision making was meant as an explication of "what the practice of mankind, wheresoever they have a clear view of their own interest, is perfectly conformable to," he was being very open about the fact that his case should be tested against the reflective judgments of ordinary human beings: if, for example, it could be shown that Bentham's account viewed certain actions as obligatory that were actually offensive to clear-thinking moral agents, he would have to accept that as legitimate counterevidence to his proposed explication. And Bentham is not alone in claiming this sort of reference point in offering a theory of moral justification. Certainly in twentieth-century Anglo-American ethical thought this appeal to reflective moral agency looms large.

For the Christian, the awareness of God's revealed moral directives should play a similar role in moral philosophical theorizing. If there is a God who has publicly announced moral preferences, then those moral publications should function as basic reference points for testing our accounts of moral meaning and value. Just as many philosophers, of both consequentialist and deontological persuasions, have taken it as very important that many clear-thinking human beings experience deep revulsion at the thought of, say, torturing a few persons in order to provide pleasure for the many, so Christians who are convinced that God has clearly condemned sexual promiscuity cannot help but take that information very seriously in weighing moral accounts—even if they cannot spell out in detail what grounds God might have for expressing this judgment.

And it is not always easy to ascertain what God's own thoughts might be when it comes to the issues of moral justification. There is an important element of mystery and awe that characterizes a healthy relationship to the God of the Bible; the distance between moral decision making and worship is not always very great in the Christian life. There are good Christian reasons for nurturing a resistance to attempts to "psyche God out" in too much detail in dealing with the issues of ethical theory.

Martin Buber captures an important biblical theme when he refers to "the true norm that commands not our obedience but ourselves."[22] Ethics, as portrayed in the Scriptures, is a dimension of the believer's relationship to God, and attempts to isolate morality from this very basic "I-Thou" context will inevitably seem artificial. There may be, for example, some sense in which God's moral commands fulfill some key Kantian requirements; it might turn out that in obeying the directives contained in the Decalogue we are in fact acting upon maxims which could be willed as universal laws of nature. But this cannot be the whole of the story, viewed biblically. Obedience to divine commands is never merely a shortcut way of discovering Kantian laws, as if the Law-giver were an incidental—and even, ideally, an eliminable—presence in the moral situation. The fact of the concrete encounter with the specific mystery of the divine presence is itself a constituting factor of the good life, including the good moral life. Philosophical speculation, both worldviewish and professional, about this factor and the way in which it shapes moral decision making is necessary and good. But it is also best thought of as taking place in the context of a moral pilgrimage. And philosophical pilgrims would do well to nurture a tentativeness about the contours of the moral landscape which they traverse. There is too much about the road ahead—to say nothing of the divine Guide who points the way—that is not yet known.

3

ON BEING FAIR TO
"INDIVIDUALISM"

AN EMPHASIS ON DIVINE COMMANDS as the central reference point for human moral decision making is often spelled out so that those commands are viewed as being issued to a human individual, standing alone, as it were, before the divine Commander. Strictly speaking, of course, one could place a very strong emphasis on divine commands without saying much at all about individuals. The most important moral commandments in the Hebrew scriptures are addressed primarily to a community: Israel's God has brought her out of Egypt, and the divine imperatives are meant to guide Israel in her communal response to this divine initiative. An ethical perspective that made much of the communal or corporate context for receiving divine directives might avoid being tainted by the label "individualism."

But such an ethic would not have captured all of the nuances of the biblical scenario. As H. H. Rowley has put it: "in no period of the life of Israel do we find extreme collectivism or extreme individualism, but a combination of both"; at specific times an emphasis is given to "the one side of this dual nature of man more than the other, but both sides belong to the wholeness of biblical thought in all periods."[1]

Most students of the Scriptures would agree that the individual and the community must both be taken into account. But there are different recipes offered for blending the two themes. Some of us are more inclined than others to put a strong emphasis on the individual's status, *qua* individual, before God. In my own scheme, ethical individuality is an important item. Since, in making my case, I intentionally draw on historical sources that are often labeled "individualistic"—Reformational Calvinism, evangelical pietism—it is important to attend here to the proper status of the individual before God. I will do so first of all by considering the "individualistic" label as such in this chapter. Then in subsequent chapters I will look specifically at the notions of the "naked self" and of "voluntarism" that are often associated with a Calvinist ethic.

"INDIVIDUALISM" AS AN ACCUSATION

On two occasions in my life, I have been called an individualist to my face: once in a friendly argument about soteriology with a European Barthian theologian, and on another occasion in a not-so-friendly argument about human rights with an Afrikaner philosopher. In each case I was unsettled by the accusation. I have been rather uninhibited myself in labeling the views of other Christians—especially fellow "conservative evangelicals"—as individualistic. When I have used that term I have not intended it as a compliment. Nor did the two persons who applied the label to me. So when the shoe was on the other foot I was taken aback.

Needless to say, I began to suspect that the term "individualist" is not always used in a precise manner, and I vowed to get clear about what the label comes to. This chapter is an attempt to promote such clarity.

Sometimes when people call someone an individualist, they mean to be saying something about that person's character: that, for example, the person is very self-centered or possesses a very independent spirit. But that is not a usage which will concern us here. Nor was it what my accusers intended in branding me as an individualist. Our focus here is not on the senses of the term which apply to the traits of specific people, but to theories, to perspectives on how individual people are meant to fit into the larger scheme of things. More specifically, we will pay special attention here to the two areas of thought which were at issue in my discussions with my accusers: soteriology and political thought.

NORMATIVE INDIVIDUALISM

Suppose someone deliberately set out to become a thoroughgoing individualist in regard to political life. Presumably it would be necessary to answer some basic questions about politics by giving a very fundamental emphasis to the place of the human individual. In thinking, for example, about the question, "What is a state or a nation?" or, "Of what sorts of things is a corporate political entity composed?" answer could be made by pointing to individual human beings. It might be said, for example, "A state is nothing but a collection of individuals," or "The basic stuff of political life is people, individual people." We might call this a "metaphysical individualism" with regard to political thought.

But such a person might also place a strong emphasis on individuals in dealing with "normative" or "ought" questions about political life. It might be taken for granted, for example, that questions of political obligation must be dealt with by referring only to the wants of self-interested individuals. It could be insisted that the value of individuals, understood in this way, is the central and controlling concept of political thought. Thus it might be necessary to struggle long and hard with the question: "How can the existence of a central political authority be reconciled with the needs of self-interested individuals?"

Steven Lukes seems to have these kinds of "normative" questions in mind (as opposed to the "metaphysical" concerns mentioned above) when he associates "political individualism" with these three notions:

> . . . first, a view of government as based on the (individually-given) consent of its citizens—its authority or legitimacy deriving from that consent . . . Second, and allied to this, is a view of political representation as representation, not of orders or estates or social functions or social classes, but of individual interests. And third, there is a view of the purpose of government as being confined to enabling individuals' wants to be satisfied, individuals' interests to be pursued and individuals' rights to be protected, with a clear bias towards *laissez-faire* and against the idea that it might legitimately

influence or alter their wants, interpret their interests for them, or invade or abrogate their rights.[2]

As Lukes spells these matters out, the normative individualist wants to stress the importance of the individual with regard to three fundamental questions in political thought: From what does a government derive its authority? What or whom do political officials properly represent? And, what is the fundamental purpose of government? In each case, the question is answered with an emphasis on the individual: Governments derive their authority to govern from the consenting wills of individuals; political officials are the representatives of individual concerns; and governments exist to serve the needs and interests of individuals. Normative political individualism, then, stresses the centrality of the individual in response to at least three different questions. My concern here is not to follow this emphasis as it weaves its way through the intricacies of political theory, but rather to look briefly at the fundamental concern for individuals and their rights, and to ask how Christians ought to assess this concern.

THE WORTH OF THE INDIVIDUAL

There are some Christians who would react strongly against talk about the value or worth of "the individual." Traditional Roman Catholicism and Eastern Orthodoxy have relied heavily on the "mystical union" motif in their ecclesiologies, and sometimes also in their perspectives on social and political patterns.[3] Similar emphases are found in some Protestant groups; for example, Afrikaner Calvinists rely heavily on "organic" metaphors from the New Testament in describing political and cultural groupings.[4]

This is an area where Christian political thought must proceed very cautiously, especially in the light of the totalitarian and authoritarian uses to which "anti-individualist" rhetoric has been put by some Christians. It may be that Christian political thought must absorb some of the crucial emphases of normative individualism before it rejects that perspective as ultimately inadequate.

Consider, for example, a common pattern of argument against

"social contract" theories of political obligation. The argument moves along these lines: political obligation cannot be grounded in a human "contract," which has been engaged in, either implicitly or explicitly, by consenting individuals. God has ordained that there be states and civil authorities; governments exist, then, not by the will of human beings, but by the will of God; therefore, we must choose: either the obligation of citizens to obey their governments is to be derived from the wills of those citizens or from the will of God.

This is much too simple, because it presents us with a false choice. Consider this question: Is my obligation to be faithful to my wife grounded in a human contractual agreement, or is it grounded in the will of God? Well, didn't God ordain the marriage institution? And aren't Christians required to live in marital faithfulness as a part of a life of obedience to God? My obligation, then, to live in marital fidelity is grounded in God's decrees.

But that cannot be the whole story. In an important sense, of course, I am obligated *to God* to live in marital fidelity—in that sense my obligation is rooted in the eternal purposes of God for creation. But in another sense, it seems obvious, I am obligated *to my wife* to offer her my continuing fidelity. And that obligation has a rather definite historical origin—I incurred that obligation ceremonially one summer evening when I stood before a gathered people and pledged my fidelity to her.

We might then say that God has ordained that there *be* marriages, and that they be characterized by loving, monogamous fidelity. But *my* obligation to live in a specific relationship to a specific person is also based on a contract or covenant between human beings. If I violate that contract, two distinct charges can be laid against me: I have disobeyed the God who ordained the institution of marriage; but I have also broken a specific vow to a specific human being, my wife.

This is no trivial point. There have been many marriages which have been sustained, especially in subcultures wherein divorce is strongly frowned upon, by a dogged and single-minded desire to be faithful to God. There is no need to debate the question here whether keeping a marriage officially intact on such a basis is better than ending it. But there can be no doubt that it is a very defective arrangement. Suppose, for example, a husband abstained from committing adultery and regularly gave his wife birthday and anniversary gifts solely on the grounds that such patterns were required by God. The wife would have legitimate reason to complain that some important elements of marital obligation were absent in this relationship.

Does the marriage relationship, then, rest on the will of God or the wills of human beings? The answer is: both. And much the same holds for the realm of political obligation. When David became king over Israel, he was reminded of a covenant that he made with God: "And the Lord your God said to you, 'You shall be shepherd of my people Israel, and you shall be prince over my people Israel,'"—but this "vertical" obligation is complemented by a "horizontal" one: "So all the elders of Israel came to the king of Hebron; and David made a covenant with them at Hebron before the Lord" (1 Chron. 11:2–3). It is difficult to see how belief in the God-instituted nature of government automatically rules out an element of contractual agreement between government and citizens.[5]

It may be the case—indeed I think it very likely—that Christians ought not to embrace a viewpoint which spells out the role of government solely with reference to the wishes and desires of individual citizens. It is not difficult to find literature in Christian political thought that makes much of "the God-ordained supremacy of the individual."[6] That kind of talk is misleading. But it is not wrongheaded to emphasize the God-ordained *importance* of the individual.

"I"-CENTERED LANGUAGE

There will be times, if we recognize the Christian importance of the individual person, when we will point to the status of the individual in such a way that our language could be construed as individualistic. The "I"-centered tone of black slave spirituality is an interesting case in point. In this situation, the black person was stripped of communal relationships, and this loss of community is poignantly expressed in black-slave spirituals: "Sometimes I feel like a mother-less child"; "I must walk this lonesome valley, I've got to walk it by myself"; "Soon I will be done with the troubles of the world."

But James Cone, in his marvelous little book on *The Spirituals and the Blues*, warns us against interpreting this kind of black spirituality as "individualistic":

> It is commonplace among many interpreters of black religion to account for the emphasis on the "I" in the spirituals and other black church expressions by pointing to the influence of white pietism and revivalism in the nineteenth century. But that assumption, while having some merit, is too simplistic; it does not take seriously enough the uniqueness of black religion . . . The existential "I" in black religion . . . did not have as its content the religious individualism and guilt of white religion or refer to personal conversion in those terms . . . The "I" of black slave religion was born in the context of the brokenness of black existence. It was an affirmation of self in a situation where the decision to *be* was thrust upon the slave . . . Thus the struggle to be both a person and a member of community was the major focus of black religion. The slave knew that an essential part of this struggle was to maintain his affirmation even—and especially—when alone and separated from his community and its support. He knew that he alone was accountable to God, because somewhere in the depth of the soul's search for meaning, he met the divine.[7]

The "I"-centeredness of slave spirituality does not constitute an individualistic denial of human community. Indeed, it is a plea *for* community. Slaves are deprived of the ability to function as familial beings, wage-earners, worshippers, students, and teachers. The "I" which is so prominent in their piety is in effect an insistence that they nonetheless possess the credentials of personhood which, if recognized, would permit them to function normally in these various social spheres. Cruelly denied the status of full personhood by other human beings, they are standing tall in the final court of appeals, affirming their dignity as created and redeemed persons.

My point here can be illustrated by a comparison of two very different expressions of individual "worth." One expression is from Fritz Perls, in his well-known "Gestalt Prayer":

> I do my thing, and you do your thing.
> I am not in this world to live up to your expectations.
> And you are not in this world to live up to mine.
> You are you, and I am I.
> And if by chance we find each other, its beautiful.
> If not, it can't be helped.[8]

My own negative reaction to this blasphemous "prayer" was captured well in a poster company's advertisement in *The National Lampoon* during the days of the Watergate scandal. The company offered a poster with Perls' "prayer" printed beneath a picture of Richard Nixon—an apt portrayal of Nixon's message to the Congress and courts: "I am not in this world to live up to your expectations. . . ."

Consider now these words penned by the ex-slave Frederick Douglass, in a letter written to the slave-owner from whom he had escaped:

> I am myself; you are yourself; we are two distinct persons, equal persons. What you are, I am. You are a man, and so am I. God created both, and made us separate beings. I am not by nature bound to you, or you to me. Nature does not make your existence depend upon me, or mine to depend upon yours . . . In leaving you, I took nothing but what belonged to me.[9]

There are fascinating similarities of language between Douglass' credo and Perls'. But the two are making very different points. Indeed, had Douglass used the very words of the Perls' "prayer," he would have still been saying something very different. Perls—in what is perhaps an excellent example of Christopher Lasch's "culture of Narcissism"—is simply proclaiming his intention to "do my own thing," come what may; but Douglass is proclaiming his created self-worth in response to the dehumanizing forces of racism. Perls is issuing an egoistic confession of faith. Douglass is saying "No" to the racist's denial of the human dignity of the black person.

The Christian emphasis on the worth of the individual is

nicely summarized by Helmut Gollwitzer, in his critique of Marxist totalitarianism:

> In Christian thought . . . an unprecedented, supreme accent is laid,
> as Marx suspected, but wrongly expressed it, on the individual life
> . . . because the content of the gospel is the victory of the love of
> God. This love is directed to every man, and further, to the individu-
> al man. It does not isolate him, but it individualizes him in the same
> way as the love of the father and mother does with each individual
> child, however large the number of children . . . For this love every
> single person is irreplaceable.[10]

Much of what we call "religious individualism"—which
might more accurately be described as a blend of soteriological and
ecclesiological individualism—is in fact a celebration of this sense
of individual irreplaceability, which is often expressed beautifully,
as in Wesley's hymn: "Died he for me/who caused his pain/for me,
who him to death pursued/Amazing love, and can it be/that thou
my God shouldst die for me?"

This sort of celebration of God's individualizing love on the
part of, say, white evangelicals, can be understood in a way that is
analogous to Cone's treatment of the "I" in black-slave spirituality.
We may come to a place in our experience where the hopelessness
of individual guilt and rebellion is realized. There is a sense of overwhelming indebtedness, accompanied by a sense of overwhelming
spiritual bankruptcy. And then the good news breaks in: "Jesus
paid it all—and he paid the debt for me. I am loved by God; I am
redeemed by his unsurpassed mercy." This experience—which can,
of course, also be expressed in very different theological terms—lies
at the heart of the Christian gospel.

We ought to be very cautious, then, about promiscuously
applying the individualistic label to any perspective which makes
significant use of the pronoun "I." There is nothing intrinsically
wrong with an emphasis on the individual when the individual is
viewed as being threatened by the forces of sin and oppression.

Needless to say, there is more—much more—to the Christian
gospel than good news for the individual. God's redemption is a
renewal of the entire creation—a creation which presently groans
for the coming of the new order. The individual is called to partici-
pate in God's work of liberation, a task which requires that she

deny herself and take up the cross—a cross that must be borne in the company of renewed humanity. And so on. The gospel is more than a message about individual irreplaceability. But it is not *less* than that.

DEFENDING THE INDIVIDUAL

We cannot afford to ignore these matters in formulating our political theories; we would do well to attempt more nuanced understandings of references to "the individual" in political thought than has often been the case in Christian discussion. It may be very appropriate to worry about an overemphasis on individuality in some North American political circles. But a similar complaint about "putting too much emphasis on the individual," uttered in South Africa or the Soviet Union or North Korea may border on the demonic.

When we hear people attacking "individualism" we must ask what alternative they are proposing. The rights of the individual can be bartered away for the sake of a variety of alternative currencies. Some will rightly insist that individual human beings must look beyond their own selfish wants to the service of the larger human community. But other attackers of individualism will intend to absorb the individual into a class or a social role; others will deny the individual integrity in favor of the interests of an emperor, a *Geist*, or a "national soul." Still others will sacrifice the individual to economic interests, or in the service of racist and imperialist designs, or out of a fear of "communism" or with a professed concern for "law and order."

In response to the worst of these anti-"individualist schemes," defenses of the individual will also vary. Some will view the individual as a virtual deity, a worthy pretender to the Creator's throne; others—and we can hope that this will be the uniform Christian defense—will defend the individual as not a "god," but as god-*like*, a bearer of the divine image. Christian arguments, proddings, and preachments on this subject will necessarily differ, in emphasis at least, from context to context. There will be times when we will issue calls to more intensive involvement in human community, insisting—as Bonhoeffer did so well[11]—that individuals must find their fulfillment in the "life together" which God intends for them. But there will be other times when we must warn individuals against an unhealthy absorption into pseudo-communities, or into unjust and oppressive social and political systems.

BIBLICAL ORGANIC IMAGERY

There can be no doubt that the New Testament does make much of a kind of "organic" relationship of the individual Christian to the larger Christian community. How ought that emphasis inform our efforts to promote clarity regarding the relationship of individuals to communities?

F. W. Dillistone provides us with a very solid guidance when he insists that the New Testament references to the community as an "organism" must be interpreted in "a metaphorical and ethical way" rather than "a metaphysical and mystical" one.[12] To put the matter in this way is not to deny the propriety of talking about a "mystical union" between the individual and God, or among individuals. But it is to insist that this union does not bring about a metaphysical elimination of individuality.

There is no need here to explore all of the ways in which the organism metaphors are used in, say, the Pauline and Johannine writings. Suffice it to note that those metaphors are employed to reinforce at least two teachings about the individual. First, the individual has *value*. The extensive discussion of the corporate "body" in 1 Corinthians 12 clearly sets forth this point. The emphasis there is on the fact that the body does indeed have *many* members and that each has to be taken seriously in its contribution to the proper functioning of the whole:

> As it is, there are many parts, yet one body. 'The eye cannot say to the hand, "I have no need of you," nor again the head to the feet, "I have no need of you' . . . If one member suffers, all suffer together; if one member is honored, all rejoice together. (1 Corinthians 12:20, 21, 26)

Second, and closely related, individuals are *accountable* to each other. In Ephesians 4 there is a strong emphasis on the body as a place in which each part works to the building up of the whole, by exercising gifts in a mutually nurturing way: "Therefore, putting away falsehood, let every one speak the truth with his neighbor, for we are members one of another" (Ephesians 4:25).

These items are at least part of what is implied by Dillistone's stress on the "metaphorical" and "ethical" uses of the organic images in the New Testament. Instead of reinforcing the metaphysical absorption of the individual into some relationship or entity, these uses actually point to the importance of individuality, albeit an individuality that requires a communal context for its health.

Christian social thought should be guided by this vision of a community of individuals who have been redeemed from polytheistic combat for incorporation into communal networks in which individuality can be preserved and enhanced. The metaphors to which we have just been referring deal primarily with the kinds of relationships that are realized in the Christian church; but they also instruct us regarding patterns that are manifested beyond the boundaries of ecclesiastical interaction. Human beings are not designed for anarchy in any sphere of life; nor is their individuality properly realized in the compulsive pursuit of "self-realization," nor by the glorifying of the "free marketeer." Rather, they are fitted for the service of a divine Ruler who calls each subject by name—but calls them nonetheless to participation in communities in which the *shalom* of God is exhibited.

My own hunch is that there is no way of spelling out the details of this Christian vision without evoking the charge of "individualism" from some quarters. But there is no need to be intimidated by that accusation. At least one of the ways in which this label functions is that in one context or another it is used to describe a position that is thought by someone to place *too* much of an emphasis on the human individual. In that case, the label never really *decides* anything. Instead it merely helps to highlight the fact that it is the place or role of the individual that must loom large in the ensuing discussion.

I do not mean to suggest that someone cannot, in one context or another, place *too* much emphasis on the place or role of the individual. There are perspectives on individuality which I believe to be "really" individualistic. But that is an assessment that one rightly makes only after careful attention to the way in which the individual's place in the larger scheme of things is being depicted.

4

THE REFORMATION'S
"NAKED SELF"

W E MUST NOW TAKE A CLOSER LOOK at the ways in which Christians have actually spelled out the vision of life in which obedience to divine directives is a central theme. More specifically, we must look at the historical embodiment of an ethic in which a strong emphasis is placed on individual accountability to a divine commander. In the previous chapter I argued that labeling a perspective as "individualist" simply because it pays a lot of attention to individuals is not adequate as a critique of that perspective. The way in which we view the individual must be assessed with reference to our larger perspective on reality—our larger worldview, if you wish.

I want to pursue that kind of investigation here by looking at some of the details of the Calvinist perspective on the individual's accountability to God. There are a number of good reasons for me to choose to focus on Calvinism. I will mention four of them. First, the Calvinist perspective is often, as we shall see, cited as an example of a Christian point of view that is much too "individualistic." Second, I am a Calvinist; thus I have a strong personal interest in testing out the merits of this perspective in response to thoughtful criticisms of it. Third, there is much to be said for a specificity of focus. It is not, in the final analysis, very helpful to try to defend a divine-command-ethic-as-such. People have different ways of understanding and expediting their obligations to God. Calvinists are one group of Christians who have made a special effort to articulate both their theological schemes and their plans of action, which makes them eminently studiable.

My fourth reason has to do with the need for ecumenical

honesty. Martin Marty once offered somewhere this sort of account of why he is a Lutheran: he finds being Lutheran a very helpful way to be Protestant; he finds being Protestant a very helpful way to be Christian; and he finds being a Christian a very helpful way to be human. This strikes me as a good account of what is involved in making a commitment to a particular confessional tradition. And once we acknowledge that it is the proper picture of the way in which our specific theological "isms" ought to be grounded, it becomes important to retrace our steps regularly, in order to see whether the more localized commitments that we have made continue to serve as helpful links to Christian humanness.

Nor can this be done adequately without looking at alternative ways of linking specific theological commitments to the attempt to be mature human beings. Retracing our steps can also be an attempt to engage in ecumenical exploration.

SELFHOOD AND MODERNITY

Having acknowledged the importance of ecumenical openness, it is safe to consider in a friendly spirit some rather harsh comments that Jacques Maritain made about Protestantism in his *Three Reformers*.

The Lutheran Reformation, Maritain wrote, brought about "the Advent of the Self." Luther's "swollen consciousness of the self" led him to celebrate the "individual will, cut off from the universal body of the Church . . . stand(ing) solitary and naked before God and Christ in order to ensure its justification and salvation by its trust."[1]

Luther is, of course, one of the three "reformers" of Maritain's title, the other two being Descartes and Rousseau. The members of this trio, he contends, "dominate the modern world, and govern all of the problems which torment it."[2] Whatever the differences in the intentions of these three thinkers, Maritain insists that their efforts converged to produce the modern understanding of selfhood.

Thus Maritain can include the Protestant consciousness in his recitation of modern spiritual ills:

Look at the Kantian shrivelled up in his autonomy, the Protestant tormented by concern for his inward liberty, the Nietzschean giving himself curvature of the spine in his effort to jump beyond good and evil, the Freudian cultivating his complexes and sublimating his libido, the thinker preparing an unpublished conception of the world for the next philosophical congress, the surrealist hero throwing himself into a trance and plunging into the abyss of dreams, the disciple of M. Gide viewing himself with gloomy enthusiasm in the mirror of his freedom: all those unhappy people are looking for their personalities; and, contrary to the Gospel promise, they knock and no man opens to them, they seek and they do not find.[3]

The Roman Catholic intellectual climate has changed significantly since Maritain wrote these words in the 1920s. One does not find any Roman Catholic thinkers these days speaking in such harsh terms about Protestantism—or about Kant, Nietzsche, and Freud, for that matter. But the kind of case which Maritain developed has not been completely abandoned. In recent years, Alasdair MacIntyre has taken up the cause, providing us with a provocative and ambitious critique of both modernity in general and Protestantism in particular.

At one point in *After Virtue*, Alasdair MacIntyre refers to Jacques Maritain as one of the "philosophers for whom I have the greatest respect and from whom I have learned the most."[4] He does not recount the specifics of his debt to Maritain, so it would be presumptuous to suggest that he has been directly influenced by Maritain's account of Protestantism's role in the development of the modern mind. But there are important similarities between Maritain's and MacIntyre's accounts of modernity. Each offers an extensive critique of the modern mind, and each insists that there is a basic unity, a coherent developing pattern, to Enlightenment and post-Enlightenment thought. Each believes that there is something very wrong with the way in which the human self is understood in the modern world. Each believes that the philosophical problems began with the abandonment of the older Aristotelian and/or Thomist understanding of selfhood. And each believes that Protestantism played an important role in producing the ills of modernity.

Whatever the influence of Maritain on MacIntyre, MacIntyre is no mere imitator of "the peasant of the Garonne." *After Virtue* is a provocative and ambitious work; it is filled with original insights and innovative characterizations of modern ethical, political, sociological, and religious thought. And it has been widely recognized to be a seminal work, not only by professional philosophers but also by practitioners in other disciplines and by popular journalists.

MacIntyre's views merit serious attention on the part of Christian ethicists. Indeed, on the face of things he might be understood to be providing much reinforcement for trends in recent Christian ethical discussion. Both Protestant and Roman Catholic ethicists have been talking much of late about "character" and "story," and about the primacy of a morality of "being" over a morality of "doing"—emphases which would seem to comport well with MacIntyre's strong case for an ethics of virtue.

MacIntyre's ethical prescriptions are grounded, however, in a larger analysis which cuts against the grain of much recent Christian ethical discussion. There seems to be a broad ecumenical agreement among Christian ethicists today that Christian moral discussion must take place within the very framework of modernity which MacIntyre criticizes. Most contemporary Roman Catholic moral philosophers, for example, show strong sympathies for one or another of the perspectives which MacIntyre attacks: analytic philosophy, phenomenology, Marxism, Kantianism, existentialism. If MacIntyre is correct, then they ought to return with considerable enthusiasm to an older perspective which many of them have either completely abandoned or significantly altered in accordance with the requirements of modernity.

But at least MacIntyre gives Roman Catholics something within their own tradition to return *to*. Protestants are left with no such choice. To return, not to Athens or Rome, but to Geneva or Wittenberg, is for MacIntyre no escape from the spirit of modernity. Protestantism is a part of the problem; it does not figure into MacIntyre's solution.

This has an important bearing on the kind of case I am attempting to develop in this book. The discussion of chapter one should make it very clear that I think that the emphasis on obedience to divine commands is at odds, in crucial ways, with much that is associated with the spirit of "modernity." It would seem important, then, to draw whatever help I can from MacIntyre's impressive critique of Enlightenment thought. Unfortunately, he makes this difficult. I want to derive both substance and inspiration from the very Protestantism that MacIntyre sees as a crucial stage in the development of the moral outlook of modernity.

The situation is further complicated by the fact that MacIntyre's account does not easily lend itself to a partial, pick-and-choose kind of agreement. He insists that the defects of modernity cannot be exposed merely by offering arguments, however sound, against various modern theories. These arguments must find their place within a larger narrative in which the "story" of modernity is told. The Protestant Reformation is only one brief episode in that overall narrative—but it is an important episode. One cannot adequately understand Hume or Kant, MacIntyre suggests, without first attempting to understand Luther or Calvin.

Even though I find much to agree with, then, in MacIntyre's critique of modernity, I find it necessary as a Reformational Protestant to tell the story of sixteenth-century Protestantism in a different manner from his account. And I judge that it is important to interact critically with his views here. MacIntyre insists that the Reformation was a significant step in the direction of the errors of modernity, and that we must return to pre-Protestant ways of thinking. I am convinced that the Reformation pointed to a legitimate alternative to both modernity and the classical scheme espoused by MacIntyre.

The Reformation and Secular Thought

MacIntyre's brief account in *After Virtue* of Protestantism's role in development of modern morality is a compacted version of the lengthier treatment which he gives to this topic in chapter ten of his 1966 book, *A Short History of Ethics*. There he views Protestantism as having stimulated the development of the major moral concepts of the modern period.

For Luther, MacIntyre argues, proper moral rules are only to be found in the divine commandments, which are understood, in turn, "in an Occamist perspective—that is to say, they have no further rationale or justification than that they are the injunctions of God."[5] In the medieval period, God's commandments were viewed as directing human beings toward their *telos*, at which their own natural desires also aim. There is no significant gap, then, between what is commanded by God and what human beings would decide to do on the basis of rational reflection on their own natural desires.

Luther rejects that medieval conception: for him, "our desires are part of the total corruption of our nature, and thus there is a natural antagonism between what we want and what God commands us to perform." To do what is right is to obey the arbitrary commands of God, which necessitates that we "act against reason and against our natural will."[6]

This emphasis is in itself a significant departure from the Aristotelian-Thomist conception of the good life. But Luther, as MacIntyre reads him, did not merely offer an alternative account of the source and range of our moral standards. He also devalued the importance of moral acting. The divine will alone reveals to us what we ought to do, but the divine commands are not construed by Luther as primarily giving us information about how we ought to live. MacIntyre sees in Luther's "faith-not-works" emphasis a downplaying of the action-evoking character of God's commandments. The divine commands make us aware of our inability to please God by means of our works.

These teachings had an effect, MacIntyre argues, of sanctioning "the autonomy of secular activity," the "handing over of the secular world to its own devices."[7] Christians are not to attempt to work out their salvation by moral activity in the secular realm. They must not rebel against even wicked princes. What really matters is the inner state—the justified condition—of the individual, who ought not to worry too much about what goes on in Caesar's realm.[8]

MacIntyre finds the same themes at work in John Calvin's thought. Like Luther, Calvin understands divine commands, not "as designed to bring us to the *telos* to which our own desires point," but as "the arbitrary fiats of a cosmic despot." And there is even an "inner identity" between the seemingly different views of Luther and Calvin regarding the secular realm. For while Calvin insisted that the princes were subject to theocratic norms as interpreted by the church, on the practical level the princes were left to their own devices. Calvinists wanted sexual behavior and Sunday observance to be regulated by secular authorities, but otherwise they allowed political and economic life to go unchecked. Thus "the history of Calvinism is the history of the progressive realization of the autonomy of the economic."[9]

In all of this, there "emerges . . . a new identity for the moral agent."[10] That agent now stands alone before God, stripped of all social characteristics: "the facts of human desires and needs can in the sixteenth century no longer provide a criterion for the choices of the moral agent, or a major premise for his reasoning." And so the person is forced to make lonely choices from among a variety of moral and social policies.[11] The Reformation has produced "the individual"—standing without a social identity before God and the secular order of society.

MacIntyre's much briefer account in *After Virtue* runs along similar lines, except that he does not explicitly repeat his contention regarding Protestantism's encouragement of secular autonomy. He outlines three main elements of the Aristotelian-Thomist moral scheme: "the conception of untutored human nature, the conception of the precepts of rational ethics and the conception of human-nature-as-it-could-be-if-it-realized-its-*telos*." Each of these elements is, he argues, necessary to a properly formed ethic: ethical precepts, which can be rationally discovered according to the dominant medieval view, are necessary to guide raw human beings toward the realization of their *telos*.[12]

Both Protestantism and Jansenist Catholicism, however, conspired to defeat this medieval consensus. Together they contended that we can have "*no* genuine comprehension of man's true end," since reason's power to discern that *telos* "was destroyed by the fall of man."[13] But while Protestants and Jansenists denied our access to the precepts of *rational* ethics, they still insisted on the availability of ethical precepts as they are communicated to us by way of divine commands.

The crucial move here is the denial of the *rational* availability of moral precepts. The "new theologies" deny that reason can "comprehend essences or transitions from potentiality to act."[14] Reason can only serve us in the moral life by calculating the means to the ends that we seek; it cannot aid us in choosing those ends. The Protestant and Jansenist can, of course, still look to divine commands for guidance in choosing moral ends. But once the will of God comes to be judged by secular thinkers to be irrelevant to the moral life, reason must serve the ends which are arbitrarily chosen by human beings.

The remainder of MacIntyre's narrative regarding Enlightenment and post-Enlightenment moral thought is devoted to demonstrating that all modern attempts to ground the human choice of moral strategies in anything but the rational grasp of a human *telos*—whether the attempt is made in terms of "custom," "pure reason," or untutored human desires—are bound to fail. To abandon a conception of a rationally comprehensible *telos* is to be left with the arbitrary choices of the human will, with the "emotivist self" whose ultimate moral decisions are "criterionless." The choice finally comes down to Aristotle versus Nietzsche. And it was Protestantism which set the stage for the appearance of the emotivist self.

THE APPEARANCE OF MODERN SELFHOOD

We are concerned here with telling the story of the emergence of the modern notion of selfhood in such a manner that Protestantism's role in the unfolding plot is adequately characterized. The formulation of the narrative requires attention to three stages: the medieval understanding of selfhood, the Reformation understanding, and the emergence of the modern view.

There is no need here to challenge MacIntyre's account of the first and third stages. Thus, the story begins with the medieval scene, as he views that situation. Here a person's understanding of his or her identity is intimately related to the person's social roles—or as MacIntyre puts it: "a man defines himself in terms of a set of established descriptions by means of which he situates and identifies himself vis-à-vis other men."[15] In the medieval setting, "I confront the world as a member of this family, this household, this clan, this tribe, this city, this nation, this kingdom. There is no 'I' apart from these."[16]

No experience of role-alienation arises here—role-conflict, perhaps, but no sense of a gap between the self and its roles as such. Nor are there any free-floating "oughts." Duties coincide with the behavioral expectations associated with social roles. There are no un-roled duties; nor are there any un-dutied roles.

And now we jump ahead to the third stage of the plot, to

recent modernity. Here we encounter the emotivist self. To be sure, we have taken a big leap, since it took a long time for modern thinkers to realize that the emotivist self could not be avoided. But we can take that leap, accepting MacIntyre's assurances that "the Enlightenment project of justifying morality had to fail."

So at the end of the story we encounter the emotivist self. This self is celebrated by Nietzsche, who

> jeers at the notion of basing morality on inner moral sentiments, on conscience, on the one hand, or on the Kantian categorical imperative, on universalizability, on the other. In five swift, witty and cogent paragraphs he disposes of both what I have called the Enlightenment project to discover rational foundations for an objective morality and of the confidence of the everyday moral agent in post-Enlightenment culture that his moral practice and utterance are in good order. But Nietzsche then goes on to confront the problem that this act of destruction has created. The underlying structure of his argument is as follows: if there is nothing to morality but expressions of will, my morality can only be what my will creates. There can be no place for such fictions as natural rights, utility, the greatest happiness of the greatest number. I myself must now bring into existence 'new tables of what is good.'[17]

We find this emotivist self everywhere today: in managerial "science," in Goffman's role-theory, in the ethical theories of both Hare and Sartre. In explicit and subtle ways we are encouraged to view our own ultimate choices as criterionless, to chisel out for ourselves the "new tables" of the Law.

Again, our question is about Protestantism's role in all of this. How shall we tell the story of the Reformation so as to characterize adequately its place in the plot?

In *A Short History of Ethics* MacIntyre argues that three

> concepts of moral import . . . emerge from the Reformation period: that of moral rules as being at once unconditional in their demands but lacking any rational justification; that of the moral agent as sovereign in his choices; and that of the realm of secular power as having its own norms and justifications.[18]

These three secularized emphases have parallels in the explicit teachings of the Reformers. The secular emphasis on the unconditionality of moral rules and their lack of rational justification echoes the Reformers' insistence that God's commands are arbitrary. The modern conception of the sovereignty of the moral agent has a parallel in the Reformation picture of the naked, un-roled self before God. And the portrayal of the autonomy of the secular realm has its counterpart in the Reformers' attempts to free the political and economic orders from ecclesiastical control.

In drawing these parallels, has MacIntyre accurately portrayed the teachings of the Reformers? It is tempting to quarrel at length here with his characterization of Reformation thought. But we must limit ourselves to a few significant critical points.

Did the Reformers view God's moral commands as "arbitrary" and "without rational justification"? Calvin, at least, does not suggest this view of God's directives. In his commentary on the Decalogue in the *Institutes* he insists that "in each commandment we must investigate what it is concerned with; then we must seek out its purpose, until we find what the Lawgiver testifies there to be pleasing or displeasing to himself."[19] Furthermore, Calvin argues, we must not treat the divine Law as if it contained "only dry and bare rudiments"—rather we must try to understand the ways in which the Law displays "all the duties of piety and love."[20]

To understand Calvin's view on whether or not God's commands have a "rational justification" we must divide the question. Does *God* have a rational justification for what he commands? If the alternative to God's having a rational justification is that his commands are—even from God's point of view—arbitrary and disconnected, then Calvin can only be interpreted as answering in the affirmative. God has a rationale for what he commands.

Do human beings *understand* God's rationale? Well, sometimes they do—although probably never in any complete sense. Calvin even believes that God has displayed his moral will apart from his explicit commands in the Scriptures. He says, for example, that "the Lord has provided us with a written law to give us a clearer witness of what was too obscure in the natural law, [to] shake off our listlessness, and [to] strike more vigorously our mind and memory."[21]

The question of how "reason" figures into Calvin's thought is a complicated one. But however that may go, one gets no impression in reading Calvin that he is asking us to respond mindlessly to "the arbitrary fiats of a cosmic despot." God's commands may strike us as arbitrary and disconnected at the outset of the Christian life; but sanctification, the process of growth in grace, leads the believer into an ever-increasing understanding of the purpose and unity of God's directives to us.

What of the second theme that MacIntyre attributes to the Reformers, the emphasis on the un-roled self's encounter with God? Much depends here on when one decides that someone has "de-roled" the human self. Was the hermit monk of the middle ages an un-roled self before God? MacIntyre thinks not. The medieval Christian believed that he or she had a role in the heavenly community, of which the earthly church was a manifestation. So, "in this sense of community the solitary anchorite . . . is as much a member of a community as is a dweller in cities."[22] Well, why can't this same analysis apply to, say, Luther? He too can be interpreted as believing that he had a role in the heavenly community— although he was very quick to establish a new churchly community in which role-harmonization could be achieved.

This response is not enough to put MacIntyre's concern here to rest. We must return to it shortly. But first we must briefly consider the third emphasis which he attributes to the Reformation.

Did the Reformers encourage that process whereby the "secular realm" became increasingly autonomous? It is difficult to understand the intent of this question unless we ask some further questions. What did Protestantism want to liberate, say, the political order *from*? And what did it want to free it *for*?

MacIntyre's answer to the first question, when he deals with this issue in *A Short History of Ethics*, is clearly unsatisfactory as an account of the actual theory and practice of the Reformers. He says that they wanted to hand the secular world over to "its own devices," so that secular authorities could "proceed effectively unchecked by any sanctions whatsoever." This is not true of Calvin, for whom theocratic norms had a very broad application to societal life—MacIntyre's claim about Calvinism's narrow interests in sexual and sabbatarian legislation notwithstanding.[23]

Calvin wanted to separate ecclesiastical and civil authority. But he did not mean thereby to remove civil authority from under the rule of God—one can only interpret him in this manner if one simply equates theocracy with ecclesiocracy. Calvin insisted that it is not the business of the gospel as entrusted to the church "to make laws which pertain to the temporal state," but that "Kings, Princes and Magistrates ought always to consult the mouth of God and to conform themselves to His Word."[24] Neither ecclesiastical nor civil authorities may follow their own devices. But this does not mean that they must follow each other's devices. Rather, each— preacher and prince—stands in direct responsibility *coram deo*.

Thus Calvin's answer to the second question is clear: What are the civil rulers to be freed for? To do the will of God without the "benefit" of ecclesiastical mediation.

Perhaps it was wise then that MacIntyre did not rehearse this particular line of argument—regarding Protestantism's espousal of secular autonomy—in *After Virtue*. On the other hand, there may still be a point to be made in this neighborhood, even if MacIntyre puts his historical case poorly. It might be possible to argue that while the Reformers did not mean to set the secular authorities free to pursue their own devices, they nonetheless made it easier for other thinkers simply to absolve civil rulers and economic agents from a sense of responsibility to anyone but themselves.

ANOTHER VERSION OF THE STORY

If we generalize this last comment we are close to the heart of MacIntyre's dissatisfaction with the Reformers: they made it *easier*, he thinks, for the modern conception of selfhood to develop. MacIntyre's case against the Reformation seems to rest on the attractiveness of certain ways of characterizing the relationship between the magisterial Reformers and modern secular thinkers. Maritain had exploited certain parallels between Luther, on the one hand, and Descartes and Rousseau on the other: Descartes liberates the epistemological self, Rousseau the moral-political self, Luther the religious self. MacIntyre exploits similar kinds of parallels: Machiavelli is Luther-without-God; Hume is Pascal-without-God; Nietzsche is Calvin-without-God. Is it not but a short step from "Here I stand . . . God helping me" of the Reformation to the unqualified "Here I stand" of the emotivist self?

To which the proper answer seems to be: Well, yes and no. Suppose we tell the story in a different way. This narrative also begins with the medieval conception of selfhood. Roman Catholic thinkers had posited a very close connection between the deliverances of divine revelation and the discoveries of natural reason, between the inscripturated Law of God and natural law. Thus the clear-thinking person, following reason where it leads, would discover many of the same things which the pious believer would accept by relying wholly on biblical revelation. Much credit, then, was given to the "natural mind."

On this version of the story, the Reformers saw the dangers of this unwarranted optimism about the capabilities of unregenerate reason. They sensed the coming onslaught against revelation from those who would attempt to grant complete autonomy to the natural mind—"today not a few appear," Calvin lamented in the *Institutes*, "who deny that God exists."[25] The Reformers sensed that the medieval church had prepared the way for a cultural capitulation to secularism by granting legitimacy to natural reason, functioning apart from the acceptance of divine revelation. So they sought to join the issue at the most crucial point: the choice must be made between reason operating independently of revealed truth and reason captivated and transformed by divine grace.

And—to continue this version of the narrative—the Reformers were correct in their fears. Secular thinkers, as inheritors of the medieval period's optimism about the ability of unaided human reason, forsook what they saw as the Thomist's unnecessary adherence to the revelational complement. In doing so, of course, they "practicalized" human reason, narrowing the scope of what it is that the natural mind can discover. Where the medievals had supplemented reason with revelation, the secular thinkers supplemented it with "custom" or untutored human benevolence or noumenal postulates. But for all of that they perpetuated a medieval-type trust in the abilities of the natural mind to function apart from revelational guidance. Thus Kant is Thomas-without-God.

Needless to say, this is much too quick. But some such story can, I think, be plausibly told.[26] I am not so much concerned here to argue that this short version of the story accurately portrays the medieval synthesis as I am to suggest that the Reformers, deeply troubled by what they saw as certain dangerous tendencies in medieval thought and practice, attempted to weave together an understanding of the human *telos*, the role of reason, the nature of God, and the moral stance of the human self in such a way that these dangers could be avoided.

In putting the matter in this way, I am insisting that the Reformers did not deny that reason can play an important role in Christian attempts to understand the human *telos*. MacIntyre takes Calvin's view to be that reason's power to discover the human *telos*

> was destroyed by the fall of man. 'Si Adam integer stetisset', on Calvin's view, reason might have played the part that Aristotle assigned to it. But now reason is powerless to correct our passions (it is not unimportant that Hume's views are those of one who was brought up a Calvinist).[27]

But Calvin seems to operate with a less gloomy view than MacIntyre attributes to him. At the very least, Calvin insists that even after the fall into sin reason continues to have an important role in the human condition: it can still be seen "among all mankind that reason is proper to our nature; it distinguishes us from brute beasts, just as they by possessing feeling differ from inanimate things."[28] Indeed, Calvin goes on, "I do not deny that one can read competent and apt statements about God here and there in the philosophers." Significantly, though, he immediately adds: "but these always show a certain giddy imagination." And this is because "they never even sensed that assurance of God's benevolence toward us (without which man's understanding can only be filled with boundless confusion)."[29]

Thus Calvin's ambivalence regarding "fallen" reason. Reason only functions effectively in a proper relationship with God, when we have "the assurance of God's benevolence toward us." In a sense Calvin's view is also more *pessimistic* than MacIntyre allows; even before the fall human reason did not on its own comprehend the truth about the good life. Proper reasoning must always flow out of a trust in God. We cannot reason toward this trust; we can only argue *from* it.

But unbelievers have not completely removed themselves from the presence of God. Calvin insists that the pagan philosopher's awareness of God is like that of "a traveler passing through a field at night who in a momentary lightning flash sees far and wide, but the sight vanishes so swiftly that he is plunged again into the darkness of the night before he can take even a step."[30] The unbeliever's reasoning about God and the good life is illuminated by these regular "flashes." In that context reason will be at best "giddy." It can be restored to stability only when a proper relationship to God is reestablished.

Calvin does not oppose reason as such; he "dynamicizes" it. The contrast is not between faith and reason, but between faithful and unfaithful reasoning. Reasoning is stabilized when the reasoner stands in a trusting relationship to God. In the context of that relationship we can again reason properly about our *telos*, in such a way that reason can once more—in a very un-Humean way—begin to correct our passions.

But this does bring us back to a Protestant idea of a pre-rational self standing directly before God—the emphasis which MacIntyre sees as a parallel to secularism's emotivist self. What shall we say about his alleged parallel?

One thing to say is that there is indeed a parallel of sorts to be drawn. David Cairns, after describing the dynamic nature of the human person's relationship to God in Calvin's theology, observes: "This whole line of thought in Calvin brings him very close to modern Christian existentialism, which pictures man's being as a life of decision in response, obedient or disobedient, to God's act of creative and sustaining love."[31] It takes little imagination to see how Calvin might be viewed as not only coming close to Christian existentialism, but also to *non*-Christian existentialism.

Similarly, in his 1898 Stone Lectures the Dutch theologian-statesman Abraham Kuyper spoke in glowing terms of the Calvinist portrayal of the individual standing alone before God

> . . . only in churches which take their stand in Calvinism, do we find that spiritual independence which enables the believer to oppose, if need be, and for God's sake, even the most powerful office-bearer in his church. Only he who personally stands before God on his own account, and enjoys an uninterrupted communion with God, can properly display the glorious wings of liberty . . . Only where all priestly intervention disappears, where God's sovereign election from all eternity binds the inward soul directly to God

Himself, and where the ray of divine light enters straightway into the depths of our heart,—only there does religion, in its most absolute sense, gain its ideal realization.[32]

Reformational Protestantism does, then, celebrate the individual person's direct relationship to God. And it is not altogether misguided to construe this emphasis in such a way that some sort of parallel can be drawn between the Reformer's views and the modern portrayal of the emotivist self whose naked will makes criterionless choices.

This parallel will be explored in more detail in the next chapter. Suffice it to note here that in MacIntyre's narrative a clear line is drawn between the classical tradition and the ways of modernity, between Aristotelianism, (or Aristotelian-Thomism) and the modern mind, for whom Nietzsche is the most consistent spokesperson. Having drawn the line in this fashion, MacIntyre has no choice but to put Protestantism on the side of modernity.

I have already suggested an alternative reading, according to which the Reformers were rejecting themes which both the classical tradition and modernity hold in common. Perhaps, however, it would be better to state the options in another, more nuanced, manner; there are not two possibilities, but three; the dialogue is not simply between the classical tradition and modernity, but among the classicalists, the modern secularists, and Reformational Protestants.

A Closer Look at "Naked" Selfhood

The need for a more nuanced way of portraying the situation is suggested by Peter Berger in his 1970 essay, "On the Obsolescence of the Concept of Honor." There Berger contrasts the ancient notion of honor—now virtually obsolete, he thinks—with what Berger takes to be a central notion of modernity: dignity.

Honor was the sort of thing that people once achieved by properly expediting those behaviors associated with specific roles in a hierarchically ordered social network. The knight, for example, achieved honor by riding "out to do battle in the full regalia of his role." In an important sense his role as manifested, for exam-

ple, in "the social symbols emblazoned on his escutcheon" provided the knight with his "true identity." But from the point of
view of modernity, which celebrates individual dignity, the knight-
ly "escutcheons *hide* the true self," for it "is precisely the naked
man . . . who presents himself more truthfully." Thus, Berger argues, "the understanding of self-discovery and self-mystification is
reversed as between these two worlds"; on one view people find
their "true" selves only in the roles which comprise their means of
social presentation, whereas for modernity an individual person
can only "discover his true identity by emancipating himself from
his socially imposed roles—the latter are only masks, entangling
him in illusion, 'alienation' and 'bad faith'."[33]

In these observations Berger seems to be reinforcing the sort
of analysis that MacIntyre details. The pre-modern self finds its
identity in its full roled-ness. The self of modernity discovers its
core identity when it is de-roled. And given this way of mapping
out the situation, it would seem that John Calvin would have to be
placed on the side of modernity.

But Berger refuses to lay out the basic options in such a stark
manner:

> Now, it would be a mistake to ascribe to modern consciousness
> alone the discovery of a fundamental dignity underlying all possible
> social disguises. The same discovery can be found in the Hebrew
> Bible, as in the confrontation between Nathan and David ("Thou
> art the man"); in Sophocles, in confrontation between Antigone
> and Creon; and, in a different form, in Mencius' parable of a crimi-
> nal stopping a child from falling into a well. The understanding that
> there is a humanity behind or beneath the roles and the norms
> imposed by society, and that this humanity has profound dignity, is
> not a modern prerogative. What is peculiarly modern is the manner
> in which the reality of this intrinsic humanity is related to the real-
> ities of society.[34]

This is an extremely important point. If there are, for example, biblical precedents for emphasizing the importance of experiencing our individuality in its un-roledness, then it may very well
be that it is impossible to point to a kind of naked selfhood without falling into the traps that MacIntyre and Berger rightly point to
in the schemes of modernity. It may be, for example, that Calvin's

understanding of selfhood, while admittedly different than the medieval conception, is also distinguishable from, to borrow Berger's formulations, the "peculiarly modern" way of relating "this intrinsic humanity . . . to the realities of society."

Some of these subtleties have been explored by William J. Bouwsma in a fascinating study of Calvin's attitude toward "hypocrisy." Bouwsma finds in Calvin a deep revulsion against the role-immersed self, the role "player" who avoids the "natural" and "spontaneous." Like many of his contemporaries Calvin yearned, according to Bouwsma, for an "openness" and a "freedom" in interpersonal relationships. Thus Calvin's hostility toward the phenomenon of hypocrisy, which "depends on and protects a discrepancy between what one is, inwardly and truly, and what one appears to be."[35]

But Bouwsma also sees an important ambivalence in Calvin's thinking about these matters. God himself, according to Calvin, calls human beings to be actors in a drama. In the final analysis we are called, not to be un-roled, but to be as it were *authentically* roled. Calvin's sensitivities on this point have to do with his keen awareness of the social upheaval that many of his pastoral charges were experiencing:

> It was one of the functions—it had others—of Calvin's doctrine of the calling that it assigned us our roles. His teaching on this point served an important social function in an increasingly mobile society in which many individuals—peasants trying to make a place for themselves in towns, young men in occupations different from their fathers', political and religious exiles—must have had troubling doubts about their social and occupational roles, feelings of the arbitrariness and absurdity of existence. The assurance that we do not choose our own roles to "play" but are called to enact them by God must, in this situation, have been profoundly helpful. Calvin intended that it should be. He commended the doctrine of the calling on the ground that it provided a remedy for the anxiety otherwise likely to surround activity in society.[36]

Calvin's ambivalence about roles was not confined to the issues of societal and occupational functioning; it extended to the sphere of intimate spirituality. Here too, as Bouwsma reads him, we are called to be actors. And we play our part in the spiritual drama properly when we avoid hypocrisy, not by shunning roles as such,

but by recognizing the need to be stern critics of our own perfor-
mances, under the gaze of the divine "spectator and critic."[37]

Unfortunately, Calvin does employ the language of "poverty"
and "nakedness" to describe this posture of exposure before the
scrutiny of God's judgment.[38] Similar images are used in Charles
Spurgeon's great Calvinist sermon on "Hypocrisy," where, for example, Spurgeon addresses the nineteenth-century British hypo-
crite in these terms:

> You may die with the name of Christ upon your lips, . . . but God
> shall not be deceived . . . by your profession . . . He shall strip the
> mask off you. Virtue is most adorned, when unadorned the most. To
> detect you, you shall be stripped naked, and every cloak shall be
> torn to tatters. How will you endure this? . . . The all-seeing God
> shall read your soul, shall discover your secret, shall reveal your
> hidden things, and tell the world that, though you did eat and drink
> in his streets, though you preached in his name, yet he never knew
> you, you were still a worker of iniquity, and must be driven away for
> ever.[39]

Like Calvin, Spurgeon here uses the language of nakedness to
describe the exposure of the "true self" before God's gaze. But this
exposed self is not naked in the sense of un-roled; rather the nakedness consists in the revelation of what that self's true role is in the
drama of life as God sees it. Spurgeon's actual contrast, if we
ignore the presence of "nakedness" and "unmasking" imagery, is
not between roledness and un-roledness, but between the insincere
role played by the sinner—say, preacher-of-the-divine-name—and
the actual role that gets exposed by God's unfailing gaze—worker-
of-iniquity.

Bouwsma's portrayal of Calvin's understanding of the spiritual drama suggests that Calvin was working with a similar contrast. Our "nakedness" is seen by looking at the true patterns of
how we play out the drama of our lives, as those role-patterns get
exposed in the light of God's judgment.

THE IMPORTANCE OF GOD'S GAZE

In considering the possible differences between the Calvinist
view of selfhood and the naked self of modernity, at least two

factors, then, must be explored. One is the matter I have been belaboring with reference to the discussions of Berger and Bouwsma: the nature of our self-nakedness as viewed by Calvinists. It may well be, as I have been suggesting, that the naked self of the Reformation is not un-roled at all. Rather, it might be better to think of the nakedness as consisting in the kind of exposed roledness that is revealed under the divine gaze.

But however that may be, there can be no ignoring the importance of the divine gaze itself in the Calvinist scheme. Once the individual self is seen as standing inescapably before the face of God, the apparent similarities between Reformation thought and the conceptions of modernity seem quite superficial. Is Nietzsche Luther-without-God? In a sense, perhaps, yes. But one strains for analogies: Is a corpse nothing but a human being without a heartbeat? Is a plucked peacock merely a peacock without feathers?

Machiavelli's Prince is not *simply* a Lutheran Prince who has lost his God. The Humean moral agent is not *simply* a Calvinist self from whom the relationship with God has been removed by some deft piece of metaphysical surgery, leaving all else intact— such clean surgery is not possible to perform on a Calvinist self whose "very being is," in Calvin's words, "nothing but subsistence in the one God."[40]

Nor can we formulate our narratives of the Reformation on the assumption that the Reformers did not know what they were getting into. The Reformers would not have been surprised by Nietzsche's account of selfhood. Calvin describes someone who "exempts himself from all judgments and wishes to rule in such a tyrannical fashion that he regards his own whim as law," adding that "such conduct . . . is utterly abhorrent not only to a sense of piety but also of humanity."[41] That he is here describing the bishop of Rome is beside the point; Calvin gives evidence of understanding the character of the emotivist self, even if he was unfair in suggesting that this self had in his day donned papal robes.

Indeed, Calvin would have recognized in Nietzsche's rallying-cry for a new humanity to write its own moral tables the echoes of an ancient manifesto. Those who tell us to trust in that which "reposes in ourselves," Calvin writes, are merely repeating the serpentine lie of Genesis 3:5 that we shall be "like gods, knowing good and evil."[42]

The modern emotivist self, whose character MacIntyre so effectively sketches, is from a Reformational perspective a very ancient self, reclothed—or perhaps it would be better to say, re-denuded. It is a self which was created for fellowship with God—a self which knows its own true identity only when it properly images the One who made it. But this self has attempted to escape the divine presence. And it is very devious in choosing its patterns of flight. Sometimes it attempts to immerse itself—to clothe itself—in this or that social role. At other times it boldly rejects all roles, positing itself to be sovereign, naked ego making its ultimate choices out of the depths of its self-proclaimed freedom.

The Reformers attempted to expose each of these devious strategies. They denounced both the medieval conception of a role-immersed selfhood and the emerging modern notion of an unroled self. Rejecting each of these perspectives, they pointed to a third understanding of selfhood: that of the human self which is inescapably a creature of God, and called by the divine Creator to assess all other choices—all other role-options—in light of revealed norms. Critics of the Reformers may still, of course, argue that the Reformers failed to establish this view of selfhood. But they may not insist—without seriously misrepresenting the Reformers' views—that Calvin and Luther simply sided with modernity as over against the medieval perspective.

Protestants—at least those Protestants who still insist on looking at the created landscape in the manner of the Reformation—can learn much from Maritain's and MacIntyre's accounts of how modernity's understanding of selfhood has come to be what it is. And they will want, in their own philosophical endeavors, to oppose that modern notion of selfhood with the same vigor which Maritain and MacIntyre exhibit. But unlike these critics of Protestantism, they will insist that the Reformers were not unwittingly preparing the way for the victory of a future enemy, but that they were effectively rearming human beings for a battle which had been going on almost from the beginning.

5

EMOTIVISM AS PLAGIARISM

I HAVE BEEN INSISTING THAT WE must not make too much of the parallels between the Reformation's understanding of self-hood and that of modernity. Whatever similarities there are between the two perspectives on naked selfhood must be treated in a properly nuanced fashion. That is the position I have been defending, and I do think that it is correct as stated. Furthermore, it seems to me necessary to defend that position, since important thinkers such as Maritain and MacIntyre have given the impression that—to put it a bit too crudely—the theological utterances of a John Calvin can be seen as the first gasp of modernity. This claim, even in the less crude versions defended by Maritain and MacIntyre, seems to me to be very misleading. Calvin was setting forth an understanding of selfhood that was very different from, and not a mere conceptual preparation for, modern emotivist selfhood.

All of this is to say that we must not make too much of the similarities between the views of the Protestant Reformers and those of Nietzsche and Sartre. But it is also necessary to say that we must not ignore the similarities that do exist. And that is what I will spell out in more detail in this present chapter. I want to insist that there is something to be gained by acknowledging and exploring the positive links between Calvinism and emotivism, especially if we have properly warned ourselves—as I tried to do in the last chapter—against viewing those links in a relatively unnuanced way.

The commonalities are worth investigating for at least two reasons. One has to do with the need for evangelizing emotivist selves. If Christians are going to present a divine command perspective as a plausible way of viewing moral reality in a modern setting, then we should search out whatever common ground it is possible to stand upon in dialogue with these proponents of modernity.

But, second, it is important that we not bear false witness against modern people, even modern people who speak in the tones of emotivist selfhood. And if the discussion of the previous chapter were to stand as it is, I fear I might be guilty of that kind of false witness-bearing. In arguing against the notion that, for example, Nietzsche's self is the Calvinist-self-without-God, I gave the impression that it is legitimate to think of the Nietzschean self as in fact *being* "without God."

In one sense, of course, it *is* legitimate to describe the Nietzschean view in those terms. Nietzsche clearly means to deny God's existence. His view of selfhood, then, is one in which the individual human being does not exist under the divine gaze.

But there is also an obvious sense in which, from a Christian point of view, Nietzsche has *not* gotten rid of God. If there is a God, then even the Nietzschean self cannot escape the divine presence. Even if the emotivist were to say, "Let only darkness cover me, and the light about me be night," there would be no escape from God's scrutiny, "for darkness is as light with thee" (Psalm 139:11–12).

These two senses, however, do not exhaust the possibilities for understanding the dynamics of God's presence-and-absence in the modern understanding of selfhood. Nietzsche, for one, is very much aware of the *idea* of God, and that idea has an important and formative role in his understanding of human selfhood. MacIntyre alludes to this fact when, in a passage quoted in the previous chapter, he supports his characterization of the Nietzschean ethic as one wherein "my morality can only be what my will creates" by citing Nietzsche's own insistence that he is producing "new tables of what is good."

It would be too simple, then, to say that Nietzsche gets rid of God. Nietzsche attempts to enlist the deity for his own purposes. More accurately, he *deifies* human selfhood. We must explore the implications of this fact for a nuanced understanding of the relationship between emotivist selfhood and the kind of conception of the self espoused by Calvinism.

The Enmity between Calvinism and Emotivism

It would be difficult to find a more harshly worded scholarly assessment of atheistic existentialism than these comments by S. U. Zuidema, a Calvinist who taught philosophy for many years at the Free University of Amsterdam:

> Sartre's teaching is . . . a tissue of plagiarism and perversion of religious ideas. His idea of freedom is a perversion of the sovereignty of God, his idea of self-election, a perversion of God's election, the idea of inter-human society as conflict, a borrowing from ancient polytheism, his idea of self-foundationing man taken from the *aseitas* of God, who is his own foundation.
>
> His idea of the power of freedom is a humanistic counterpart of the Occamistic idea of God, his idea of man's project of self-salvation a travesty on the gospel, his teaching on contingency an adulterated reproduction of divine creation (and also checkmate to freedom's power). His cult of man's self-worship is a twisted version of divine worship; his teaching on society, a radicalization of this cult of self to include the subjugation of one's neighbor; his existential tension corresponds to divine leading and ruling; his salvation the walling-in of man behind the barriers of auto-eroticism; his idea of man in flight before God; and his deepest intent is an apostate *Eritis Sint Deus*, you shall be as God, by forsaking God and justifying that which the Bible teaches as the fall into sin.[1]

Again, these are harsh words. But the assessment to which they give expression is, for the most part, an accurate one. Indeed, Sartre himself might endorse the characterization of his philosophical project as a "plagiarism and perversion of religious ideas."

Certainly Nietzsche would not be insulted to have his own work described in those terms; the Nietzschean revision of the "Old and New Tables" of the divine law in *Thus Spake Zarathustra* has been aptly portrayed by Eric Bentley as a "naturalistic ethics" that is "vitiated by [Nietzsche's] utterly religious view of nature."[2] Surely the Sartrean project deserves to be portrayed in a similar vein.

Like Nietzsche, Sartre saw the need for a way of viewing the world that did not merely embody an alternative to Christian thought—it must in a profound sense *replace* the Christian perspective. In employing the categories of "plagiarism and perversion," Zuidema is providing labels that identify a deep impulse in atheistic existentialism.

Which is not to say that Zuidema's characterization of the Sartrean project serves as a model of polite philosophical discourse. His remarks exhibit an obvious sense of affront, even outrage. But Zuidema is not alone in his expression of hostility toward Sartrean thought. Sartre seemed to have a knack for irritating his fellow philosophers. Anglo-American analytic philosophers have often chided him for his metaphysical obfuscations. And Marxists have regularly attacked him for what they see as his obsession with the alienation of bourgeoise individuals.

Understandably, though, many of the more energetic and spirited attacks on Sartre have come from religious quarters. Roman Catholics have certainly singled him out for special critical attention, especially Catholics in places like France, where Sartre was a symbol of the intellectualized resistance to Catholicism's longstanding cultural hegemony. Sartre seemed to have felt the sting of that kind of negative Catholic attention when he prepared his well-known lecture, *L'existentialisme est un humanisme*, in 1946. Indeed, he seemed rattled enough by Catholic criticisms to lapse momentarily into what many of his interpreters view as the "bad faith" of a Kantian-type universalizing.[3]

Zuidema's angry reaction, however, seems to be motivated by different concerns than those which have often been at work in the minds of Sartre's Catholic critics. According to Sartre's own account in 1946, for example, the Catholic party line on his philosophy seemed to feature the accusation that he denied "the reality and seriousness of human affairs."[4] But Zuidema is hardly worried about a lack of seriousness in Sartrean thought. On the contrary, Zuidema's complaints stem from a conviction that Sartre treats human affairs with an ultimate seriousness that only God deserves.

Zuidema represents a strain of Dutch Calvinist thought in which a strong emphasis is placed on the "antithesis" between belief and unbelief, on the radical oppositional nature of the differences between a biblically based understanding of reality and the kind of thinking that celebrates "human autonomy." Sartre's philosophy represents, for Zuidema's way of viewing the situation, one very bold and consistent expression of sinful thought. Maritain and MacIntyre may think that Reformational Protestantism and atheistic existentialism are merely two different ways of presenting the same core notion of selfhood. But Zuidema seems to know nothing of this kinship. When Zuidema encounters Sartre, the Calvinist self is standing face to face with the radically secularist self of modernity—and the mood is clearly one of angry confrontation.

Of course, there are many different varieties of angry confrontation. And it may be that this one—the one between Zuidema and Sartre—is best understood as a family quarrel. Or perhaps it is even more intimate than that: perhaps we have here a glimpse of the experience of self-hatred that occurs when the naked Reformational self catches its own reflection in the mirror of modernity. Perhaps. But I doubt it. There is nonetheless, something worth exploring about the very obvious—and, I think, special—sort of enmity that we see displayed here in the encounter between Calvinism and emotivism.

SERPENTINE AUTONOMY

Zuidema attributes serpentine designs to Sartre. Atheistic existentialism is, thus interpreted, a reissuing of the rebellious manifesto of Genesis 3: "You shall be as God."

Suppose we follow Zuidema in characterizing Sartre's thought in serpentine terms. Sartre's philosophical formulations are, then, one very bold way of giving intellectual expression to the manifesto of Genesis 3. These same sinful designs can also be seen operating in Kant's insistence that moral agency must be viewed in autonomous terms: the moral self must view itself as self-legislating, producing universal laws which have their origin in the individual human will. Iris Murdoch employs imagery similar to Zuidema's when she observes that "Kant's man had already nearly a century earlier received a glorious incarnation in the work of Milton: his proper name is Lucifer."[5]

But Sartre carries the autonomy program a step further than Kant. He insists that we must not even see ourselves as bound by the laws of universalizing rationality. We do not legislate out of a sense of duty to conform to the rational "givens" of our common "nature." Rather, we must view ourselves as the creators—*ex nihilo*—of human nature as such: we are "condemned at every instant" to invent our own humanness.[6] The understanding of "autonomy" at work here is very un-Christian. Zuidema was right to condemn it. The fundamental desire to act as a moral creator-legislator stands in sharp contrast to the biblical scheme: "There is a way which seems right to a man, but its end is the way of death" (Proverbs 14:12).

The Sartrean endorsement of radical autonomy, then, is worthy of our vigorous rejection. It must also be said, however, that the special vigor with which Calvinists reject the Sartrean scheme has something to do with an odd sort of affinity between atheistic existentialism and what Calvinists often set forth as the right way to understand human nature. The Calvinists may detest the explicit spirit of religious rebellion that the existentialists display, but they also sense that the existentialists have at least located the point of rebellion in the right place.

Modern and post-modern secularizing thought is united in its endorsement of the notion that human consciousness is the ultimate measurer of the issues of moral and spiritual reality. But to decide that the human person is the ultimate measurer of all things is only a first step. The secularizer must then choose that dimension of human nature which will function as the means of measuring.

Arthur Holmes has distinguished four varieties of what is popularly referred to as "secular humanism": scientific, romanticist, existentialist, and Marxist.[7] If we set aside Marxism as a special case, because of its "collectivist" understanding of human reality, the differences among other three options can be seen as having to do with differing preferences regarding which aspect of human consciousness is to be construed as the primary "measuring" device. We might think of scientific humanists as emphasizing the cognitive, romanticists the affective, and existentialists the volitional.

To put it in these terms is to see something of why Calvinism views atheistic existentialism with special hostility. The Calvinist reads the serpentine challenge to divine authority as primarily a confrontation between *wills*. Human beings were created to submit to the divine will. And the serpent tempts them to look to their own wills as the ultimate source of moral authority.

Existentialism as Volitionalism

Before going any further with this analysis, though, we must ask whether it is all that obvious that Nietzsche and Sartre *are* volitionalists.

Nietzsche does present us with somewhat of a problem in this regard, since he can be found writing scornfully of the will as an invention of the "priests."[8] However, as Patrick Riley points out in his insightful study of the idea of will in political thought, Nietzsche operates with two different notions of will in his writings, one negative and the other positive. Riley nicely summarizes Nietzsche's negative treatment of will:

> Christian and Kantian good will is really bad in that men are counted as free so that they can be found guilty ("responsible") and then punished. Will as the capacity to be guilty is nothing but "the metaphysics of the hangman." The "moral world order" that one ought to will, according to the "calamitous spider" Kant, is the "foulest of theologian's artifices". . . .[9]

The good sense of will for Nietzsche is, as Riley puts it, "will as power, as creation, as mastery, as assertion"[10]—and this volitional activity is central to Nietzschean (super-) humanness.

It is also central to Sartrean selfhood. Sartre makes it clear, in his 1946 lecture, that creative will, will as mastery and assertion, is prior to both the affective and the cognitive:

> We are left alone, without excuse. That is what I mean when I say that man is condemned to be free. Condemned, because he did not create himself, yet is nevertheless at liberty, and from the moment that he is thrown into this world he is responsible for everything he does. The existentialist does not believe in the power of passion. He will never regard a grand passion as a destructive torrent upon which a man is swept into certain actions as by fate, and which, therefore is an excuse for them. He thinks that man is responsible

for his passion. Neither will an existentialist think that a man can find help through some sign being vouchsafed upon earth for his orientation: for he thinks that the man himself interprets the sign as he chooses. He thinks that every man, without any support or help whatever, is condemned at every instant to invent man.[11]

Emotivism as Consistent Modernity

It should be obvious by now why Zuidema posits an intimate link between Sartrean thought and the Serpent's manifesto. By insisting that the human will is the ultimate locus of moral creativity, Sartre is, like the snake of Genesis 3, challenging divine authority in a very direct and unambiguous manner.

But I want to push my examination of Zuidema's sense of outrage even a little further to point out some elements of agreement between Zuidema's complaints about Sartre and MacIntyre's critique of the Nietszchean emotivist self. There is an important point that Zuidema is making which might well be obscured by the heavy rhetoric he employs, a point that can be stated more effectively if it is seen in relationship to the more careful formulations offered by MacIntyre. I also want to suggest that, in the final analysis, Zuidema's sense of what the basic error of emotivism is takes a different form than MacIntyre's.

Both Zuidema and MacIntyre view the Nietzschean-Sartrean perspective as the most consistent scheme to emerge out of the intellectual environs of modernity. MacIntyre's case is compelling on this point, especially as it is expressed in his much discussed "Nietzsche or Aristotle?" chapter in *After Virtue*. There he argues that

> it was Nietzsche's historic achievement to understand more clearly than any other philosopher—certainly more clearly than his counterparts in Anglo-Saxon emotivism and continental existentialism—not only that what purported to be appeals to objectivity were in fact expressions of subjective will, but also the nature of the problems that this posed for moral philosophy.[12]

To be sure, MacIntyre is focusing exclusively on Nietzsche here. Indeed, he implies here, as he does elsewhere,[13] that Sartre (one of

Nietzsche's "counterparts in . . . continental existentialism") may not have been as consistent a thinker as Nietzsche was. I have no quarrel with this analysis. It may well be that Zuidema should have directed his tirade against Nietzsche rather than Sartre. But for my purposes here I will treat Zuidema's Sartre and MacIntyre's Nietzsche as emotivist bedfellows.

In insisting that Nietzsche is the one who saw most clearly where the various philosophical projects of modernity must lead, MacIntyre endorses—albeit in more reasonable and cautious terms than Nietzsche himself was capable of—the Nietzschean critique of other Enlightenment and post-Enlightenment thinkers. And in doing so, MacIntyre joins Nietzsche in viewing these other thinkers as operating with serious misunderstandings of the real character of their own projects and accomplishments.

Paul Ricoeur has given the title of "masters" in "the school of suspicion" to the trio composed of Nietzsche, Freud, and Marx,[14] and MacIntyre would undoubtedly concur in this way of characterizing Nietzsche's genius. But in MacIntyre's scheme Nietzsche has an advantage over Freud and Marx in that Nietzsche's assessments of the thinkers whom he criticizes are basically correct. Not that Nietzsche is always fair in the states of mind that he attributes to specific thinkers. When he refers, for example, to "that most deformed conceptual cripple there has ever been, the *great* Kant,"[15] Nietzsche can be taken to be suggesting at least two things about Kant: one, that Kant's views, considered in the context of the overall philosophical project which they were meant to expedite, were intellectually "crippling"; and the other, that Kant was in some personal sense insincere, an intellectual deceiver of sorts. MacIntyre concurs in the first kind of judgment, but he does not join Nietzsche in the latter sort of name-calling.

To be sure, MacIntyre does seem to come close to the second sort of practice at times, as when he treats the contemporary claim to "managerial effectiveness" as a "masquerade" that serves "to sustain and extend the authority and power of managers."[16] But McIntyre does not seem to think that the claim to managerial expertise is necessarily a part of a conscious deception. Contemporary claims to bureaucratic effectiveness are, he thinks, systematically false—or at least they are "rarely" true. But their falsehood has to do with the fact that they rest on more basic claims which are in fact ill-founded.[17] Contemporary people, including the managers themselves, have a difficult time acknowledging the falsehood because these more basic claims are the stuff of an Enlightenment-type project that they very much want to succeed. Nietzsche is to be admired, then, not for the contempt he shows for people who perpetrate Enlightenment confusions, but for his ability to identify bad arguments.

It may not be obvious that Zuidema has the same kind of respect for Sartre as MacIntyre has for Nietzsche, but in an important sense he does. Like MacIntyre, Zuidema views the emotivist's portrayal of the isolated, "sovereign" human self, a self whose ultimate choices are of necessity criterionless, as an exhibition of modern secularity at both its best and its worst. Best, because it is stripped of all the pretensions of earlier Enlightenment thinking—Sartre may be, for Zuidema, a spokesman for the Serpent, but it is at least a serpent who has come out of the closet. And worst, because it reveals a modernity that has no means of resisting, in MacIntyre's words, "the new dark ages which are already upon us."[18]

Thus far I have discussed the similarities between the ways in which Zuidema and Sartre evaluate emotivism. But there is an important difference. They offer different assessments of the *way* in which emotivism is fundamentally misguided.

For MacIntyre, Nietzsche's volitionalism is the most consistent expression of the modern spirit. But Nietzscheanism is nonetheless a false perspective. To recognize that Nietzsche's stance is the only consistent outworking of the Enlightenment project is, for MacIntyre, to see that we must go back to a very different view of human nature if we are to avoid emotivism.

But while Zuidema rejects emotivist volitionalism, he does not reject volitionalism as such. The Nietzschean-Sartrean version of existentialism, more than any other version of Enlightenment or post-Enlightenment thought, joins the issue between belief and unbelief at precisely the right point. The basic conflict is one of wills. It is this conviction, that in confronting Sartrean thought Christians are encountering sinful rebellion in its purest form, which accounts for the intensity of Zuidema's outrage against Sartre.

For both MacIntyre and Zuidema, emotivism is a lie, a masquerade. But for MacIntyre it is a lie in the sense of a rather straightforward falsehood, a claim that fails to comport with the way things are. For Zuidema it is a lie-as-perversion, a subtle twisting of the basic truths about moral and spiritual reality.

EMOTIVIST SELFHOOD AS *Imitatio Dei*

'Consciousness of God is self-consciousness, knowledge of God is self-knowledge," wrote Feurbach in *The Essence of Christianity*. "By his God thou knowest the man, and by the man the God; the two are identical."[19] Feurbach's formulations bear a striking resemblance to the opening lines of the *Institutes*, where Calvin argues that the knowledge of God and the knowledge of self are intimately related—indeed, Calvin says, "while joined by many bonds, which one precedes and brings forth the other is not easy to discern."[20]

Needless to say, there is grist in this comparison between Feurbach and Calvin for the mills of those who find "short steps" between the Reformation and blatant secularism. But I have already given my reasons for insisting that what may look like a short step to some thinkers is a very long distance for others of us. For Feurbach the knowledge of God and the knowledge of human selfhood are actually one thing; they are, he says, "identical," since God is in reality nothing more than "the expressed self of a man." For Calvin, of course, they are two distinct knowings which are directed toward two distinct realms of personhood—albeit realms that are "joined by many bonds."

The two ways of viewing the relationship between the knowledge of God and knowledge of self, as represented by the perspectives of Feurbach and Calvin, are in fact rival hypotheses for accounting for a datum that is recognized by both sides as begging for explanation: the intimate link between the ways in which deity and human selfhood are understood. Crucial to the disagreement between the two perspectives, as already noted, is the question of whether or not God exists. Each hypothesis is grounded in a very strong conviction on this issue, which has often made it very difficult for the two sides to draw upon each other's analyses.

But there *is* much for each to learn from the other. This is certainly true on the Christian side of things. Feuerbach insists that our ways of talking about God are really ways of talking about ourselves. Even though Christians disagree with this basic contention, we might still learn from the ways in which Feuerbachian analysis can illuminate what is going on when, from the believer's perspective, people confuse the worship of the true God with the service of those idols which they manufacture out of the stuff of their own anthropocentric designs. Thus Merold Westphal encourages Christians

> to recognize in the diatribes of Marx, Nietzsche, and Freud . . . the powerful parallel between their critique of religion and the biblical critique of religion. One has but to mention Jesus' critique of the Pharisees, Paul's critique of works righteousness, and James' critique of cheap grace to be reminded that the Christian faith has built into it a powerful polemic against certain kinds of religion, even if they are practiced in the name of the one true God.[21]

A similar theme is expressed by José Miguez Bonino, specifically with regard to the relationship of biblical religion to Marx's critique of religious belief. "Christianity and Marxism (in their original and most authentic intention)," he argues, "do not confront each other as respectively the defender and the accuser of religion and the gods"; rather they "share the same uncompromising rejection of 'mystifications' of the product of man's activity, whether material, mental or religious"—although, unlike Marxism, the biblical writers are "not primarily interested in rejecting atheism but idolatry."[22]

Martin Marty has observed that Calvin's insistence that "the human mind is an idol factory in constant operation" requires a correlative recognition that "the responsible believer's mind is also an idol-smasher."[23] The knack for idol-smashing must be exercised diligently in the Christian life, and not only because of the pull of depravity. The very fact that the knowledge of God and the knowledge of self are so closely, even inextricably, bound together means that even under the best of conditions our attempts to understand God will be closely intertwined with other very intimate impulses and relationships. It is not surprising, for example, that the love of God is sometimes described in ways that hint strongly of sexual erotic love, nor that our feelings toward God seem so closely bound up with the ways we experience parental authority in our lives.

These facts may seem to some to serve as strong evidence for various versions of the Feurbachian hypothesis. But they fit Calvin's formulation equally well: if the knowledge of God is closely bound to knowledge of ourselves, it would be strange indeed of our relationship to God showed no kinship with other forces and factors that have shaped our most intimate experiences of social reality.

The argument I have just been outlining is one that has been attended to by a number of writers in recent years, as is evidenced, for example, by my references to the helpful comments by Westphal and Miguez Bonino. What is not made as much of, though, is the way in which the argument can also be turned around. If what atheists say by way of criticizing religion as such can be used to understand the varieties of idolatry, then why can't what Christians say about the varieties of idolatry serve to illuminate the varieties of atheism? This is by no means an original proposal.[24] But it strikes me that it is the atheism-illuminating-idolatry flow that has gotten the most attention in recent years.

If we know that our relationship to God is so bound up with other intimate forces and relationships that it requires vigilance to keep ourselves from diluting or misdirecting the devotion that belongs to God alone, then it would seem plausible to think that people who deny God's existence will do so by confusing the religious impulse with some other force or relationship. If this is the case, then atheistic accounts can be expected to come in a number of versions, since atheists will differ among themselves over which force or relationship they will use as a means of "reducing" religion. Thus the varieties of "nothing but" claims about religion: "religion is nothing but suppressed sexuality"; "religion is nothing but disguised economics"; "religion is nothing but the reification of our deepest fears," and so on.

Sometimes, of course, these atheistic accounts are given credence by the ways in which they match up to notions of God that have become culturally prominent. Where God is viewed in highly rationalistic terms, it is tempting to argue that God is nothing but a mythic reinforcement for what can otherwise be known by reason alone. Or when God is viewed as the supreme Egotist whose psychic needs must be fed at all cost by everything and everyone in the universe, then it will probably not be long before someone suggests that God is nothing but an idea invented by powerful human egotists to keep the rest of us from concentrating on the feeding of our own psychic appetites.

In the 1960s when the union of the Unitarian and Universalist denominations was being consummated, there was a joke of sorts going around to the effect that the merger was a marriage of convenience, bringing together a group who believed that God is too good to damn us with one who insisted that we are too good to be damned. Actually, such marriages of conceptual convenience are not all that rare, and I am suggesting that they even take place, in subtle disguises, among people who claim not to believe in God. Very often the God whom the unbeliever is rejecting bears a very close resemblance to the image of humanness which that unbeliever is commending for our consideration.

Which brings us back to Nietzsche and Zuidema. Nietzsche is not *merely* discarding belief in God. He is extracting from a certain conception of God a key attribute which he then reinvests in human beings. The attribute in question is the one formulated, as already noted, by Patrick Riley: "will as power, as creation, as mastery, as assertion."

Actually each of these four terms used by Riley to describe Nietzsche's conception of will is helpful for understanding the ways in which Nietzsche's anthropology is parasitic on a specific theology. The will-to-power is, for Nietzsche, a deep power, the power of *creation ex nihilo*—which in turn frames his understandings of "mastery" and "assertion." The proper exercise of power for Nietzsche is not simply shoving others aside in the pursuit of self-interest, or the employment of the skills of "assertiveness training" in the search for personal happiness. It is the kind of being-in-command that dares to issue the creative divine *fiat*. As Nietzsche's Zarathustra boasts in discussing the writing of a new table of the law:

> I taught them all *my* art and aims: to compose into one and bring together what is fragment and riddle and dreadful chance in man—
>
> as poet, reader of riddles, and redeemer of chance, I taught them to create the future, and to redeem by creating—all that *was* past.

> To redeem that past of mankind and to transform every 'It was,' until the will says: 'But I willed it thus! So shall I will it—'
>
> this did I call redemption, this alone did I teach them to call redemption.[25]

And from *Twilight of the Idols*: "We deny God; in denying God, we deny accountability: only by doing *that* do we redeem the world."[26] Or as Nietzsche wrote to Burckhardt: "Dear Professor, when it comes right down to it I'd much rather have been a Basel Professor than God; but I didn't dare be selfish enough to forgo the creation of the world."[27]

Will-to-power also looms large in the Calvinist scheme. That sovereign will is central to Calvin's understanding of God's nature hardly needs arguing. And when that God turns to the conversion of human beings, it should come as no surprise that it is the human will that is the primary target of divine grace. Calvin introduces the chapter of the *Institutes* entitled "How God Works in Men's Hearts" by citing Augustine's comparison of the human will to a horse that gets its direction from its rider. Either God is giving the commands to the human will or the devil is doing so; and when the will is under Satan's control, the mind of the human being is "blinded":

> The blinding of the impious and all iniquities following from it are called "the works of Satan." Yet their cause is not to be sought outside man's will, from which the root of evil springs up, and on which rests the foundation of Satan's kingdom, that is, sin.[28]

Here we see the core of what is often thought of as Calvinist volitionalism. Will is central to humanness, the foundation on which sin itself rests. From it springs the roots of both righteousness and unrighteousness. And because will cannot be neutral, neither can the other human capacities which are often viewed as the roots of our most basic designs. When volition is in rebellion against God it draws the cognitive and the affective into its apostasy; intellect is blinded and feeling is corrupted.

Nietzsche's quarrel with Christianity is a dispute about who has the basic right to say, "I willed it thus!" in determining the course of human affairs—indeed, of the patterns of reality as such. His universe, like that of the Calvinist, is ordered by commands.

There is no dispute between the two parties about the appropriateness of a command ethic. An honest look at the brutal realities makes it clear that there could be no other kind of ethic. The question is not about whether commands constitute and sustain the cosmos. It is a deep confrontation over the question of who gets to do the commanding. The enmity between the Calvinist and the emotivist should come as no surprise.

A Gentler Portrayal

Does this mean that only Calvinist volitionalists can genuinely appreciate the stark contrast between emotivism and the Christian Gospel? The answer is no, and it is an important answer to be clear about.

It is difficult to find a better book about the character of contemporary, post-modern godlessness than John Courtney Murray's *The Problem of God*. Murray, like Zuidema, sees atheistic existentialism as getting at the heart of the matter in its portrayal of the differences between belief and unbelief. Father Murray sets the stage for understanding this portrayal by means of an insightful discussion of God's response to Moses' query about God's name in Exodus 3—the divine answer that is most commonly rendered in English as "I am who I am."

Murray rejects two traditional interpretations of this divine self-designation. One is the suggestion that God is making an ontological claim as "the Absolutely Existent One to whose being there is no limit or restriction," as one whose "very Name is Being." The other account sees God as offering a brief formula for understanding his causal relationship to the cosmos—"I make to be whatever comes to be."[29]

Murray's preferred interpretation sees God as promising his own supportive presence to those who trust him: "I shall be there, with you, in power," or more literally, "I shall be there as who I am shall I be there."[30] This divine pledge captures a theme that is, for Murray, at the heart of biblical religion. The "problem" of God as it is raised on the pages of the Scriptures, both Hebrew and Christian, is not primarily one of "essence and existence" but of "the historical-existential order."[31] When the biblical writers worry about God it is not about whether God exists as such, but whether God is existentially present, whether the divine power is available for those who have put their trust in the Lord's mercy.

With this as background, Murray insists that for the thinkers of post-modernity, of whom Nietzsche is a key figure, "the problem of God has come back in its biblical mode of position."[32] Murray's own summation of the religious accomplishments of post-modern thinkers cannot be improved upon:

> We who say we believe in God have some reason to be grateful to these men, the heirs of modernity, who have managed to better modernity's instruction. They have done us the service of bringing to the surface, so that it is all but palpable, our own problem, the religious problem, the human problem. They have stated the issue with rather appalling clarity, in a phrase calculated to shock us into awareness of its urgency. They have said that God is dead. So the affirmations clash. For we say that God is living.
>
> The issue is drawn. Which is the myth and which is the reality? Is the myth in Nietzsche or in the New Testament? Is it in Marx or in Moses? Is it in Sartre of Paris or in Paul of Tarsus? Is God dead, as the prophet of the post-modern age proclaimed, or is he still the living God of more ancient prophecy, immortal in his being as He Who Is, deathlessly faithful to his promise to be with us all the days, even to the end of the epoch within which both the modern and the post-modern ages represent only moments in a longer dialectic of history?[33]

It is interesting that there is nothing in these remarks of commands and wills. Murray chooses instead to view the dispute as an argument about the divine *presence*. When Zuidema confronts the emotivists his first impulse is to say, "You are not in charge." Murray's is to respond with, "You are not alone."

To be sure, there is no need to choose between these modes of approach; they need not be seen as radically opposed accounts of the differences between Christian faith and emotivism. The reason why human beings are not in charge of the universe is because they are not alone in it; and one very fitting way of responding to the divine presence is by an act of submission.

But is there something even more telling in the way that Murray makes his case? Is it possible that while the emotivist and

Calvinist might be strongly inclined to see their conflict as having to do with a dispute about wills, this way of viewing the situation does not really probe to the heart of the matter?

There is something to be said for this line of questioning, although it is not necessary to abandon completely the Calvinist emphasis on volition. Indeed, I am convinced that Calvinism, at least healthy Calvinism, does just that: it places an *emphasis* on volition without endorsing a thoroughgoing volitionalism. It is also important, I think, to be clear about this fact. A divine command perspective that is presented in terms of pervasive volitionalism runs into many problems, not the least being the appearance of harshness and arbitrariness.

The Calvinist movement, from its beginnings, was aware of this danger and did a number of things to avoid it. It was not always successful—much that has gone by the name of Calvinism deserves to be accused of harshness and arbitrariness. But it is significant that efforts were made to provide a larger, and "softening," context for the stress that is placed on will-to-will encounter. This context will be explored in the next chapter.

6

GOD THE POLITICIAN

IN THE ACCOUNT OF REFORMATION political thought that he wrote for *The Cambridge Modern History*, J. N. Figgis suggested that John Calvin and Thomas Hobbes can be seen as operating with similar conceptions of authority, in which "theology . . . goes hand in hand with politics." Calvin's God, Figgis insisted, "is the ideal type of absolute monarch" and Hobbes's Leviathan "owed more of his non-moral attributes than the author knew" to such an idea of God. Indeed, Hobbes's scheme "is the political counterpart of the Calvinistic theology."[1]

This is not an especially shocking suggestion. We have become accustomed in recent years to accounts of Reformation social thought which highlight continuities with other periods. A noteworthy effort in this regard is that of Quentin Skinner, who portrays a continuous movement of political thought from Marsiglio of Padua through the Reformers to John Locke.[2] Indeed, such continuities are often emphasized in a manner these days that makes it difficult to find any places to insert the traditional period-markers.

The proposed connection between Calvin and Hobbes has a fascination, though, for reasons that do not hinge on the acceptance of any elaborate thesis about historical continuities. The apparent fittingness of placing Calvinist and Hobbesian conceptions of authority side by side has strong similarities to the linking of Calvin to Nietzsche, which we have already discussed. But it is worth pursuing the Hobbesian connection in its own right, since it affords a better reference point than Nietzscheanism does for considering the explicitly political dimensions of Calvinist thought.

And it is important that we do look directly at the political agenda in considering this particular strand of Reformation think-

94

ing about divine commands. We are all indebted—at least those of us who study ethics in the Anglo-American world—to Alasdair MacIntyre for his consistent emphasis on the need to evaluate ethical theories by taking into consideration their correlative sociologies. Ethical accounts of duty, goodness, and virtue inevitably suggest (even if only implicitly) ways of organizing social reality; these accounts must be assessed by looking at, among other things, the social practices and institutions which would be the appropriate incarnations of their theoretical prescriptions.

As a religious ethic, Calvinism is eminently studiable in this regard, since Calvin and his followers have seldom been shy about giving concrete institutional shape to their intellectual accounts of the good life.[3] Their efforts to influence and shape societal practices provide us with important evidence to consider in our attempt to understand and evaluate Calvinism as a concrete manifestation of divine command ethics.

But there is another good reason to look here at Calvinist political themes. It is in this particular area of thought and practice that we can observe Calvinists actually charting out how far they are willing to go in following through on their undeniably voluntarist impulses. This is what we will be especially looking for in this chapter; it will also be necessary, of course, to sketch in some of the details of the overall political perspective in order to be sure that we have an accurate grasp on the context in which they were testing their own limits in this regard.

THE HOBBESIAN "FEEL" OF CALVINISM

Figgis is surely right in noticing that Calvinist thought has a Hobbesian "feel" to it. An obvious point of comparison lies in the fact that both Hobbesian politics and Calvinist soteriology feature the concept of sovereignty. The Calvinist answer to the question, "How does an individual get right with God?" can be plausibly viewed as a vigorous attempt to celebrate the unimpeachable control of the divine will over the salvific process from start to finish. The classic formulae of the Synod of Dordrecht (1618–19), popularly summarized by the "TULIP" acronym (for: Total depravity, Unconditional election, Limited atonement, Irresistible grace, Perseverance of the saints) can easily be spelled out in these terms: human beings are totally incapable of initiating the redemptive operation; that operation, if it is to get started at all, is a divine elective option; when God chooses to negotiate the atoning arrangement there is no salvific "waste factor"; God's efforts are irresistible; and no divine transaction ever gets cancelled. In short: what God wants, God gets; and what God gets, God keeps.

Thus the rudimentary soteriological picture in Calvinism: God's sovereign will overwhelming the human will; naked divine power confronting naked human powerlessness. With this picture before us, it is difficult to fault Figgis for offering his suggestion. There is surely something fitting about the observation that such a view is very Hobbesian, and that Calvin and Hobbes set forth a conception of authority in which it is difficult to untangle the theological from the political.

In conceding this much to Figgis, though, I mean to be placing considerable weight on the notion of *rudimentarity*. The picture of Calvin as a proto-Hobbesian makes excellent sense when we focus on some of the unadorned basics in the Calvinist scheme. I want to insist, however, that in this case first impressions are somewhat deceptive, especially if we want a fair assessment of the Calvinist contribution to political thought.

The fact is that Calvin—and certainly many of his early disciples—regularly pushed the Reformed account of things beyond that which was suggested by a focus on the mere rudiments of Calvinism. This seems obvious in the case of Calvin's assessment of the noetic capacities of unregenerate human beings. It is not at all difficult to find Calvin offering very dismal accounts of the ability, or the inability, of the unsaved thinker to comprehend the basic contours and issues of created reality. But Calvin is usually quick to qualify these negative assessments in significant ways.[4] Even a very cursory survey of Calvin's citations in the *Institutes* reveals the great respect he had for the writings of, say, Aristotle, Cicero, and Seneca.

Similar kinds of qualifications are introduced as Calvin and his disciples develop their understanding of political authority. While the initial Calvinist accounts of political life exhibit Hobbesian tones, Calvinist political theory develops along very non-Hobbesian lines. Nor is this due to any blatant contradiction between rudimentary Calvinism and its more developed formulations. Rather, while the Calvinist, or Reformed, scheme begins with an impulse that has a similar "feel" to the Hobbesian picture, that impulse turns out to be more complex than it might appear to be on first impression.

THE VOLUNTARIST IMPULSE

In his illuminating study of Calvin's political thought, David Little employs the notion of a "new order" as his organizing theme. Calvin was exploring the possibilities for the re-ordering of both "the organization and understanding of social life."[5] In so doing, it was necessary for him to depart from the conceptions of "order" contained in the Stoicism and humanism with which he was very familiar, to say nothing of the teachings of much of medieval Catholicism. Calvin rejected the kind of view of reality, Little argues, where human beings "in ethical obedience can only adjust to the inexorable, eternal law of nature," the sort of view which lacks "any kind of basis for a revolutionary reordering of things."[6]

In spelling out Calvin's alternative conception of moral and political order, Little rightly makes much of the strong *voluntarism* in Calvin's thought, assuming the same understanding of "voluntarism" that Francis Oakley employs when he places Calvin in the camp of those who see "the moral or judicial natural law as grounded in the will rather than the reason of God."[7] As Little puts it, proper obedience is, for Calvin, directed toward "the 'free will' of God as the source of order," and this human response of obedience is *itself* a voluntary one which "'mirrors' the freedom of God."[8]

This emphasis on the naked will-to-will character of the central divine-human encounter is necessary for seeing clearly how Calvin was distancing himself from the sort of medieval account associated with, for example, Thomism. Skinner describes St. Thomas's scheme as a "vision of a universe ruled by a hierarchy of laws."[9] But this is a bit too imprecise to serve as a helpful basis for contrasting the Thomist and the voluntarist perspectives, since Calvinists also tended rather quickly to fill their universe with laws. It is more accurate to say that the Thomist vision features a hierarchy of legal *systems*. While Calvinist voluntarism featured a revelatory encounter in which a naked divine will issued legal commands to a naked human will, the Thomist preferred a picture in which both the divine and human wills were already immersed in law prior to the presentation of the biblical imperatives: the revealed legislation in the Scriptures, that which comprises the *lex divina*, is itself a specification of that primary law, the *lex aeterna*, which is God's own everlasting normative point of reference; and the biblical laws are in turn understood by human beings in light of the *lex naturalis* to which they have extrabiblical noetic access.

As a voluntarist, Calvin wants to focus on the revealed legislation of the Scriptures as a free and direct address from sovereign divine will to defenseless human will. The proper human response in the context of this will-to-will confrontation is not so much understanding as it is surrender.

It is not surprising, then, that we find in Calvinism an impulse toward a political account in which surrender to empowered will is a highly valued ethical commodity. But the proper nature or character of Christian surrender in the political arena becomes a central concern for Calvinism. There is a very good reason why this gains the status of a problem requiring a solution: the kind of surrender required in the political arena is not an unmediated obedience to the *divine* will; here the immediate object of surrender is the will of the *human ruler*. The Calvinist fondness for the surrender of human wills allows for no easy detour, it seems, around the question of the proper relationship between biblically revealed law and the positive laws of a specific human society.

The theme of surrender of will is obviously very much on Calvin's mind in those concluding pages of the *Institutes* where he writes about political authority. And the voluntarist strain in his thought makes a rather simple formulation of the case very attractive to him: since the Scriptures call human beings to surrender to the divine will, and since the divine will as expressed in the Scriptures calls us to surrender to the will of human political authority, then surrender to earthly rulers is simply one of the ways in which we are called to surrender to the will of God.

But as tempting as this simple formulation is for Calvin, it will not do. In order for Calvin to see its inadequacies he does not even need to step out of his voluntarist framework. The simple-minded insistence on uncritical surrender to human rulers is unsatisfactory precisely *for* voluntarist reasons. The scriptural call is for human beings to obey the revealed will of God. The human rulers are themselves human beings who must surrender to what God has commanded in the written Word. Since it is a matter of empirical observation that human rulers commit serious offenses against the divine will, it is important to be aware of the fact that Christians can sometimes be faced with unavoidable choices between obedience to the divine will and subjection to political authority. There is no mistaking Calvin's verdict on this subject, as he expresses it in the opening sentences of the last section of the *Institutes*:

> But in that obedience which we have shown to be due the authority of rulers, we are always to make this exception, indeed, to observe it as primary, that such obedience is never to lead us away from obedience to him, to whose will the desires of all kings ought to be subject, to whose decrees all their commands ought to yield, to whose majesty their scepters ought to be submitted. And how absurd it would be that in satisfying men you should incur the displeasure of him for whose sake you obey men themselves! The Lord, therefore, is the King of Kings, who, when he has opened his sacred mouth, must alone be heard, before all and above all men; next to him we are subject to those men who are in authority over us, but only in him. If they command anything against him, let it go unesteemed.[10]

Skinner claims to find at least four arguments that the Reformers and their immediate disciples utilize to justify various resistance-strategies: the "inferior magistrates" theory of the Lutherans, the Calvinist appeal to "ephoral" authority, the "private law" defense of individual resistance, and the constitutionalist argument.[11] But earlier in his exposition Skinner notes that Calvin also employs the "exception" argument quoted above, and that Calvin's use of this notion pre-dates the more elaborate account suggested by his notion of "ephoral" authority.[12]

It is no accident that this "exception" argument serves to express the initial Calvinist impulse toward resistance. This appeal to exceptions in the pattern of submission to earthly authorities is unavoidable for voluntarists, precisely because it is an argument that can be formulated in voluntarist terms. Indeed, it can be thought of as a kind of "weightier will" argument. No human will, even that of the most powerful earthly potentate, can rival the authority of the divine will. And this lesson is spelled out explicitly in the Scriptures: biblically informed voluntarists can hardly avoid the implications of the stories of the acts of resistance performed by Moses' mother and Daniel or, to cite Calvin's own example, of Hosea's complaint against the citizens who obeyed the wicked commands of King Jeroboam.

But Calvin does not stop with the appeal to strictly voluntarist premises. He points to a pattern of thought that takes the case well beyond any sort of simple-minded voluntarism.

Softening the Voluntarism

Little's study of Calvin illuminates the voluntarist strain in Calvin's thought. It is interesting to note, though, that Little chooses to employ the idea of a voluntarist "moment" in Calvinism.[13] This apt characterization conforms nicely to Frederick Carney's wise counsel that we not be too quick to read the consistent voluntarism and individualism that we find clearly exhibited in Hobbes and Locke back into the early Calvinist political writings.[14]

Beginning with Calvin himself, Calvinist political thinkers did much to soften the impact of the voluntarism that seems to dominate their rudimentary formulations. I will point to four softening factors in their writings here. The first two items, which I will not deal with in as much detail as the second pair, serve a parallel function in Calvinist soteriology, and it will be helpful to introduce them with a brief look at the soteriological context.

Earlier I described Calvinism's rudimentary soteriological depiction as featuring a naked will-to-will encounter, with sovereign divine power confronting human defenselessness. One factor which serves to hold the voluntarist impulse in check here is the Reformed emphasis on *covenant*. To be sure, the covenant idea can itself be spelled out in thoroughly voluntarist terms, as any Hobbesian will insist. But this is not the pattern of its use in the mainstream of Calvinism. What the covenant theme accomplishes is to surround God's sovereign will with a divine character in which fidelity is a prominent feature. The God who overwhelms our depraved wills with sovereign grace is a deity who honors commitments and who calls human beings to exhibit consistent patterns of behavior. This emphasis has the effect of virtually eliminating any notion of arbitrariness in the way the divine will deals with those who are the beneficiaries of electing mercies.

There can be no doubt that the doctrine of the covenant of grace had this "taming" effect in Puritanism. Perry Miller notes that the covenant concept had the effect of removing from Puritan theology

> the practical difficulty of conceiving of the Deity as a definite character . . . for in His contracts with man He has, voluntarily, of his own sovereign will and choice, consented to be bound and delimited by a specific program . . . For all ordinary purposes He has transformed Himself in the covenant into a God vastly different from the inscrutable Divinity of pure Calvinism.[15]

A passage which Miller quotes from Preston's *New Covenant* is especially striking in this regard:

> how great a mercie it is, that the glorious God of Heauen and Earth should be willing to enter into *Couenant*, that he should be willing to indent with vs, as it were, that he should be willing to make himselfe a debtor to vs. If we consider it, it is an exceeding great mercie, when wee thinke thus with our selues, he is in heauen, and wee are on earth; hee the glorious God, we dust and ashes; he the Creator, and we but creatures; and yet he is wiling to enter into Couenant, which implyes a kinde of equality betweene vs.[16]

The second softening factor is *law*. The special emphasis that Calvinists place on the role of biblical law as a positive guide in the Christian life, as evidenced in the famous "third use" of the law, has done much to mitigate the effects of soteriological voluntarism. There is no mistaking the fact that the God who is associated with this emphasis on law is very fond of lawlike consistency in the lives of the elect. And it is difficult to acknowledge the premium placed on lawfulness in one's own life of obedience to the divine will without also gaining the impression that the lawlike consistency to which human beings are called corresponds to a lawfulness that resides in the very heart of the divine Redeemer.

The important functions performed by these two themes—

covenant and law—in mainline Calvinism become obvious when we look at the varieties of Calvinism from which they are absent. There is a strong strain in British and North American Puritanism in which God's redemptive dealings with human beings are viewed as a thoroughly unpredictable business. This way of construing divine agency is preserved, for example, among contemporary adherents to that brand of Dutch Reformed thought that describes itself as "experiential" (*bevindelijke*) Calvinism. These worshippers cannot find any "objective" reference points for gaining the assurance that they are numbered among the elect, since any such criteria would limit God's free—read: arbitrarily dispensed—grace.[17]

It is no accident that proponents of this brand of Reformed thought object to the way in which the ideas of covenant and law function in mainstream Calvinism. To be sure the two terms show up in their own theological formulations. But for them "law" and "covenant" tend to be associated with a God who issues rather disconnected fiat-type commands which exhibit little by way of a unifying, rationally coherent, pattern.

The themes of both covenant and law are put to important political use in early Calvinism. Carney illustrates the social use of the covenant theme nicely in his succinct summary of the way in which this theme functions for Althusius:

> Basically, covenant is the agreement of an association, or its leaders, to conduct the life of that association in keeping with the primordial essence of all true group life, as well as with the particular expressions of this essence as adopted by the association in respect to the circumstances of its time and place. Thus the social and political covenants are agreements to conform to common law, and to establish and conform to such proper laws as shall seem best designed to express and fulfill the common law.[18]

Note that as Althusius views the situation, the covenant is not an agreement on the part of human beings that they will obey the arbitrary commands of a divine despot. Instead, it commits them to abiding by laws that facilitate the realization of prevenient social designs. God's commands are viewed as directing people toward a lawful conformity to creational purposes.

As Carney observes, most early Calvinist writers operate with some sort of appreciation for the role of "natural law" in political life, although their formulations suggest a variety of metaphysical and epistemological nuances. A careful reading of the Calvinist literature reveals a broad consensus regarding what Calvin himself described as the "fact that the law of God which we call the moral law is nothing else than a testimony of natural law and of that conscience which God has engraved upon the minds of men."[19] Calvinist reactions to other sorts of natural law doctrines are not motivated by any obvious desire to deny this fact; rather they are energized by an eagerness to grant at least equal attention to the fact that human depravity impairs our ability to grasp and honor the dictates of natural law. What may appear at first to be a strong bibliomonism in the Calvinist treatment of law turns out to be more accurately characterized as bibliocentrism.

As noted earlier, Skinner's description of Thomism as a "vision of a universe ruled by a hierarchy of laws" is not helpful for distinguishing between the Thomist and voluntarist perspectives. Certainly many Calvinists, especially those with a fondness for the idea of "creation ordinances," have depicted the basic mode of God's relationship to the creation as essentially a legislative one. Theirs too is a law-filled universe. On such an account, divine law extends far beyond the confines of a decalogic legislation—although, again, proper noetic access to the broader sweep of divine law must begin with humble submission to the Sinai law-giver.

And it is this premium placed on humble submission to the divine Sovereign who speaks to the church through the Scriptures which brings my next two softening factors to the fore. The first is the Calvinists' interpretation of the thirteenth chapter of Romans, which was for them the Bible's central political passage. The second is their own experience of authority and decision making in the context of the worshipping community.

There are other items which could also be considered. But these two matters deserve more careful and nuanced attention than they have often received in studies of Calvinist politics. And they represent the kinds of issues that ought to be viewed with special seriousness by those of us who are convinced of the integral and formative role of theological conviction in Calvinist political thought.[20]

In a sense, both of these items that I choose to focus on here have to do with the relationship of ecclesiology to political thought.

I will not review here the detailed discussion—conducted by Figgis, Oakley, and others[21]—of the degree to which Calvinist political accounts were directly influenced by earlier debates regarding the merits of conciliarism. I do want to suggest, however, that the kinds of ecclesiological perspectives that had been considered prior to the Reformation manifest a typology that can also be used to sort out the various options which Calvinist thinkers considered as they attempted to ascertain the proper locus of political authority. And I want to insist, finally, that the most "direct" influence of ecclesiology on their political thought had to do with something much more intimate than the attractiveness of ideas that had been debated in previous centuries. Their efforts to articulate a theory of political organization had profound links to their experiences as Christians who were themselves seeking to be re-formed by the "polity" of the ecclesial Body of Christ.

Patterns of Government

There can be no doubt that Romans 13:1–6 is the key biblical reference point for Calvinists as they attempt to discern the will of God for political life. Calvin refers to it eleven times in chapter 20 of the *Institutes*, and it figures prominently in the political writings of Beza, Knox, Buchanan, Gillespie, Rutherford, and others. Indeed, even though I will not pursue such an investigation here, I am convinced that a detailed study of the history of Reformed interpretations of this passage would be a fruitful project. I will limit my attention here, however, to the fact that Calvinist reflection on the political implications of Romans 13 dealt with a framework of options similar to the one generated by earlier ecclesiological disputes.

The question of the primary locus of churchly authority had been debated for several centuries prior to the Reformation. To be sure, all parties agreed that in one crucial sense of "primary" Christ alone is the primary authority of the church. But they found much to argue about in considering this question: When Christ imparts his authority to the human ecclesial community, where—in the most basic sense—does that authority reside? Where is it directly deposited?

Reduced to its simplest terms, the discussion produced four possible candidates: the pope, the larger company of ecclesial officials, the even larger company of the faithful, and the individual Christian. This last option was usually raised for the sole purpose of denying its attractiveness. Each of the others, though, had serious defenders.

Needless to say, each option lends itself to different nuances: advocates of an absolute papacy might argue among themselves over the person-versus-office distinction; conciliarists can divide over the question whether, say, cardinals always actually possess their authority or whether it only reverts to them from the papacy when they are meeting in council; and advocates of "whole church" authority must decide whether the only thing the broad company of the faithful can do with its power is to delegate it to ecclesial officials. But even given the variations that result from introducing these assorted delegatings and revertings, the four-option typology remains intact if we keep our focus on the basic question of where the divinely deposited authority primarily resides.

The political version of that question was a very important matter for early Calvinist thinkers. J. D. Douglas introduces his narrative of the Scottish Covenanting tradition by observing that when the Scottish Reformers turned from the narrower soteriological agenda to a broader address to political issues they added to their basic watchword, "None but Christ saves," the political corollary, "None but Christ reigns."[22] However, Douglas seems to forget his own helpful characterization here when he raises the "curious point," later in his discussion, that the same Scottish Calvinists who show such disdain for actual human kings often exhibit strong royalist notions in their theorizings about political authority.[23] But isn't it likely that it was precisely because of their high understanding of the character of Christ's reign that they could display both an affection for the royal office and a distrust of human beings who surround themselves with the trappings of regal power? One way of opposing monarchical government is by having a conception of royalty that is so exalted that no one less than a deity could rightly lay claim to the title.

But the same recognition of human failings that made some Calvinists wary of human monarchies also reinforced their conviction that human government is not dispensable. The fact of human depravity, then, makes the delegation of power to human beings both a necessary and a problematic matter for Calvinists. It is necessary because sinful humanity needs coercive authority for the proper ordering of communal life. And it is problematic because only the divine sovereign can be expected to put strongly concentrated power to consistently righteous use. (Unlike those who make promiscuous use of Lord Acton's dictum, Calvinists are not likely to believe that it is absolute power *as such* that corrupts; but they do have grounds for worrying about the placing of absolute power into *human* hands.)

One way of reading the development of Calvinist thought on the question of the locus of political authority might employ a model of "progressive descent" through the four levels suggested by the analogy to the ecclesiological debate. It might be argued that Calvin was by instinct a strong monarchicalist, but that in the final pages of the *Institutes* he turns to the ephoral option, where the second layer of decision-makers is viewed as the primary source of the monarch's delegated authority. Then the next generation of Calvinists—especially the Huguenots and the Scots—came to insist that the ephoral officials themselves receive their authority from the larger populace. And it might even be argued that for some Calvinists this people-as-a-whole populism soon gave way to a thoroughgoing individualism.

This picture seems to be, roughly, the one with which Skinner operates. He depicts Calvin as only very reluctantly acknowledging limits on obedience to monarchs[24] and then, after detailing the views of those Huguenot, Scottish, and English Calvinists who view the primary locus of authority in the ephor-populace range, Skinner seems eager to celebrate what he sees as the "almost anarchic" elements in George Buchanan's account of authority.[25]

But this is not a satisfactory picture of the development of Calvinist thought. There are better reasons for adopting what I will call a "middle range" account, a view that sees the Calvinist movement committed at every point to an understanding of government which presupposes that the primary locus of authority is found somewhere in the middle region—between monarch and the individual citizen—occupied by second-rank magistrates and the people-as-a-whole.

For one thing, Skinner's "progressive descent" type account requires him to insist on a tone of "concession" and "conditionality" in those passages where Calvin advocates something less than full obedience to monarchs. Skinner notes, for example, that Calvin says that "aristocracy, or a system compounded of aristocracy and democracy, far excels" any other form of government.[26] But Skinner acknowledges this comment only by way of insisting that Calvin "concedes" the point here in an "Aristotelian vein"[27]—thus treating Calvin's observation as both reluctantly offered and highly derivative.

But Calvin actually seems to make his point with considerable enthusiasm, and with an appeal to the authority of, not Aristotle, but the God of the Old Testament. The preference for aristocracy-democracy, he insists, is not only "proved by experience," but "also the Lord confirmed it by his authority when he ordained among the Israelites" a pattern of government characterized by "aristocracy bordering on democracy."[28]

When Skinner turns to the penultimate paragraph of the *Institutes*, the "ephor" passage, he seems willing to grant the integrity of Calvin's "antimonarchical sympathies." But even here Skinner sees Calvin as manifesting a "characteristic caution" in a passage that is "extremely oblique and conditional in tone."[29] Skinner obviously does not intend here to move far from his earlier insistence that "Calvin is at all times a master of equivocation, and while his basic commitment is unquestionably to a theory of nonresistance, he does introduce a number of exceptions into his argument."[30] Having established that as his framework for sorting out the data, Skinner deals with apparent counterexamples by making much of Calvin's grudging "concessions" and the reluctance of his "tone."

On the other end of the scale of "descent," it is necessary for Skinner to make much of individualistic tendencies that he finds in George Buchanan, whom he treats as the Reformed thinker whose thought serves as a kind of Calvinist threshold into Lockeanism. Skinner finds Buchanan saying at one point, for example, that the right to oppose tyranny is the possession of "every individual citizen"—a claim that Skinner interprets as a move toward an "almost anarchic" position. It is not clear, however, that Buchanan is doing anything more in this comment than appealing to the

long-standing "private law" type argument for individual resistance. It *is* clear, though, that Buchanan also insists that the
authority to depose a ruler is, in Skinner's own paraphrase of
Buchanan, "lodged at all times . . . with the whole body of the
people"—an insistence that Skinner manages to downplay by as-
serting that Buchanan is here "[r]everting to his more scholastic
mood."[31]

Furthermore, the impression given by Skinner that Buchanan's "almost anarchic" view is the logical-historical preparation of
a Calvinist threshold to Lockeanism would have been much more
difficult to sustain had he clearly placed Buchanan in the proper
historical sequence, where Buchanan's contribution is followed by
the extensive, and decidedly non-individualistic, writings of Althusius, Gillespie, and Rutherford.

For these and other reasons, the progressive-descent model is
less than convincing. The fact is that all early Calvinist writers on
the subject, from Calvin through Rutherford, located the primary
depository of human political authority in the middle range. And
their interpretations of Romans 13 reflected this fact. They certainly did not think that the Apostle was advocating strong mon-
archism. Nor did they hold to the view that the citizenry was required to submit in an unquestioning manner to a political power
that is transmitted directly from God to monarchs or second-level
magistrates.

What, then, was the Calvinists' understanding of Romans 13?
Several aspects of their viewpoint can be highlighted. First, they
took the Romans passage to be teaching them that political authority, wherever it resides primarily, has its origins in God. They did
not view this text as telling them *where* God primarily deposits this
authority—that is a matter to be decided by appeals to experience
and other passages of Scripture. But wherever that power resides, it
is a God-given power.

Second, they viewed God's "ordaining" of specific officials as
a transaction that makes use of human processes of decision making, even of exercises in popular sovereignty. Samuel Rutherford
makes this point nicely:

> all Royal power . . . is only in *God*; but it is in the people as the
> instrument: and when the people maketh *David their King at*

Hebron, in that very same act, *God* by the people using their free suffrages and consent maketh *David King at Hebron*.

Nor is this to be understood, Rutherford continues, as Israel consenting to the "prior act of *God's* making David King"; rather it is *in* "Israel's act of freely electing him to be King" that God achieves the king-making.[32]

Third, there is a Calvinist consensus that the idea of an "ordained" magistrate can in no way be used to justify tyrannous rule. Rutherford expresses this consensus well when he affirms "with Buchanan, that Paul, Rom. 13, [is] speaking of the office and duty of *good magistrates*, and that the text speaketh nothing of an absolute *king*, nothing of a Tyrant."[33]

Fourth, there is nonetheless a kind of God-given dignity to political office that is not merely transmitted to it by acts of human delegation. This is a difficult point to get clear about, but it is important to acknowledge. B. Katherine Brown is helpful in this regard in her analysis of the understanding of authority in American Puritanism. She reports that John Cotton strongly insisted that "the ultimate power should be in the people"; but he also expressed the clear conviction that officials in the Bay Colony, "once chosen, were . . . spokesmen of God, and the laws, once made, were a reflection of divine guidance." Brown contrasts this view with "modern politics" where elected officials "are looked upon as the spokesmen of the people and the laws are the reflection of the social and economic fabric of society."[34]

The Puritan theme she is illuminating here is also clearly present in earlier Calvinism. Again Rutherford:

> There is a Dignity materiall in the people scattered, they being many representations of God and his Image, which is in the King also, and formally more as King, he being indued with formall Magistraticall and publick Royal Authority, in the former regard this or that man is inferiour to the King, because the King hath that same remainder of the Image of God that any private man hath, and something more, he hath a politicke resemblance of the King of the Heavens, being a little God, and so is above any one man.[35]

Political officials derive their "glory" from three factors, all of which are touched upon here by Rutherford. The ruler as an individual human being bears the divine image. And she or he also receives something of the collective image possessed by the people-as-a-whole and delegated to those who exercise public authority. But there is also a sense in which human rulers reflect, in their exercise of political power, the glory of God's authority. To be sure, this last kind of imaging, this "politicke resemblance of the King of the Heavens," does not serve to justify blind submission to rulers on the part of the citizenry. But its recognition does manifest a Calvinist sense of the dignity of political office that is, as Brown rightly observes, missing in much of contemporary political life.

LEARNING THE LESSONS OF POLITY

In his 1979 Presidential Address to the Canadian Political Science Association, Kenneth D. McRae complained about the contemporary influence of Hobbes's understanding of politics as "a science that suppresses or subordinates every major source of human variation: ethnic identity, social orders and classes, individual temperament."[36] McRae pleaded for a recognition of alternative currents in political reflection: "Should we," he asked, "devise an alternative curriculum in political thought that would stress Althusius over Bodin, Montesquieu over Rousseau, von Gierke over Hegel, Acton over Herbert Spencer, Abraham Kuyper over T. H. Green, Karl Renner and Otto Bauer over Marx and Engels? In short, have we been studying the wrong thinkers, and even the wrong countries?"[37]

It is no accident, I think, that at least two professing Calvinists made it onto McRae's list of non-Hobbesian theorists. But the recent literature on Calvinist political thought provides abundant evidence that it is not enough simply to begin *studying* such thinkers. We must also be willing to alter the agenda of political questions that we bring to such a study if we are to avoid the very real sin of treating a movement like Calvinism as a mere bridge, or threshold, to highly secularized thought.

The tyranny of asking the wrong questions is nicely illustrated in J. W. Gough's classic study of social contract theory. A decision about the merits of the social contract idea rests, Gough argues, on a fundamental choice: "In the last resort the issue is between those who regard the rights and powers of government as ultimately derived from the inherent rights and powers of individuals, and those who would deny this and maintain that authority belongs of right to the state itself."[38]

For the early Calvinists this is clearly a false choice. For one thing, the populace as a candidate for the primary locus of political authority cannot, in their schemes, be collapsed into either the state or discrete individuality. But even more poignant would be Calvinism's insistence on the kind of richness of associational life that Carney has so helpfully explicated. The plurality of associational forms—family, guild, university, and the like—cannot be correctly viewed as gaining the right to exist from the suffrage of political authorities; such entities exist by virtue of God's extrapolitical, and extra-individual, creating designs.

God's social purposes in the world go far beyond the relationship between individuals and political governments. And this is nowhere more obvious for Christians than in the life of the ecclesial community.

I have already touched on the scholarly discussions of the influence of previous ecclesiological debates on Calvinist analyses of political authority. This way of exploring the links between ecclesiology and politics is a welcome diversion from the almost exclusive attention given by many scholars to "church-versus-state" conflicts when dealing with Calvinist social thought.

This is not to say that there are no historical reasons for attending to the ways in which Calvinists tried to coordinate churchly teachings with political programs. But to focus myopically on the way in which Calvinists attempted to reduce the tensions between churchly and governmental *policies* is to miss out on some basic matters that cannot be subsumed under that heading. One such issue is the way in which Reformed Christians sensed a call from God to integrate the *roles* associated with a variety of communal contexts.

The question of how to coordinate the ecclesial and political roles, for example, seem to be very much on the minds of the early Calvinist writers. Sheldon Wolin sees the Calvinists as working on this issue in a manner that was very different from that of the Lutherans and the Anabaptists. These other groups, Wolin argues, worked at "de-politicizing" the church, which was meant to be, on their accounts, a voluntary fellowship in which coercion and domination had no proper place. The Calvinists, on the other hand, insisted on a church *polity* undergirded by coercive, disciplinary power. But they were not content merely to politicize the church; they also wanted to "socialize" the political community so that civil authority embodied more than a coercive power.[39]

Wolin does not mean to suggest that the Calvinists were bent on erasing all differences between ecclesial and civil associations. The two communities were viewed as promoting different objectives,[40] with the church being

> the better society on several counts. Its mission was loftier, its life more social, and its virtues of a higher dignity. The sacramental bond provided a kind of unity which the civil order could never attain: "every one imparts to all in common what he has received from the Lord."[41]

There are points to quarrel with in Wolin's case. It is not clear, for example, that he has set out the differences between the Calvinist and Anabaptist perspectives in a way that is fair and helpful. For those of us who are convinced by John Yoder's formulation of the Anabaptist position in terms of "the politics of Jesus," it is not satisfactory to characterize the differences between Calvinism and Anabaptism as if they rested on a disagreement over the very possibility of a Christian "polity."[42] It seems better to argue that the debates between the two groups had much to do with the degree to which, and in what sense, the internal polity of the ecclesial community could be "exported" into the larger society.

Nonetheless, Wolin is correct in seeing the concept of a righteous polity as central to the Calvinist vision for both ecclesial and civil society. Indeed, this case has now been made in great detail and in a very convincing manner by Harro Hopfl in his recent study of Calvin's social thought.[43]

In addressing the question of how the two "polities"—ecclesial and civil—could be synchronized, the Calvinists were speaking to a crucial problem of modernity, namely, the growing danger of a complete "segmentation" of social roles. Wolin nicely describes the Calvinist project here:

> The individual was to be reintegrated into a double order, religious and political, and the orders themselves were to be linked in a

common unity. The discontinuity between religious obligations and restraints and their political counterparts was to be repaired; Christian virtue and political virtue were to move closer together. The order that emerged was not a "theocracy," but a corporate community that was neither purely religious nor purely secular, but a compound of both.[44]

There is much evidence in the Calvinist literature to support this characterization. I cite only one example here, from George Gillespie's prefatory remarks "To the Candid Reader" of his book *Aarons Rod Blossoming*; Christ's church, he says, is "a visible politicall ministeriall body, in which he hath appointed Laws, Ordinances, Censures . . . This was the thing which Herod and Pilate did, and many Princes, Potentates, and states do look upon, with so much feare and jealousie, as another Government coordinate with the civill."[45]

Nor would those fearful princes and potentates have their anxieties greatly reduced by reading Gillespie's book. To be sure, he makes much of the differences between the ecclesial and the civil, and between their respective officials. But there is also no doubt in Gillespie's mind that, say, both clergy and magistrates are required—admittedly, in different ways and contexts—to honor Christ's kingship in their exercising of their authority.[46]

It is difficult to read these Calvinist writers without sensing the strong tension that they feel in dealing with the two polities. It is clear that they want to keep the spheres distinct in very important respects. But neither can they refrain from drawing analogies between the ways in which authority is exercised in these different associational contexts—which is not surprising, given the Apostle's own use of the language of "ministry" in Romans 13 to describe the work of civil authorities.

Their willingness to draw analogies between church and state had implications for the ways in which the Calvinists viewed both the structures and the style of authority in the civil realm. Beza, for example, explicitly appeals to conciliar ecclesiology—the view that is held, he says, by "the more sensible part of those who call themselves Roman Catholics"—in criticizing a strong monarchical conception of political rule.[47] And Gillespie discovers a whole arsenal of arguments for the thesis that "Presbyterial Government is the most limited and least arbitrary Government of any other"—

a claim whose implications he is willing to draw out for both spheres of decision making.[48]

All of which should be enough, by itself, to release us from any initial inclination we might have had to link Calvinist and Hobbesian politics. But Calvinist reflections on the style of political authority are even more poignant in this regard. Rutherford gives expression to a common theme in the tradition, for example, when he points to what he views as a divine requirement that kings function as "fathers, nurses, protectors, guides."[49]

This serious reliance on parenting-nurturing images in spelling out the nature of political rule draws on at least two sources. One is the Old Testament, to which the Calvinist writers turned for guidance in explicating the notion of political "ministry" set forth in Romans 13. Citing the political literature of Israel, they made much of the image of a shepherd ruler, commissioned by God to defend the cause of the poor and the helpless by means of an administration of justice that would be like showers watering the parched earth (Ps. 72:6).

The second source is the actual experience of authority in the church, where as Gillespie puts it, the "kingly office of Jesus Christ," which "is administered and exercised by the working of his spirit in the soules of particular persons" is manifested "outwardly also and visibly" in the ecclesial fellowship.[50] It is here, where believers experience the righteous administration of Christ in a very intimate way, that they learn the patterns of virtue which they must somehow translate into attitudes and actions appropriate to the political life of the larger society.

I have no desire to argue here that these Calvinists always did this well. Indeed, they often failed miserably in both their ecclesial and their civil roles. But our focus here is on what they wrote in their reflective moments; and those writings manifest a commitment to ecclesial and political sanctification that is at odds, in many important ways, with a Hobbesian understanding of authority and virtue.

This is not to deny that there was something like a Hobbesian "moment" in their ecclesial and political experiences. Not only is such a strain to be acknowledged in their thought and experience; it is to be celebrated. Crucial to the Calvinist vision of things is the moment when the human will surrenders to the power of the divine sovereign. Such surrender must be unconditional, a bowing in awe before God's overwhelming majesty.

Preston King has observed that for Hobbes the world's order "does not so much reflect an ultimate Reason as an ultimate Will," so that "command is the essence of order in the universe as a whole."[51] It is not necessarily unfair to attribute a similar view to Calvinism. But it is one thing to see command as of the "essence" of reality and another to insist that everything in the universe is held together by despotic imperatives. The commands of the Hobbesian sovereign never lose their arbitrary character; thus Hobbes's insistence that the *"mortal God"* who rules us "under the *immortal God*" secures both domestic and international peace by means of "terror."[52]

It is not so with the Calvinist God, whose imperatives aim at the creation of new possibilities for cultivating those virtues that God intended in creating human beings. And the necessity of that pursuit of virtue means that the Hobbesian moment—however appropriate and necessary it is as the occasion for the initial act of surrender, and even as a posture to which Christians must return on occasion for reliving the moment of surrender—is not sufficient to nurture and sustain the process of sanctification.

It was no Hobbesian God that these Calvinists addressed when they sang the words of Calvin's hymn: "Thou hast the true and perfect gentleness,/No harshness hast Thou and no bitterness;/Make us to taste the sweet grace found in Thee/And ever stay in Thy sweet unity." Nor could they endorse, at least in their times of careful reflection, any political account in which the harshness and bitterness of Hobbesian politics was thought to be compatible with Christian virtue.

7

NARRATIVE, CHARACTER, AND COMMANDS

W HEN I WAS STUDYING ETHICS as a Philosophy graduate student in the 1960s we were all very much caught up in the debates between consequentialists and deontologists. We took it for granted that ethics, or at least what we called normative ethics, was primarily a matter of thinking about the making of decisions. We also assumed that when ethicists think properly about the best way to make moral decisions they are confronted with three philosophically interesting options. The first option is the view that actions are judged to be right or wrong simply with reference to the consequences they are likely to produce. The second option is to view various kinds of actions—for example, promise keeping and truth telling—as being intrinsically right or obligatory, quite apart from any consequential states of affairs they might bring about. A third option is to attempt some combination of these two approaches, as for example, in William Frankena's "mixed deontology."[1]

Our philosophical discussions in the 1960s were consciously shaped by the moral perspective associated with post–World War II Anglo-American analytic philosophy. We were very much aware of the fact, of course, that not everyone who talked about ethical matters with a scholarly focus viewed the moral situation in the same way that we did. Indeed, our discussions were regularly interrupted, on the particular campus where I was studying, by the students of Hannah Arendt, Leo Strauss, and Richard McKeon, and a number of wandering mystics and watch-dogging Marxists, and even by (to use Ralph McInerny's delightful label) a "peeping Thomist" or two—all people who for various reasons thought it important to tell us that we had a very narrow-minded understanding of the ethical enterprise.

We philosophers would typically handle all of these critical souls with bemused condescension. But we reserved a more direct response—open mockery—for the ethics students from the Divinity School, who would baffle us with their talk about an "ethics of being" and the "Christomorphic structure of the moral life."

The mood among Anglo-American philosophical ethicists began to change, however, during the next decade. Some philosophers began to suggest that there are important questions to ask prior to making decisions about specific moral actions: What kind of person do I want to be? What kind of character am I trying to build? What sort of narrative am I in the process of composing as I weave together the actions and habits and attitudes and responses that make up the life that I live?

I remember reading, in the early 1970s, a specific paragraph which forcefully impressed the importance of these questions on my thinking. It was in an essay by Robert L. Holmes, for which he had won an award in the Council for Philosophical Studies Competition on the topic of violence. Holmes was defending nonviolence in a way that fit neither consequentialist nor deontological categories:

> To live nonviolently and to encourage others to do the same *is* the end, and the question is not whether nonviolence is effective (though one might ask whether it is effective in achieving other ends) but whether this or that person is successful at living nonviolently. Here means and ends collapse into one another . . . Rather than being steps on a ladder to a lofty and remote destination, means on this view are more akin to ingredients in a recipe, the end or final product of which is made up of what is put into it.[2]

The view which Holmes was sketching out in these brief comments struck me as being much closer to many of the concerns I had as a Christian ethicist than the options which I had been trying to accommodate to my convictions. And I was not alone in finding such a perspective attractive. Well-known philosophical ethicists began to pay closer attention to the themes of virtue and character and narrative[3]; most notable here is Alasdair MacIntyre, whose *After Virtue*, which appeared in 1981, was anticipated in the previous decade by a number of essays in which MacIntyre had explored these issues.[4]

In the process, some traffic lanes between the theological and philosophical discussions of ethical matters began to become unclogged. MacIntyre's philosophical efforts, for example, have close affinities to the theological work of Stanley Hauerwas.[5] Philosophically sensitive theological studies of the ethics of virtue have also been contributed by Gilbert Meilaender[6] and James W. McClendon, Jr.[7]

I will not review here all that has been set forth in these writings. Nor will I offer much by way of negative criticism.[8] My main purpose in my brief comments on these explorations of the relevance of narrative and virtue for Christian ethics is to suggest that they have much to offer by way of fleshing out a divine command perspective.

This suggestion does need a little explaining, though, since the people who have done the most in recent years to develop the virtue and narrative themes have sometimes given the impression that their views do not sit well with a strong emphasis on divine commands. Hauerwas, for example, rejects a deontological ethic that focuses primarily on "God's commanding presence"[9]; and McClendon offers a detailed critique of "decisionism" in Christian ethics, which sees the good life in terms of making decisions in response to "a few *propositions* about persons, evil, ideology, and the like," which are provided to us for the purpose of fulfilling "the Christian responsibility to *organize the world.*"[10]

But a careful examination of their developed cases shows that these writers are complaining, in the remarks just cited, about an undue emphasis on such things as commands, duties, and decisions; they are not insisting that such items have no place at all in a Christian moral perspective. Thus, Hauerwas:

> There is nothing about an emphasis on narrative and the virtues that in itself denies that we must still make decisions or that we are often rightly required to justify why we have acted as we have. However, it is true that those decisions do not have the same status they assume in ethics that ignore the significance of the virtues.[11]

And Meilaender, in suggesting that a virtue ethic "is dominated by the eye" because cultivating the appropriate character traits requires that we "*see* our world and human nature rightly," is nonetheless reluctant to abandon completely an ethical emphasis that encourages us to listen to divine directives and correctives:

> No ethic of virtue will be safe without a spirit of confession always ready to hear the divine word which—seeing us whole—condemns even the best of our virtues, and again—seeing us whole in Christ— says, even with reference to much that does not get into the self-conscious life stories we narrate, "well done."[12]

It is tempting to take these qualified comments as reasons for treating the ethics of virtue and narrative, not as a strict alternative to a divine command perspective, but as a set of reminders regarding important factors that are sometimes ignored in Christian moral thought. Indeed, McClendon seems to concede something of this sort when he notes that while the explorations of

> narrative, character, practices and virtue . . . have not displaced the decisionist focus, they have at least softened or widened it. Moral decisions cannot be seen merely as the isolated acts of a natural (or rational, or society-regarding, or obedient) will; they must as well be seen as the display of character with its virtues and vices, or as the unfolding of an integral vision, or as participation in practices whose goals are the goods that the practices evoke—in a word, as elements of an ongoing narrative in whose episodes the moral agent is a character, and against whose setting the values of these decisions can be weighed.[13]

It would be wrong, though, simply to commend these ethicists for their important reminders regarding the significance of narrative and virtue. They are asking for more than that and, as I view things, they deserve more. What McClendon describes as the softening and widening of the decisionist focus is, when rightly conducted, more than a mere dose of cosmetic medication; it is corrective surgery that probes the deep causes of a syndrome whose harmful effects have been all too obvious in Christian moral thought.

My own sense is that divine command ethics has regularly

needed this surgery. A healthy version of the divine command perspective will pay attention to the themes and emphases associated with the recent discussions of narrative and virtue. But divine command thinking has not always been as healthy as it should be. To be sure, there have been healthy displays of the divine command perspective in the past; I have already given some evidence for this assessment, and will provide more in the following pages. But my primary concern here is not so much to engage in historical defense as it is to show that divine ethicists today must pay serious attention to recent discussion of narrative and virtue.

The Cultural Attractiveness of "Narrative"

Professional ethicists are not the only ones who have been thinking much about narratives during the past few decades. "Narrative" and "story" have, for example, also figured prominently in popular discourse, especially among those people most affected by the therapeutic (sub)culture.[14] The popular use of these themes may give the impression of being yet another display of ethical relativism; but it actually serves, in its cultural setting, as a corrective to relativistic tendencies.

There was a time in the late 1960s and early 1970s when the therapeutic culture seemed to be committed to a thoroughgoing "process" discourse. Healthy communication was understood by many to be the reporting and comparing of subjective states in non-evaluative ("non-judgmental") terms; people talked much, for example, about what they were "comfortable with" and what "threatened" them.

Again, much of this talk gave the impression of a blatant relativism at work. Individuals were viewed as psychic processes, flowing from one subjective state to another with no criteria for declaring one set of feelings—whether those presently experienced by another person or even one's own previous subjective states—to be better or worse than any other. "Good" was a term that was used primarily to assess a person's willingness to describe his or her feelings ("I feel good about your openness"); it was not as likely to be used to assess those feelings themselves.[15]

But even during the heyday of this kind of discourse serious efforts were made within therapeutic culture to avoid a thoroughgoing relativism. In "transactional analysis," one of the better known "self-help" programs of the period in question, the language of subjective states was linked to role-patterns that people were seen as "acting out." This emphasis was, in effect, a counterweight to the more relativistic "process" picture. Certain "scripted" roles, such as Victim or Rescuer, were considered unhealthy, in need of being replaced by more "adult," consciously chosen, patterns of behavior.[16] And these dramatic categories of role and script soon gave way to a widespread use of "journeying" and "life-story" themes.

My account here is, admittedly, impressionistic; but I have no doubt that the sketch can be fleshed out in a convincing manner. A more detailed analysis might well explore the links between the quest for "roots" by Afro-Americans and other ethnic groups in the 1970s and the increasing tendency within the therapeutic culture to view subjective experiences as episodes in a patterned "journey" which can be recounted as a "story" that has an overall plot.

The narrative ethicists, then, have focused on a theme that has come to have an appeal in the larger cultural context. And there are genuine continuities between their treatment of narrative and the individualized use of that motif in the therapeutic culture. McClendon suggests a helpful way of viewing the connection when he briefly describes two convictions that undergird his interest in narrative. The first is the sense "that my own story is inadequate, taken alone, and is hungry for another to complete it"—thus the need for the individual to find a community narrative as a means of making sense of his or her personal story. But the second conviction is the recognition that

> *our* story is inadequate as well: The story of each and all is itself hungry for a greater story that overcomes our persistent self-deceit, redeems our common life, and provides a way for us to be a people among all earth's peoples without subtracting from the significance of others' peoplehood, their own stories, their lives.[17]

McClendon is proposing an account in which the quest for a story which can make sense out of an individual's own life cannot be considered complete until the narrative of a single person's pilgrimage is viewed in the context of a larger story about humankind's relationship to ultimate reality. And not just any sort of cosmic story will do. The quest for an intelligible story, McClendon insists, cannot be divorced from a concern for "truth"—a concern that "involves us, *necessarily* involves us, in the story of God."[18] To be sure, truth cannot be found, McClendon also insists, apart from "a community that is of necessity story-shaped."[19] But this in no way denigrates a concern for the truth of the gospel. Rather it highlights the importance of a communal context for finding and appropriating the truth about reality.

Hauerwas also gives a strong statement of the need for this communal realization of truthfulness when he notes that

> Christian convictions do not poetically soothe the anxieties of the contemporary self. Rather, they transform the self to true faith by creating a community that lives faithful to the one true God of the universe. When self and nature are thus put in right relation we perceive the truth of our existence.[20]

The quest for links between an individual story and larger communal, and even cosmic, narratives cannot avoid the questions of truth. Indeed, MacIntyre finds narrative to be an important and helpful theme precisely *because* it avoids those accounts of theoretical diversity which are characterized by an indifference to questions of truth. He argues that instrumentalist and skeptical accounts of theoretical change in the natural sciences refuse to allow a role to reason in choosing between rival paradigms; Kuhn and Feyerabend, for example, portray "the history of epistemological crises as moments of almost total discontinuity without noticing the historical continuity which makes their own intelligible narratives possible."[21]

A conscious awareness of the nature and role of narrative allows us, MacIntyre argues, to assess rival theoretical perspectives with reference to the questions of truth and intelligibility. And this assessment is itself a rational activity:

> It is more rational to accept one theory or paradigm and to reject its predecessor when the later theory or paradigm provides a standpoint from which the acceptance, the life-story, and the rejection of the previous theory or paradigm can be recounted in more intelligi-

ble historical narrative than previously. An understanding of the concept of the superiority of one physical theory to another requires a prior understanding of the concept of the superiority of one historical narrative to another. The theory of scientific rationality has to be embedded in a philosophy of history.[22]

Even though MacIntyre's case here is formulated specifically with reference to the natural sciences, he intends his account to have broader application. Indeed, his *After Virtue* is an elaborate demonstration of its applicability to ethics.

It should also be obvious that MacIntyre is not implying that later perspectives are always preferable to earlier ones. His own well-known negative assessment of modernity provides ample evidence for the claim that moving from later back to earlier perspectives can count as rational progress. The proper defense of any perspective, whether an earlier or a later one, takes the form of the construction of a narrative which gives an intelligible account, not only of why the preferred view is plausible, but also why people might nonetheless be led to accept the view that is being criticized. For example, to show why Christianity is a better moral perspective than, say, Marxism, I must tell a story in which I make sense out of the attractions of Marxism, even while I am showing that Christianity provides a more coherent account of moral reality. In fact, the Christian explanation of the lure of Marxism is an important element in the demonstration of Christianity's coherence.

NARRATIVE, WORLDVIEW AND PRESUPPOSITIONS

In an earlier chapter I discussed the notion of a worldview. I noted that people who take the analysis of worldviews to be an important Christian enterprise think of these sorts of questions as crucial ones: How are we to account for humanness? How does that account relate to our larger understanding of reality as such? What is basically wrong with the human condition as we presently experience it? What could remedy this defective situation?

Reformed thinkers, especially those in both the conservative Dutch Calvinist community and in North American evangelicalism, have often linked an interest in worldview analysis to a strong emphasis on the role of basic presuppositions in human thought. One common way of construing this relationship is to see a world-view as a set of presuppositional beliefs or convictions or dispositions which operate in a very basic and formative manner in the way in which people think about and assess reality.

Cornelius Van Til gives a bold formulation of the presuppositionalist case:

> the argument for Christianity must . . . be that of presupposition. With Augustine it must be maintained that God's revelation is the sun from which all other light derives. The best, the only, the absolutely certain proof of the truth of Christianity is that unless its truth be presupposed there is no proof of anything. Christianity is proved as being the very foundation of the idea of proof itself.[23]

Van Til treats presuppositions as items that are strongly cognitive in nature. While the basic sin of the fall involves the acceptance of "the idea of autonomy,"[24] regenerated thinking reasons from a different starting point, which Van Til often designates as the "principle" of "the self-contained ontological trinity,"[25] or the "conception" of the triune God as "the absolute personality."[26]

Other Reformed thinkers employ less intellectualized conceptions of basic presuppositions. Herman Dooyeweerd uses the term "ground motives" to refer to the standpoints from which human beings view the world. Dooyeweerd's notion of "ground motive" is not an easy one to give a concise account of, and I will not make any effort in that direction here; but it is clear that Dooyeweerd does not want to construe it in primarily cognitive, or what he calls "analytic" or "logical," terms.[27]

The most nuanced formulation of the presuppositionalist perspective has been detailed by Nicholas Wolterstorff in his *Reason Within the Bounds of Religion*. It is not enough, Wolterstorff argues, to proclaim that "everyone has a 'set of presuppositions' or a 'perspective on reality' to bring to a theoretical inquiry. That may be true. But saying such things cannot be the end of the matter. It must at best be the beginning." [28]

Wolterstorff goes on to clarify the presuppositionalist perspective in a number of important ways, including these three. First, he distinguishes among several kinds of beliefs that influence the ways in which people interpret reality, pointing to the importance of what he labels "*control* beliefs," which guide us in the rejecting and devising of theories.[29] Second, unlike Van Til, he is careful to note "that the propositions included within the belief-content" that guides Christian thought "are not just about 'the supernatural.' They are as much about this world and its inhabitants as they are about God."[30]

But third, and most important for our purposes, Wolterstorff refuses to limit that which guides Christian theorizing to the propositional. Our assessments of reality are to be shaped by "authentic Christian commitment," and this "is not to be identified with the believing of propositions, dogmatic or otherwise"—although it surely "does *incorporate* this in several ways."[31]

Even though Wolterstorff does not deal explicitly with the role of narrative in discussing the factors that shape Christian thought, it is very obvious that his formulations allow for a *rapprochement* between presuppositionalist and narrativist perspectives, especially in the way in which he views Christian theorizing as being guided by something that includes, but is not coextensive with, a set of propositions. In insisting that for Christians "authentic assent" is offered *in* the context of a community and to a "complex of action and belief," Wolterstorff echoes the themes of the narrativists. Indeed, in sketching out the shape of this communal assent, he employs the narrative mode:

> From times most ancient man has departed from the pattern of responsibilities God awarded to him at creation. A multitude of evils has followed. But God was not content to leave man in the mire of his misery. In response to man's sin and its resultant evils he resolved to bring about renewal. Indeed, he has already been acting on that resolve, centrally and decisively in the life, death, and resurrection of Jesus Christ, but more generally by calling out a people who will make decisively ultimate in their lives the challenge to be witnesses, agents, and evidences of his work of renewal.[32]

Wolterstorff seems, then, to be endorsing something very much like a narrativist perspective. He recognizes that the propositions that are often associated with the content of a worldview are dependent upon a larger "complex"—on a way of connecting belief and action, past and present, in such a manner that these propositions cohere in the context of a broader unity. Even his suggestion that "authentic Christian commitment as a whole, but also the belief-content thereof, is relative to persons and times"[33] can be seen as an acknowledgment that a community's narrative is a dynamic entity, developing through time—so that the complex of beliefs and actions that constitutes authentic Christian commitment can be rearranged as new chapters are added to the story of a community's believings and doings.

From the narrativist's point of view, of course, Wolterstorff is merely being more conscious than other presuppositionalists have been of the narrative-dependency of the presuppositions that are held to be central to authentic Christian commitment. The narrativist holds that even where there is no acknowledgment of the formative role of narrative, people are nonetheless operating within a narrative framework. An examination of Van Til's presuppositionalist case bears this contention out. While Van Til continually claims that it is the *belief* that there is a triune God that is the presupposed "foundation of everything else that we hold dear,"[34] he himself seems rather eager to place this cognitive claim in a narrative context. For example, he moves rather quickly from the claim that proper Christian thinking finds its "final reference point" in "the self-contained ontological trinity" to a recounting of the narrative setting for this "principle":

> When man became a sinner he made of himself instead of God the ultimate or final reference point. And it is precisely this presupposition, as it controls without exception all forms of non-Christian philosophy, that must be brought into question. If this presupposition is left unquestioned in any field all the facts and arguments presented to the unbeliever will be made over by him according to his pattern.[35]

It seems clear that what Van Til is presenting here as properly presuppositional is not really a "principle" at all but a way of recounting both the biblical saga of the fall into sin and the development of secular philosophical thought in such a way that they are linked together in a single continuous narrative. To observe this is not so much to criticize Van Til as it is to show that his account is richer than he himself describes it as being.

The affinity between narrativism and Reformed presuppositionalism can also be seen by tracing the movement in the other direction. Narratives do after all contain or imply propositions which can be assessed with respect to truth and falsity. Certainly the sorts of Christian narratives which Hauerwas and McClendon deem to be important have this propositional core to them; they are truthful narratives, even if their truth can only be properly received and lived out in community.

The narrativists, then, are not denying the importance of propositions. Nor does anything that they say prohibit us from listing the specific cognitive claims that can be associated with a worldview as a way of viewing and assessing reality: claims about, say, the metaphysical composition of a human person or the nature of divine transcendence. In setting forth these worldview accounts in propositional form, though, we must constantly remind ourselves of the narrativist insistence that such propositions have to be regularly traced back to the narrative contexts on which they are dependent.

And we must also keep in mind that these narratives are not themselves *merely* sets of propositions. When we encounter the scene where the resurrected Jesus asks the disciple who had betrayed him three times, "Simon, son of John, do you love me?" (John 21:15–17), it is undoubtedly important to our proper Christian grasp of this story that we believe the proposition that it was the case that Jesus asked Peter a question. But it is also necessary that we hear the question itself in all of its dramatic poignancy, in a manner that goes far beyond the offering of cognitive assent to the claim that the question was actually asked.

At many points in our Christian narrations the propositions which are either directly stated or implied are often the least important items being presented for our consideration and response. And even when specific cognitive claims can be rightly singled out for special attention because of their significance to a community that is called to live truthfully, it is necessary nonetheless to remember that they are but distillations from a much richer and more textured drama—and that to distance them for too long from that narrative context is to deprive them of the source of their life-directing power.

THE ETHICS OF BEING

But the narrative ethicists have not only emphasized the importance of narrative, they have also written much about virtue and character. And in doing so they have been quite critical of ethical schemes in which other items are viewed as having priority over virtuous character. Meilaender lays out the issues nicely:

> Not whether we should frame one innocent man to save five—but on the virtue of justice, with its steady, habitual determination to make space in life for the needs and claims of others. Not whether to lie to the secret police—but on that steady regard for others which uses language truthfully and thereby makes a common life possible. Not whether abortion is permissible in an extreme case— but on the ancient question Socrates raised, whether it is better to suffer wrong than to do it. An ethic of virtue turns away not only from an overemphasis on borderline cases but also from the concept of duty as the central moral concept. *Being* not *doing* takes center stage; for what we ought to do may depend on the sort of person we are. What duties we perceive may depend upon what virtues shape our vision of the world.[36]

Actually there are at least three points which Meilaender is making in this passage. One is that it is bad to spend too much time thinking about borderline cases. A second is that the kind of moral decisions we make often depends on the kind of moral people we are. And the third is that moral being and not moral doing must take "center stage" in Christian moral thought.

The first two points need not be viewed as incompatible with an ethics of "doing." Each of them can be interpreted as good advice for people who place a premium on the making of the right kind of moral decisions. But the third point calls into question the decisionist emphasis as such.

Now, strictly speaking, this anti-decisionist stance does not seem to be required by a narrativist perspective. It seems quite plausible, for example, to hold to a divine command perspective which places obedient human actions at the center of things, morally speaking, and yet still hold that narrative is crucial for understanding the intent of the divine directives. James Gustafson has insisted that Karl Barth's divine command ethic was based on the requirement that the divine commands be viewed as fitting into the overall patterns of biblical theology.[37] Even though some of Barth's comments do not inspire confidence on this point, Gustafson does seem to capture the overall thrust of the Barthian ethic when he argues that while the Barthian deity "gives specific commands on each occasion, he is not capricious; thus his commands are likely to be consistent with the Decalogue and the Sermon on the mount."[38] This way of viewing things comports well with Calvin's comment, quoted earlier, that a proper understanding of the Decalogue must see these commandments as containing more than "only dry and bare rudiments"; we must view them as a unified display of "all the duties of piety and love."[39]

One obvious way of interpreting these comments by Gustafson and Calvin is to view them as emphasizing the need for a narrative that will tie together what might otherwise be mere "dry and bare rudiments" (at best) or a series of capricious fiats (at worst). This seems not only a plausible interpretation of, say, Calvin's remarks—it also seems to be true. To belabor the obvious: God himself seems to insist on a narrative context for the Decalogue, prefacing the list of imperatives with a reminder of the drama within which they appear: "I am the Lord your God, who brought you out of the land of Egypt, out of the house of bondage" (Exodus 20:2).

A divine command theory that emphasizes, then, the larger dramatic context from which God's imperatives derive their significance will want to support the narrativists' contention that narrative is basic to biblical morality. To understand the meaning of divine commands is to grasp something of God's character, of the divine intentions in providing moral guidance to human creatures. And this in turn requires that we know the story of God's dealings with the creation.

Obedience to God's commands can also be seen as intimately connected to a concern for developing moral character in the human commandee. If God's imperatives to us are not to be viewed as arbitrary and disconnected, neither should our acts of obedience to those directives. A divine command perspective ought not treat discrete acts of surrender to divine fiats as intrinsically valuable. Emphasis should be placed on the value of cultivating a pious disposition to trust God by obeying his commandments. Here it is not obedience as such that is treasured, but an obedience that is grounded in—that is a manifestation of—a patterned godliness.

Not that obedience must be postponed until character is cultivated. Obedience can itself be an important instrument for cultivating virtues. To obey a divine directive when one is not inclined to do so can be an effective means of developing a disposition to trust God. Surrendering to a command from God when doing so has the feel of an arbitrary act of obedience can be a helpful way of becoming a more patient and less self-centered person. It is not without reason that monastic communities portray submission to directives as itself a moral and spiritual "discipline."

Similarly, the development of character need not be treated as an alternative to an emphasis on decision making; it can itself be an important part of the preparation *for* decision making. How I behave in a supermarket checkout line, or while driving in bumper-to-bumper traffic during rush hour, or when negotiating the arrangements for a speaking trip—these do not have the status of full "ethical decisions." But they are, as virtue ethicists like to argue, important sequences in my moral pilgrimage: they involve the seemingly insignificant moments when the state of my character development will be displayed.

I agree that these patterns of character are important for their own sakes. It is important simply to be a friendly, patient, and good-hearted person, and it is in the "little" situations of life where we often show very clearly "what we are made of" morally. But one can grant this and still think that the making of proper decisions is also a very significant matter for the good life. Furthermore, one can view the moral "stuff" that goes into the display of character in seemingly insignificant situations to have a very important relationship to the making of good decisions: such situations can be viewed as the moral training-ground for decision making.

The Necessity of Moral Preparation

A perspective that views moral decision making as applying divinely authorized directives to specific situations will be greatly impoverished if it ignores this important topic of the character-forming preparation for the making of decisions. Consider, for example, the application of Just War criteria to situations requiring military decisions.[40] Many of us who subscribe to Christian teaching regarding Just Wars believe that the norms associated with that tradition of decision making—proportionality, just cause, last resort, discriminate use of violence, etc.—are principles for implementing divine directives, such as "Protect the innocent," "Do justice," "Defend the weak and the powerless," and so on.

Critics of the strict advocacy of Just War criteria point out, though, how difficult it is to engage in the calm deliberate application of such considerations when immersed in the passions and agonies of actual warfare. This is a legitimate consideration. But it is not a good reason for dismissing the Just War criteria.

For one thing, it may mean that the guidelines associated with Just War doctrine should not only be utilized in actual situations of warfare. It may be that military planners should think long and hard about Just War considerations during more tranquil days. Consider a parallel in marriage relations. Marital fighting can often be an element of a very healthy marriage relationship. But there are fair and unfair ways of fighting with one's spouse. It is even possible to spell out some rules for fair fighting in marriage.[41] Even if people have such rules available, however, they do not necessarily think very clearly about them in the actual process of a marital argument, when marital partners are not always in the best mood to think about the rules of fair play.

Rules for fairness in marital fighting, then, might be more useful when the arguments are not yet being waged. In calmer moments, spouses could think about those rules, attempting to "internalize" them in order to have their attitudes and instincts shaped by the concerns that they embody. In that way the rules may serve a marriage well even in those confrontational moments when people are not consciously attending to them.

But we can be even more explicit about the importance of moral character in fleshing out an adequate Just War doctrine.[42] While Just War theorists have sometimes given the impression that their perspective is primarily a story about the *how* and *what* of military strategy, with little interest in the *who* of decision making, some of the classical defenders of Just War doctrine have pointed the way to a more comprehensive theory, in which moral and spiritual dispositions have an important place. For example, moral character is an obvious concern of John Calvin when he comments about the kinds of attitudes which civil authorities should bring to their deliberations regarding military policy, an area of activity which Calvin sees as justified insofar as it is a legitimate extension of the magistrate's task of punishing wrongdoers:

> . . . it is the duty of all magistrates here to guard particularly against giving vent to their passions even in the slightest degree. Rather, if they have to punish, let them not be carried away with headlong anger, or be seized with hatred, or burn with implacable severity. Let them also (as Augustine says) have pity on the common nature in the one whose special fault they are punishing. Or, if they must arm themselves against the enemy, that is, the armed robber, let them not lightly seek occasion to do so; indeed, let them not accept the occasion when offered, unless they are driven to it by extreme necessity . . . [And] let them not allow themselves to be swayed by any private affection, but be led by concern for the people alone. Otherwise, they very wickedly abuse their power, which has been given them not for their own advantage, but for the benefit and service of others.[43]

There is an interesting and important reversal in these comments of the usual ways of dealing with us-versus-them realities of warfare that we often find among Christian patriots. Instead of celebrating "our" virtues as over against "their" vices, Calvin asks civil authorities to look very carefully at their own sinful tendencies while at the same time focusing on the humanness of the enemy. Consider, for example, how Calvin's comments might be translated into concrete advice to Ronald Reagan prior to the bombing of Libya: "Be careful," Calvin would say, "to guard against giving vent to your passions in this situation, even in the slightest degree. If you must punish Kadaffi, do not be carried away by headlong anger, or be seized with hatred, or burn with implacable severity. Work hard at having pity on the common nature that you share with the one whom you are attacking—do not be carried away, for example, by that sinful rhetoric about 'mad dogs' and 'evil empires' that so easily dehumanizes the enemy. And do not lightly seek occasions to attack; indeed, do not accept the occasion when offered, unless you are driven to it by extreme necessity; trying every other means of resolving the conflict before resorting to the dropping of bombs.

Above all, seek to honor all human beings, for if you are swayed by private affections—say the desire to be tough, or to appear to be in charge—you very wickedly abuse the power which is given to you by the Sovereign Ruler of the universe."

Calvin rightly points us to the need to apply the doctrines dealing with human depravity more evenhandedly than is often the case in Just War deliberations. We too are sinners, and the exercising of political power and military might are all too obviously the kinds of activities in which our depraved natures are easily lured into unrighteous schemes.

Sinful people do not need to be told to look for faults in their enemies. But we do need to be encouraged to engage in the careful examining of our own motives and intentions. For Calvin the Just War doctrine is an important pastoral instrument for encouraging this sort of self-examination.

Given some common conceptions about Calvin's theology, it is perhaps even more surprising that he admonishes rulers to "have pity on the common nature in the one whose special fault they are punishing." But this is a very serious matter for Calvin, who believes that all human beings, Christian and non-Christian, continue to be bearers of the divine image; to desecrate that image is to insult the God in whose likeness each woman and man is created.

It is on this important matter of theological anthropology that Calvin appeals in the passage quoted to the authority of St. Augustine. And Augustine is no less forthright on this matter in his letter to Marcellinus, to which Calvin is alluding. There is a danger, Augustine warns, that in punishing evildoers the civil authorities will conquer their external enemies only to be destroyed by "the enemy within," namely, by their own "depraved and distorted hearts." We can avoid such corruption only by developing "those kindly feelings which keep us from returning evil for evil." If these requirements are observed, Augustine argues, "even war will not be waged without kindness, and it will be easier for a society whose peace is based on piety and justice to take thought for the conquered."[44]

Calvin and Augustine are aware of deeper spiritual issues that are at stake in dealing with the questions of war and peace—issues that go far beyond making the right sorts of strategic decisions. They are insisting that we employ Just War considerations as instruments of basic moral pedagogy. Who are we and who is our enemy? To what degree are our actual military policies shaped by the prompting of the depraved "enemy within," who wants nothing more than for us to look for vices in the external foe rather than to examine our own motives and passions? How have we decided who our enemy is? And what are we doing to preserve the necessary awareness that our military foes continue to bear in their persons the image of the God who has drawn near to humankind in Jesus Christ.

Needless to say, it is not only military decision-makers who need to attend to the business of character development. The considerations that Calvin raises with reference to the use of violence have application to a much broader moral and spiritual territory.

Once again, then, it is important to remind ourselves of the crucial links between the developing of character and narrative structure. Moral and spiritual development is not simply a matter of uninterrupted "growth." The coherence that we must strive for in the formation of character is not the coherence of a logical argument, nor of a smooth-flowing movement from one stage to another. Rather it is a coherence of a *story*, the telling of which may well include attempts to make sense of tragic failures, seemingly gratuitous detours, bothersome mysteries, and breath-taking surprises—a story that will even feature commands from a God who graces our pilgrimages with much-needed guidance along the way.

NARRATIVE, CHARACTER, AND INWARDNESS

Have we succeeded in closing the distance, then, between the narrative-character approach and a divine command perspective? Are there any significant differences left to worry about?

My primary interest in the discussion of this chapter is to show that it is wrong to make too much of the differences. In arguing this I am merely echoing, from a divine command perspective, the observation already made in the writings of Hauerwas, McClendon, and Meilaender, that narrativism is not intended as an exclusive alternative to an ethic of commands and rules. Recent narrative ethicists see themselves as recovering themes that have been around for a long time in the Christian tradition, but which were almost completely ignored by many ethicists for several decades in this century. It would not surprise the narrativists to find out that, for example, John Calvin paid some attention to narrative and character.

Nor do the recent narrativists deny the propriety of making moral decisions or of paying attention to divine commands. The question for them is what belongs in "the center stage" of Christian ethical discussion.

Do the differences between the command ethicists and the narrativists, then, come down to little more than a mere matter of emphasis? Not quite. There are some substantive disagreements at stake—although again, not as many as it might seem at first glance. Two such disagreements deserve some attention here. The first has to do with the criticisms of ethical "inwardness" that surface from time to time in narrativist discussions. The second is directly related to the "center stage" question.

It might strike some people as odd that the ethicists who are interested in character would accuse divine command theorists of a preoccupation with ethical inwardness. Shouldn't it be the other way around? Isn't it the character theme that most tempts us to focus on our subjective "being," while command theories call us away from introspection to an involvement in "doing"?

The facts suggest otherwise. That the character ethicists are not preoccupied with subjective states is rather easy to explain. Character should not be identified with private inward being. The deemphasizing of ethical "doing" does not mean that it is ethical passivity that is being prescribed. The ethics of character, as propounded by the writers I have mentioned, is a celebration of the dynamic development of the virtues. The "action" orientation that these ethicists criticize is not ethical action as such, but the moral life viewed as a series of discrete "doings." In a sense, these writers are *very* interested in moral "doings"—but it is the doings, both big and small, that comprise a coherent narrative that they mean to emphasize.

A command ethic, on the other hand, has indeed often been linked to a fondness for introspection. That this is the case can be clearly seen in the Puritans, whom E. Brooks Holifield has described as the "cartographers of the inner life."[45] Sydney Ahlstrom portrays Puritan subjectivism nicely in his account of "the anxieties produced by the doctrine of election":

> The problem of assurance became existentially central. When neither professions of faith, nor attendance on the ordinances, nor outward evidences of sanctified living could assuage this concern, only an inward experience of God's redeeming grace would suffice. And in the tradition of pastoral care that shaped this accent on conversion and in the vast devotional literature that arose to sustain it one discerns an emphasis on a subjective criterion of salvation that is unmistakably modern—and proleptically "evangelical."[46]

Nor are the Puritans an aberration from Calvinism in general on this point. A similar emphasis on the subjective experience of election is obvious in this passage from the Canons of the Synod of Dordrecht (1618–19).

> The elect in due time, though in various degrees and in different measures, attain the assurance of this their eternal and unchangeable election, not by inquisitively prying into the secret and deep things of God, but by observing in themselves with a spiritual joy and holy pleasure the infallible fruits of election pointed out in the Word of God—such as, a true faith in Christ, filial fear, a godly sorrow for sin, a hungering and thirsting after righteousness, etc.[47]

It is not difficult to see how this invitation to cultivate a habit of "observing in themselves" could lead some Dutch Calvinists to experience the same "anxieties" which Ahlstrom finds in the Anglo-American Puritans. The anxieties get to be especially acute when the traits referred to by the Dordrecht synod become the primary objects of introspective focus: granted that one experiences a faith in Christ and a sorrow for sin—but is it a "*true* faith"? a "*godly* sorrow"? Many Calvinist pietists have been plagued by genuine fears that their subjective experiences were "counterfeit" versions of the genuine thing.[48]

These anxieties can also take a specifically moral shape, as when, for example, a distinction is made between a mere "outward" conformity to the commands of God and a sincere and wholehearted surrender of one's being to the Lord's will. We encountered this theme earlier in a reference to Spurgeon's sermon on "hypocrisy." There is no need to document here the long-standing pietist fear of a religion that consists in a merely "formal" worship and an "external" conformity to the patterns of right living. Such concerns are already prominent in the Reformation's charges against the "outward show" of religion that it associated with Roman Catholicism, and the charge was repeated against the Protestant varieties of "dead orthodoxy" which were to be rejected by those pietist movements which have been so sensitively chronicled by Ernest Stoeffler and others.[49]

McClendon is on solid ground, then, when he notes that the decisionist perspective in Christian ethics has often been associated with communities who "emphasized the inner struggles of the soul."[50] I am not as convinced as McClendon is that Krister Stendahl[51] has shown, as McClendon puts it, "how little this interiorization is biblical and how much it is due to Augustine and Luther."[52] Even if Stendahl is right in his overall account of Pauline psychology (which I doubt), there are certainly other biblical materials which could be taken into account, such as the "Search me and know me" prayer of Psalm 139 and Jesus' reiteration of Hosea's insistence that the Lord looks for the heart of mercy rather than external sacrifices (Matt. 12:7).

Of course, the real issues have to do with the best way of construing these Christian calls to self-examination, and the narrativists have rightly raised the question whether pietist introspection has been nurtured by an acceptance of unhealthy views of selfhood. McClendon himself acknowledges that the "*inner* contest" is undeniably "a recurrent feature of human life." But he is troubled by the fact that

> in modern Christianity, the new exaltation of the will, together with the interiorization of the Christian life, made it seem that such struggles are not part but the whole of morality—as if being continually divided against itself were the soul's main business, as if a self divided were the normal moral status of the Christian life.[53]

Hauerwas also wants to avoid a divided self; "it is our nature," he insists, "to be historic beings,"[54] not Kantian noumenal selves that are transcendentally separated from the dynamics of involvement in the world.[55] To view ourselves in the Kantian fashion is to treat our historic selves as mere "instances" of a "truer" selfhood that is best understood by stripping ourselves of our peculiarities. On the contrary: "because the self is historically formed we require a narrative to speak about it if we are to speak at all . . . [O]ne understands in what his or her selfhood consists only insofar as he or she learns to tell that particular story."[56]

Here the concern about the "naked self" is resurfacing. Hauerwas's historically particularized self is the role-immersed self of MacIntyre's scheme. It is a self that is, in Hauerwas' words, "subordinate to the community rather than vice versa, for we discover the self through a community's narrated tradition"[57]— where the communal narration necessarily involves an understanding of the social practices which are the stuff of a community's life.

My own response to the narrativists' critique of Christian introspectivism is basically to accept their philosophical framework while denying that their criticisms of the inwardness of pietism are conclusive. As a critique of transcendental egos and similar metaphysical entities, their case is compelling. But I do not think that their efforts at linking Christian "interiorization" to secular conceptions of selfhood are convincing. At the very least it seems quite plausible to me to restate the Christian introspectivist case in terms of the narrativist framework itself.

Let me illustrate. In the early 1970s two sociologists published a report on their study of a group of "Jesus people." They were very negative about this religious phenomenon, as is obvious from these comments:

> Instead of progressing toward adult ethics, the Jesus person clutches tenaciously to childhood morality, with its simplistic black-and-white, right-and-wrong judgments. Rather than developing behavior oriented towards reality, he flies into ideational, ideological abstractions to numb his awareness of his newly arisen needs.[58]

One does not have to be an apologist for the "Jesus people" movement to sense a strong bias in this account. The contrast between "behavior oriented toward reality" and the flight "into ideational, ideological abstractions" is, for example, especially poignant. If there really is a God, and if the Jesus person has actually entered into a speaking relationship to that God (however childish the involvement in that relationship might presently be), then praying to God actually counts *as* "behavior oriented toward reality"—

and indeed the denial of the reality of that relationship by means of sociological jargon turns out to be a flight "into ideational, ideological abstractions."

Assuming a Christian way of viewing the behavior of the Jesus person, let us suppose that such a person, who, prior to her conversion spent most of her waking moments actively communicating with other human beings, now devotes much time to prayer and spiritual reflection. Perhaps she even takes the advice given to her by the Synod of Dordrecht, taking care to observe in herself, with a spiritual joy and holy pleasure, those infallible fruits of election which are pointed out in the Word of God.

These spiritual patterns might well be thought of as introspective in nature. But are they best thought of as efforts on her part to get beyond her historic being into a transcendental ego of which her phenomenal self is at best a mere instance? Probably not. In fact, assuming that her prayer and contemplation involve talking to God and thinking about various things that Jesus did and said, it seems more plausible to think of what she is doing as yet another activity *of* her communal self *in* its historic being. In short, it is quite reasonable to think of these introspective events as being as much a part of her narrative as anything else that she does in life.

We need look no further than to Alasdair MacIntyre to gain support for this interpretation. As I noted in chapter four, MacIntyre acknowledges that medieval Christians included in their repertoire of social roles those roles that they filled because, as members of the earthly church, they were members of the heavenly community; thus, says MacIntyre, "in this sense of community the solitary anchorite . . . is as much a member of the community as is a dweller in cities."[59]

Members of Jesus people communes should fare at least as well as solitary anchorites in such a scheme. Christian introspection, whether in the desert of the Syrian Fathers or in northern California in the 1970s, can be one legitimate way of doing what Hauerwas describes as discovering "the self though a community's narrated tradition."

This consideration of the narrativists' critique of inwardness provides yet another occasion to urge that we not be too quick to accuse those Protestants who call for individual accountability and introspective obedience of aiding and abetting the cause of the emotivist self. To be sure, some Puritans and pietists have aligned themselves much too closely with the obsessions and formulations of secular modernity. Ahistorical conceptions of the transcendental ego have, without doubt, had a powerful influence on Christian thought in recent centuries. But not every soul that spends much time looking inward upon itself is seeking to escape narrated history. Introspection can itself be one very important way of taking our roles—*all* of our roles, including those which are most obvious when we are thinking very intensely about the God who creates and redeems us—with utter seriousness.

And it may even be that an acute awareness of the fact that we are "historically formed" may lead us to a strong sense that the "divided selfhood" which McClendon views as unhealthy for the Christian life is indeed a part of our "normal moral status"—at least given the present opportunities for realizing moral normalcy.

Imagine a young man who has come from an African country to study ethics with a leading narrativist. Surrounded by the sights and sounds of Berkeley or Durham he feels like a new and very different sort of person than he was in the culture that nurtured him. But periodically he receives letters from his family, and sitting in his dormitory room he reads those epistles from the homeland with an intense longing to be where he "really belongs." In such moments the lures of his present environs grow strangely dim; but they do not dissipate altogether. He is, as it were, a divided self. And he comes to think that, given the circumstances in which he finds himself, this sense of dividedness is healthier than any of the alternatives. So he nurtures that awareness of role-dividedness—by spending much time, for example, re-reading and reflecting upon the letters from home—as the only way that he can with integrity acknowledge the fulness of the narrated reality in which he is immersed.

I need not draw out the pietist parallel in any detail. For many Christians, life in the world in which they find themselves can only be pursued in a healthy manner if they nurture the sense of being a divided self. Bible-reading, prayer, and contemplation are for them like reading letters from the homeland; these are the means of maintaining the awareness of the larger social reality in which they are immersed as earthly creatures who are also servants of the God whom they worship in the company of an invisible cloud of witnesses.

But it is not simply that many Christians feel torn between two homelands. They also have an experience of being torn between two selves: one self is often content to move about in the world, comfortably garbed in the roles whose correlative practices comprise what many modern folks think of as "the good life"; the other self occasionally sees this worldly self as nothing less than a "wretch," a bearer of a "burden of death." Again, this is a sense of being torn, and with it comes a longing for unity—or, to put it differently, for a coherent narrative in which the tensions and anxieties of divided selfhood are resolved. This longing even takes on—more and more, for some of us—the nature of a strong hope: for "we know that when he appears we shall be like him, for we shall see him as he is" (1 John 3:2).

To disagree with this endorsement of a kind of sense of divided selfhood, it is not enough to assume simply that dividedness is a bad thing for selves to experience. To be sure dividedness can often be very destructive; it is not good to call oneself "Legion." But sometimes the conviction that one is divided is the healthiest way of dealing with a divided reality. If a proper debate on the merits of divided selfhood is to proceed in a productive manner, then, some attention must be directed toward the differences which characterize various Christian attempts to make sense out of the complex social reality in which we live as historically formed selves.

THE SPECTER OF LABADISM

In the weeks prior to his twentieth birthday in 1830 Andrew Bonar, soon to become one of Scotland's best known preachers, was struggling with the state of his soul. On March 13, for example, he reported in his dairy that he was once again filled with "deep sorrow"—but "I see," he continued, "that all this is not godly sorrow." We have no way of knowing whether Bonar had yet read Dordrecht's checklist of divine election's "infallible fruits," but it is obvious that he considered the absence of a godly sorrow for sin to be a matter of eternal significance. Witness the two poignant sentences that comprise his diary entry for May 30: "Yesterday was my birthday. I am not born again."[60]

Before the year was out Bonar received the assurance of his salvation. Within a decade he would be a prominent figure in a widespread spiritual awakening in the Scottish churches, and he was later to become an enthusiastic supporter of the evangelistic efforts of Dwight L. Moody and Ira Sankey. Even though he can always be found complaining in his diary that he had spent too little time in prayer and fasting, the cultivation of broader revivalistic sympathies was clearly accompanied by expressions of increasing confidence about the health of his soul. By the time he reached his eightieth year he could express strong misgivings about the kind of Calvinist piety that had shaped his earlier struggles, as evidenced in his comments upon reading a Puritan spiritual classic:

> Reading *Brainerd's Life*, it seemed to me that he did not hold fellowship with the *living Savior* as he might have done, and did not see himself covered with Christ's merits whereby God's eye was turned away from his imperfections, corruptions, ignorance, failures, because the obedience of Christ was imputed to him. I would be like Brainerd every day, mourning and sad, if I did not see myself so covered with the obedience of Christ that the Father saw me in Him to be beautiful and attractive, because of the garment of righteousness.[61]

Bonar considered himself a good Calvinist to the end. And with some justification: he does not deny, after all, that he continues to be afflicted with "imperfections, corruptions, ignorance, failures"; he only claims that these defects are hidden from God's gaze by the garment of Christ's righteousness. But the imputed merits of Christ seem to "take" remarkably well in his Calvinist soul. The "beautiful and attractive" person whom Bonar presents for divine scrutiny is, one suspects, more than a mere masquerade as Bonar has come to view things.

Bonar claims Christ's perfection as a matter of subjective appropriation in a fashion that is not typical of mainstream Calvinism. It is certainly not typical of the mainstream among the Reformed people of the Netherlands; his kind of spiritual confidence has often raised worries about "Labadism" among the Dutch Calvinists. Their reference here is to the teachings of Jean de Labadie (1610–

1674), a Jesuit whose Jansenist sympathies led him into the Calvinist fold. As a Reformed pastor in the Netherlands, Labadie established small conventicles (*gezelschappen*) which supplemented the ordinary workings of Reformed congregational life; but these intimate fellowships soon became full-fledged house churches (*huiskerken*) for Christians who, like Labadie, had become scornful of the "worldliness" of the orthodox churches.[62] "Labadist" became a term of derision applied to any individual or group who attributed too much righteousness, imputed or earned, to the elect.[63]

Labadism was closely linked with antinomianism in the minds of Dutch Reformed. And this suggests yet another worry that they might have about Bonar's pattern of piety. While Bonar pays much attention in his diary to what it means to live the Christian life, he seldom makes any reference to divine commands. Explicit reliance on divine directives is closely related in Calvinism to an awareness of the very "imperfections, corruptions, ignorance, failures" which Bonar wants to divert attention away from. When these defects are attended to there is also a requisite sense of the necessity of a rescue operation from the outside. If, on the other hand, a person's spirituality permits the hope that he can be invaded, not by mere corrective information but by an actual dose of correcting righteousness, then the other-directedness of a command morality will seem less than fitting.

BEING HONEST ABOUT LABADISM

Why rehearse these old Calvinist polemics? One reason for doing so is that the debates are not merely "old" ones. The issues raised by the Labadists are very much alive in Christian ethical discussion. In an important sense the recent narrativist explorations that we have been referring to in this chapter are, if not a full-blown Labadist revival, at least a contemporary restatement of some key Labadist themes.

The plausibility of viewing recent narrativism as a manifestation of Labadism can be strengthened by reminding ourselves of yet another detail of past Calvinist polemics: "Labadism" functioned among the Reformed as a virtual synonym for "Anabaptism." Both labels stood for the same distasteful ideas; a Labadist was basically an Anabaptist trying to disguise himself—or herself, as in the case of Labadie's gifted co-worker, Anna Maria van Schurman[64]—as a Calvinist.[65]

Recent narrativism has strong and explicit Anabaptist connections: both Hauerwas and McClendon make a point of emphasizing those leanings, and a hard-line Calvinist would be quick to note that in Hauerwas's case the Anabaptism gets added to the perfectionist strains of his birthright Methodism.[66] And while Meilaender works within a Lutheran framework, it is a Lutheranism that is based on the understanding—which he argues for, it must be immediately added, in a very convincing manner—that the *simul peccator* side of Luther's famous maxim was not intended to discourage the sort of "soulcraft" that would seek "to transform and reshape the person at his innermost core."[67]

In pointing to these connections I am not leading up to the dismissive observation that, while the narrativists have been saying some interesting things about story and character, they are after all Labadists and therefore a dangerous breed among contemporary ethicists. Nor do I shrink from making this polemical move merely out of an awareness of the requirements of ecumenical courtesy.

Traditional Calvinism was wrong to condemn Labadism. Not that my theological ancestors were wrong to *argue* with the Labadists. But they were wrong to condemn them, for in doing so they misconstrued the nature of the argument. They insisted that they were combating an external foe who was importing alien themes for the purpose of destroying or polluting Calvinist teaching. Labadism, as they viewed this foe, was fed by very different theological and ethical impulses than those of Reformed Christianity. This portrayal was of a piece with their assessment of the Anabaptists, and it has contributed to the deeply entrenched practice of treating Reformed and Anabaptist perspectives as two very different types of Christian thought and practice.

I will not present a detailed case here against this portrayal of the differences at stake in Reformed-Anabaptist polemics.[68] The specifically ethical dimensions of those polemics, though, do provide much support for a more plausible portrayal, which sees the disputes between Calvinists and their Anabaptist-Labadist opponents as intra-family tensions rather than as battles between very different theological tribes.

To say that Calvinism is a religion that makes much of the radicality of human sin and the overwhelming power of divine grace is to risk understatement. But these twin themes are most prominent when Calvinists are announcing the rudiments of their system. At an earlier point in our discussion we noted some instances of the pattern whereby rudimentary Calvinism quickly gathers nuances and qualifications when subjected to the systematizing efforts of Reformed theologians. This is true with reference to these two themes as well. For a system of thought that insists that divine grace, and divine grace alone, conquers the radical rebelliousness of the human soul, Reformed theology can issue forth in surprisingly optimistic assessments of the capacities (especially the political capacities) of the reprobate and surprisingly pessimistic portrayals of the moral potential of the elect.

And this is precisely where the Anabaptist-Labadist challenge has been so difficult for Calvinists to deal with, since it probes Reformed thought at a very vulnerable point: the Anabaptists and Labadists have low expectations regarding the unbelieving world and high hopes for the believing community—a set of attitudes that seem to flow directly out of rudimentary Calvinism.[69] The debate between the Reformed and their more "perfectionist" opponents probes, then, at the very stuff of the Reformed system, raising the question of how radical the sin is that permeates the patterns of the unbelieving world and how powerful the grace is that touches the life of the believing community.[70]

For me to offer this assessment of what goes on in those debates is not to side with the Labadists against traditional Calvinists, but it is to insist that we be clear about the nature of the Labadist challenge. The Labadists and Anabaptists pose questions that are native to Reformed territory; they are not importing an alien ethical agenda. Labadist criticisms of Calvinism probe at very real Reformed vulnerabilities—even though, as I am inclined to argue, it is best to live uneasily and honestly with the tensions and nuances that give rise to that legitimate sense of vulnerability.

This is not to say that Labadists are people who cannot live with the experience of vulnerability or are incapable of dealing with nuances and qualifications. That would certainly be an unfair characterization of Anabaptist thought; there are many precedents to be found in that tradition for the recent narrativists' frequent reminders that since we do after all continue to struggle with sin in our lives, we must ever be alert to those divine directives which challenge the best of our inner-directed programs of sanctification.

Both the traditional Calvinists and their Labadist critics have operated with a vision of the Christian life in which correcting grace confronts the radicality of human sin with a power that aims at nothing less than the transformation of human life at the very core of its being. Both groups are constructing their narratives out of the same plot-components; they differ in the way in which they put these pieces together into a coherent story. It could even be said that their differences come down to matters of emphasis. But not "mere" emphasis, since they are each attempting to tell the kind of complicated story in which the whole plot can be significantly altered by placing a different emphasis on a seemingly minor detail of character-development.

HEARING UNTIL WE CAN SEE

For Calvinism the good life is very much a matter of "hearing and doing," of learning to "trust and obey." A high value is placed in this scheme on conforming to obligations that we may not fully understand or, if we should happen to understand them, that we are not fully inclined to fulfill.

Obedience is obviously an important moral commodity here. But obedience is itself a manifestation of a deeper posture of surrender to the will of God. Surrender takes place in battle, and the Christian life is viewed by Reformed Christians as a warfare in which our own intimate spiritual spaces are an important part of the battleground. Sanctification is a series of surrenderings.

This is a way of telling the story of a Christian life in which much attention is paid to volitions. Holifield has described the main goals of Puritan-type piety as "introspective watchfulness, strenuous inner discipline, and self-control."[71] This brief list could also double as an account of some of the more important psychological attributes of the Puritan God. And for human beings to develop the patterns of godliness in which those God-like characteristics would be prominently displayed they must first surrender to the divine will. There can be for us mortals no cultivation of watchfulness without a willingness to be watched ("Search me, O God, . . ."), no exercise of discipline without the passive reception of the severe mercies of the divine disciplining, no being-in-control without first being-controlled.

Again, the alternative ways in which Calvinists and Labadists spell these details out is not a question of "mere" emphasis. There is value, of course, in talking about the role of emphasis in sorting out these differences; it helps us to see that we will not get to the heart of the differences between the two sides simply by looking at how their premises bear on their conclusions. The disagreements here will not be illuminated by looking at arguments that are abstracted from the narratives in which they are embedded. The different stories told by Calvinists and by Labadists are due to (among other things, of course) diverse ways of plotting out the expectations that each side nurtures regarding the continuing role of sin in the Christian life.

It is typical of Reformed Christianity for the believer to expect that the struggle which takes place on the inner battleground will continue, with some degree of intensity, until a time that will always be not-yet as we reckon things in this life. Obeying commands that do not-yet sit comfortably with our thoughts and desires is a moral pattern that looms large in our foreseeable futures.

There are very real dangers that accompany this way of assessing our present condition. We run the risk of fostering the notion that it is somehow "normal" for our willings to be at odds with our thinkings and feelings. This is why such a viewpoint desperately needs eschatological reminders and yearnings.

In some autobiographical comments that he appended to a collection of his ethical essays William Frankena reported that he began his graduate study in 1930 "with a Calvinistic background and Hegelian sympathies." Then he adds: "Paul Henle later remarked that he could see the Calvinism in me but not the Hegelianism, and I suppose this is still true."[72] The Calvinist influence seems unmistakable in the "decisionist" tone of much that Frankena has written about the moral life. But there are also strong hints at some key points in his formulations of a recognition of the necessary role of a kind of eschatological yearning in a properly formed moral perspective. Perhaps this is a Hegelian remnant that Henle failed to discern; but one can hope that it too comes with the Calvinism.

Frankena's view that in making moral judgments we are implicitly claiming conformity to, or vindication from, the standpoint of an ideal consensus may have similarities to the Rawlsean appeal to an "original position" and even to Mannheim's depiction of the "free-floating intellectual" and to Habermas's projected "ideal speech situation." But Frankena's version of the ideal consensus is a state of affairs that he sees us as wanting very much to realize; to appeal to this ideal consensus is to seek, as it were, its approval, to claim its vindication in the end—"which never comes or comes only on the Day of Judgment."[73] It is to press on in the awareness of the not-yet aspects of moral fulfillment.

Frankena's awareness of the "ideal" nature of the consensus to which we appeal in our moral assessments means that his portrayal of our present moral situation is characterized by a kind of personal fragmentation, wherein our volitions do not match up well with the cognitive and affective components of the good life. But Frankena seems very much concerned to remedy that brokenness, even if the cure only comes with the realization of an ideal consensus. The ultimate consensus that Frankena describes is no mere intellectual agreement. It is a consensus of "being" in which moral thoughts and feelings and choices come together in a harmonious display of character. It is not insignificant that in his presidential address to the American Philosophical Association he cited as "rough evidence" for the falsity of ethical relativism the fact that "religious people who have theological beliefs of certain sorts tend to adopt the ethics of love."[74] Frankena seems more sensitive than some other philosophical advocates of an "ideal consensus" perspective to the dynamic *yearnings* that are crucial to the good life. He even seems more sensitive to the importance of eschatological longings than many traditional Calvinists have been. Not that the Calvinists have been unaware of those yearnings; but they have often treated them as mere reminders of the not-yet-ness of the moral present.

It is no accident, then, that Labadists and Anabaptists have preached a "realized eschatology" to the Calvinists. They have been right to do so. Some degree of eschatological realization must characterize any Christian's story. To be sure, some of us will also insist that our personal narratives must tell about the ways in which we constantly listen for signals that travel to us over long moral distances—signals that regularly compel us to choose courses of action that do not sit well with our actual thoughts and our desires. These moral reports will be dull and uninspired, however, if they are not also accompanied by testimonies of at least partial realizations of the unity of personhood for which we long.

On my own account of what goes into a good Calvinist ethic it is crucial to attend to the question of how best to plot out the patterns of our moral pilgrimages. And this way of characterizing the ethical enterprise is best thought of, I think, as an advocacy that occurs *within* the narrativist camp. To recognize this will not make all of our arguments go away. But it will be no small achievement if we can gain a better sense that the arguments are, after all, discussions about how best to write the stories that tell of our character-forming moral efforts.

8

THE TRIUNE COMMANDER

CHRISTIANS PLAY FAVORITES WITH THE members of the Trinity. Some Christian groups find it most natural to pray to God the Father; their hymns and other expressions of spirituality seem to dwell mainly on the First Person of the Trinity, an emphasis that is also carried over into their theological reflection. Other groups find it very appropriate to employ "dear Jesus" prayers and songs and to center their theological discussions on the Second Person of the Trinity. And there are also Holy Spirit oriented Christians; because of the recent charismatic renewal their numbers have been increasing, as more and more Christians have been invoking the power and the presence of the Third Person of the Trinity.

That there is a selective pattern of this sort at work in the Christian community seems to be an undeniable fact. And it is also important to take this fact seriously if we are going to be clear about many theological and ethical differences that divide and confuse the Christian community.

Consider, for example, the kinds of moral disagreements that conservative Protestants argue about. Why is it that Christians who claim to accept the Bible as their infallible guide in matters of faith and practice can nonetheless disagree vigorously with each other about what the Bible teaches regarding moral matters? My own sense is that these arguments cannot be properly understood without taking intratrinitarian preferences into account.

To be sure, there are also other factors. People come to the Bible with different cultural experiences; they bring different questions and expectations to their readings of the Scriptures. In making moral use of the biblical literature they often show distinct genre preferences: some are attracted to the legal materials of the Old Testament; others are fond of the Wisdom literature; others place a very special emphasis on the accounts of Jesus's ministry; still others, such as the black slaves in North America, have made much use of the apocalyptic themes of Daniel and Revelation.

Many of these differences are linked to different moral styles or temperaments in the Christian community. I am convinced, though, that these style-temperament factors are themselves very closely connected to the preferences people show for one or another of the members of the Trinity.

One way of testing out these preferences is to ask Christians a question of this sort: When you think about *obeying* God which member of the Trinity do you view yourself as relating to primarily? Which of the divine Persons calls you to, or directly mediates, the strategies for your response of, obedience to the divine will?

There certainly seem to be Christian groups whose ethical style is strongly oriented toward God the Father. An obvious example of such a style is Calvinism, in which God as Law-giver occupies a very central place in worship and moral decision making. In my own Reformed denomination, for example, the reading of the Decalogue is required at each Sunday worship; in much of Dutch and Scottish Calvinism, the worship service has traditionally been experienced as a regathering at Mount Sinai.

Of course, Sinai need not be viewed as the only locus for the divine Law-giver's deliverances. Natural law can be considered to be a legitimate means of packaging divine legislation; magisterial Catholicism is also a variety of Christianity wherein the First Person receives much ethical attention.

But there are other groups of Christians who would respond to the "Which Person?" question by referring to the second member of the Trinity. Jesus-centered emphases in worship and ethics come in many different varieties; there are many more subcategories here than with either of the other two options. This variety is due to the fact that the person and ministry of Jesus are subject to very different interpretations in the broad Christian community, and this diversity has spawned a wide variety of ethical programs.[1]

There is, for example, a strong *imitatio Christi* strain in Roman Catholicism, which stands alongside of the more dominant natural law emphasis. Although there is surprisingly little about Jesus in Thomas a Kempis's classic, *The Imitation of Christ*, the "following Jesus" theme is dominant in Franciscan piety.[2] On the Protestant side, *imitatio* patterns appear in a number of subcommunities. It is certainly strong in Mennonite morality.[3] And, ironically, both the fundamentalists and the liberals in North American Protestantism have developed a significant "be like Jesus" emphasis; each camp has promoted a moral style in which the question "What would Jesus do?" is a central reference point for moral deliberation—although, to be sure, the two sides disagree very much as to what Jesus would actually do in a variety of situations.[4]

What unites these various Second Person ethical programs is the conviction that significant guidance for living the good life can be received by attending to the person and ministry of Jesus. Indeed, not only *can* guidance for the moral life be received by way of devotion to Jesus, but proper and adequate moral guidance *must*, on this view, be received in this manner. The Torah is not enough; nor are other ethical materials—Wisdom, prophetic, devotional, historical—from the Hebrew Scriptures. The person and ministry of Jesus provides us with new moral materials, a new moral content, which goes beyond the deliverances of the Older Covenant. The mountain on which the Beatitudes were uttered is on a loftier ethical plane than the heights of Sinai.

Our third ethical style is grounded in the insistence that the ministry of the Holy Spirit brings with it important elements of moral newness that go beyond even those contained in *imitatio Christi* patterns. Here Christians understand "doing the will of God" primarily in terms of following the leading of the Holy Spirit, or as acting in the power of the divine Comforter. For these believers, a moral program that focuses exclusively or primarily on the deliverances of the Old Testament or the contents of the Gospels is seriously defective. The Christian moral life is to be lived with a conscious awareness of the Spirit's presence and guidance. In our attempts to be obedient to the God of the Bible the Person of the Trinity with whom we are to deal most directly is the indwelling Spirit.

A TYPOLOGY OF UNITARIANISMS

There is nothing startlingly new about these observations. Using ways of thinking about the members of the Trinity as a scheme for sorting out differing styles and emphases is a practice that goes back at least as far as Joachim of Fiore's proposal of a Trinitarian account of the flow of history.[5] In recent decades Christian thinkers have proposed Trinitarian models—often in very illuminating ways—for everything from urban social theory[6] to patterns of congregational ministry.[7]

One especially provocative typology was set forth in an essay published in the 1940s by H. Richard Niebuhr.[8] Niebuhr suggested that there are three kinds of unitarianisms at work in the Christian community, each of them focusing on one of the divine Persons. In sorting out these three strands, Niebuhr was not thinking so much about churches which officially endorse a unitarian dogma. Rather he meant to be sorting out what he referred to as "practical monotheisms," functional unitarianisms which characterize the lives of Christian groups who might nonetheless claim to be strongly trinitarian in their credal commitments. This phenomenon is displayed wherever a group directs its attention or devotion toward one of the Persons of the Trinity in a manner that is for all practical purposes unitarian in scope.

As Niebuhr sorts out the three basic varieties of functional unitarianism, he seems to be suggesting that the favoritism shown in each case is itself guided by a certain kind of motive that takes cognitive shape. For example, a "unitarianism of the Father," he says, is attractive to Christians whose traditions have been shaped by the questions that are generated by philosophy and natural theology. First Person unitarians seem to be, on his understanding, people with a strong speculative bent. They are looking for answers to cosmic questions—questions which are satisfied by a belief in a deity who is, for example, "the first cause and the great designer."[9]

Second Person unitarians, on the other hand, seem to be preoccupied with questions about personal redemption, as Niebuhr reads their concerns. They want a God who has entered into their history, who has drawn near to them in order to save them. Whereas the First Person unitarians have a speculative bent, this brand is more oriented toward historical revelation.[10]

The unitarians of the Spirit are, in Niebuhr's scheme, interested in religious experience. The primary object of spiritual attention is neither a Creator God, who is available to speculative thought, nor a Redeemer God, whose incarnational ministry is presented to us in a historical revelation. They want an indwelling God, a contemporaneous deity who is directly available—"in the inner life"—"through spiritual awareness."[11]

There are things to quibble with in the way Niebuhr sets forth his typology. For one thing, he seems much too content to allow these unitarianisms to continue to function in their unitarian forms. He sees each group as lodging a legitimate protest against the reductionistic tendencies of the other groups. By recognizing the utility of these protests, theologians can be the ones who maintain and protect "a synthesized [trinitarian] formula in which all the partial insights and convictions are combined." Such a formula, he is convinced, "will never please any one part of the Church but it will be an ecumenical doctrine providing not for the exclusion of heretics but for their inclusion in the body on which they are actually dependent."[12]

My own instincts are much more reformist than Niebuhr's. If a specific group has a weak grasp of the reality of God's trinitarian workings, than I would be inclined to encourage them to improve their theology and practice on this point, rather than viewing their imbalance as a helpful corrective to the larger ecclesial whole.

On the other hand, neither am I convinced that the unitarian tendencies in the Christian community are quite as pronounced as Niebuhr claims them to be. There do seem to be Christian groups— the Eastern Orthodox are a good case in point—who manage to function in fully trinitarian ways; they succeed in this by following a trinitarian-structured lectionary which provides for conscious liturgical attention to each member of the Trinity on a regular basis. Furthermore, even where specific groups do not successfully nurture a trinitarian consciousness, they often operate more as binitarians than as unitarians; people develop "hyphenated" theologies in which one Person is dominant, with another Person also playing a significant functional role. Thus Calvinists are often Father-Son oriented, while many Pentecostals operate with a Spirit-Son theology.

FIRST AND SECOND PERSON MORALITIES

While Niebuhr does seem a little too eager to formulate his sociological case in such a manner that the existence of unitarian "heretics" is par for the course, his typology is nonetheless provocative and useful. He is certainly right in pointing to *tendencies* in the direction of functional unitarianisms, and his probing of the moods and motives associated with these tendencies is quite helpful. It is perhaps best to think of his scheme as pointing to Weberian ideal types (even if it is a little awkward to suggest that a unitarian pattern can somehow function as an "ideal"!)

The fondness for questions of philosophy and natural theology, for example, is clearly discernible among groups who have a strong First Person orientation. It is significant that an interest in "Christian philosophy" has been almost exclusively limited to the Roman Catholic and Reformed traditions of western Christianity. Anglicanism has, to be sure, also fostered this interest, but Anglican philosophers have tended to be either Catholic or Reformed in their philosophical dispositions. On the other hand, one finds very little interest in philosophy in the Holiness or Pentecostal traditions; when the spiritual descendents of John Wesley have turned to philosophical speculation, they have tended to develop their own version of a First Person orientation, one that can serve as an alternative to the systems of Calvinism and Catholicism—as in the case of Boston Personalism.[13]

The speculative interest in creation on the part of Roman Catholic and Reformed philosophers takes the form of a strong interest in *law*. Niebuhr's observation that First Person thinkers prefer to ground the Christian vision in a speculative conception of the nature of reality rather than on historical particulars is nicely illustrated in Abraham Kuyper's response to the proposal that our understanding of the good life should center on Jesus's historically revealed teachings. His remarks are worth quoting at length:

> Can we imagine that at one time God willed to rule things in a certain moral order, but that now, in Christ, He wills to rule it otherwise? As though He were not the Eternal, the Unchangeable, Who, from the very hour of creation, even unto all eternity, had willed, wills, and shall will and maintain, one and the same firm moral world-order! Verily Christ has swept away the dust with which man's sinful limitations had covered up this world-order, and has made it glitter again in its original brilliancy. Verily Christ, and He alone, has disclosed to us the eternal love of Christ which was,

from the beginning, the moving principle of this world-order. Above all, Christ has strengthened in us the ability to walk in this world-order with a firm, unfaltering step. But the world-order itself remains just what it was from the beginning. It lays full claim, not only to the believer (as though less were required from the unbeliever) but to every human being and to all human relationships. Hence Calvinism does not lead us to philosophize on a so-called moral life, as though *we* had to create, to discover, or to regulate this life. Calvinism simply places us under the impress of the majesty of God, and subjects us to His eternal ordinances and unchangeable commandments. Hence it is that, for the Calvinist, all ethical study is based on the Law of Sinai, not as though at that time the moral world-order began to be fixed, but to honor the Law of Sinai, as the divinely authentic summary of that original moral law which God wrote in the heart of man, at his creation, and which God is rewriting on the tables of every heart at its conversion.[14]

Kuyper's comments here exhibit a strong aversion to any kind of focus on historical particularity. This passage is heavily laced with references to "order," the "unchangeable," "principle," and "law"—terms which would show up with similar frequency in comparable passages from many Roman Catholic writings.

To be sure, it would be unfair to characterize Kuyper's thought, as illustrated in these comments, as exclusively First Person oriented. References to the Second Person do have a place in the scheme which he outlines. It is interesting, though, that his formulations focus on "Christ" rather than "Jesus." As John Bolt has pointed out, Kuyper's "cultural-ethical vision" features "the *kingly* (but not the *priestly*!) rule of Christ";[15] thus the Second Person referred to in the above passage is very much the eternal Logos and the ascended Lord; there is little here of the Suffering Servant.

Bolt also rightly points out that Kuyper's deemphasizing of the need for Christians to imitate the historically particular patterns of Jesus' example is not essential to Calvinism. Bolt finds *imitatio* themes in Calvin's *Institutes* as well as in the writing of Kuyper's close associate, Herman Bavinck—Bavinck even wrote, Bolt informs us, a somewhat sympathetic review of Charles Sheldon's *In His Steps*![16]

There can be no doubt, however, that the call to imitate Jesus' historically particular example is not as pronounced in Reformed ethics as it is in, say, the Anabaptist tradition. It is no accident that Kuyper, after expressing the thoughts quoted above, very quickly turns to a condemnation of the Anabaptists' "avoidance of the world."[17] Nor is it irrelevant to point out that Kuyper gave his Stone Lectures, from which this passage is quoted, at Princeton in 1898, just three years before his own "kingly" ascent to the office of Prime Minister of the Netherlands. This was hardly a time in his career when he was interested in building bridges to the Anabaptist position. Broad political coalitions of the sort that Kuyper had been encouraging for decades are more easily justified by speculative appeals to "world-order" and creational "laws" established by the First Person Creator, than by insisting that we direct our Christian attention to the specifics of Jesus' earthly ministry.

PRINCIPLES AND NARRATIVES

It should be obvious that in sorting out the differences between a First and Second Person orientation we are getting at some of the same issues already discussed in the principles-versus-narratives debate. As Niebuhr sketches out the unitarianisms of the Father and the Son, the former approach features creational generalities while the latter focuses on redemptive-historical particulars. The ethical emphases of each, then, can reasonably be expected to emphasize principles and narratives, respectively.

Earlier when I discussed the differences between the narrativists and divine command ethicists I argued that a *rapprochement* was possible. I noted, for example, that the narrativists do not deny the appropriateness of the kinds of considerations emphasized by divine command theories; but they do insist that those considerations are themselves dependent upon a narrative structure. I offered evidence for this contention by insisting that the Calvinist writers who put so much stock in constructing systems based on "principles" and "presuppositions" actually offer narrative contexts for the cognitive claims that serve as the premises for their arguments. And, I suggested, even when they do not actually acknowledge that they are employing these narrative frameworks, they are nonetheless taking them for granted.

The same line of argument can be employed here. Kuyper

wants to ground his cultural-ethical perspective in a recognition of God-as-Creator and Christ-as-King. In doing so, he purposely distances himself from perspectives which feature the imitation of the historical Jesus; that kind of approach, he argues, mistakenly appeals to historical particularities rather than to an unchanging creation-order.

But a careful look at Kuyper's actual argument, in the lengthy passage quoted above, reveals that he is not simply pointing to a self-evident "firm moral world-order." What he is doing is telling a *story* about that world-order. In this narrative, God created the world-order in the beginning, but sin soon entered into the picture. Sin did not, however, destroy that order; rather, it covered it up. In the earthly ministry of Jesus of Nazareth the eternal Christ "has swept away the dust with which man's sinful limitations had covered up this world-order, and has made it glitter again in its original brilliancy." We are, as the disciples of Jesus, thereby given new strength "to walk in this world-order with a firm, unfaltering step."

Again, Kuyper is not so much providing us here with a direct appeal to creational generalities as he is offering us a narrative which is designed to encourage us to take creational generalities very seriously. And once we are clear about what his story is, it is not difficult to imagine alternative stories which place the creational materials in a different perspective.

For example, we could construct a narrative that begins by pointing to the moral confusion, ignorance, and perversity that characterize our lives as human beings who live in the kind of moral world that we presently inhabit. We could acknowledge that the Bible tells us that things were not once this way, that there was a time when human beings lived in obedience before the face of God. But we could also express some skepticism about our present abilities to imagine what that situation was like, or to gain much moral help from those imaginings.

In this alternative narrative, then, we could make much of the appearance of Jesus on the scene: in his earthly life he modeled obedience to the divine will for us, and he died on the Cross to make it possible for us to grow into that pattern of obedience. We could even acknowledge that in following Jesus we may be recapturing something of that original situation about which we know so little; but we could also insist that it does not help much to try to guess what that original situation was like. The important thing is to look to the New Testament's narratives about Jesus for our signals as to what God wants us to be.

This line of argument is typical of Anabaptist thought.[18] And the fact that it sounds in certain ways more "Calvinistic" than Kuyper's account—with its emphasis on the radicality of sin and the need for total reliance on God's redemptive initiatives—is another indication of the ways in which the Anabaptists present a special challenge to Reformed thought by probing Calvinist vulnerabilities.

The important thing to underscore here, however, is the fact that when we dig beneath the surface of First Person versus Second Person tensions (along with the subsidiary tensions between emphases on Jesus as priest and Christ as king), we once again encounter two differing narratives. And for some of us of Calvinist persuasion, the Anabaptist narrative makes more Reformed sense than Kuyper's triumphalist appeals to creation-order and kingship. In this regard, Bavinck is a more sensitive Calvinist guide, as is obvious in these comments from his review of *In His Steps*:

> The true imitation of Christ occurs when, freely and independently as children of God, in our circumstances and relationships, even when it demands of us the most severe self-denial and a bearing of the heaviest cross, we do the same will of God which Christ explicated and at the cost of His glory and life, even to death on the cross, perfectly fulfilled, since whoever does the will of God is Jesus' brother and sister and mother.[19]

THIRD PERSON ETHICAL CONCERNS

The emphases that Niebuhr associates with the differences between First Person and Second Person unitarianisms have figured prominently in recent ethical discussions: philosophical versus historical interests, principles versus narratives, obedient action versus godly character. And in the past the same kinds of questions have often dominated the debates between Calvinists and Anabaptists, Jesuits and Franciscans, Barthians and liberals.

The ethical relevance of the Holy Spirit has regularly been ignored in all of this. Or if pneumatology has not been completely neglected in moral theological discussion the unique contribution of a Holy Spirit focus has often been downplayed by collapsing the Spirit's ministry into the work of one of the other two divine Persons—as in "the Creator Spirit" or the "Spirit of Jesus."

In order better to appreciate the ethical benefits of attending to the unique ministry of the Holy Spirit we can use Niebuhr's characterization as our point of departure. Third Person unitarians, he suggests, emphasize the indwelling God, a deity who is very much present in our inner lives and is known to us not primarily through speculation or historical investigation but by means of direct awareness.

There are at least two ways of exploring this ethical emphasis in a contemporary Christian context. One obvious way is to look at the ethical styles associated with classical Pentecostalism and the more recent charismatic renewal, to see how an explicit emphasis on the Holy Spirit bears on ethical teaching and practice. The other is to look at various "liberation" type themes on the contemporary scene, to see how their immanentist orientation might relate to the kind of ethical style that Niebuhr associates with Third Person unitarianism.

Neither of these phenomena lends itself conveniently to a brief discussion. Yet there are aspects of each of them that have a direct bearing on my concerns here. Surprisingly little has been done by way of exploring the potential contribution that Pentecostalism might make to the ethical thought and practice of the larger Christian community. I will make a few suggestions along these lines shortly. But it is also necessary at least to take note of the relevance of liberationist explorations for my discussion here.

Kenneth Hamilton overstates the case when he insists that liberation theology as a movement shares the hostility expressed by the Young Hegelians and Ernst Bloch toward the First Person of the trinity—the liberationists' "Saviour or Christ of the liberated future," Hamilton argues, is the spirit of humanity awakened to combat the repressive structures ordained and sustained by the Creator God."[20] Again, this is too unnuanced; but Hamilton is certainly correct in portraying liberationist thought as having a special interest in the workings of a God who is immanently at work in the present historical process—a God whose purposes cannot be ascertained apart from a proper awareness of "the spirit of humanity," especially the consciousness of those segments of humanity who experience various forms of systemic oppression.

There is a genuine difficulty involved in any attempt to characterize what liberation theology as such does or does not affirm, and Hamilton should have been more aware of this problem. For one thing, there seem to be no canonical criteria for deciding just who is or is not to be included within the proper boundaries of "liberation theology." If, for example, the South African "black theology" movement is included in the liberationist movement, then Hamilton is far off the mark in his insistence that liberation theology is hostile to that which the Creator God ordains and sustains.[21]

There is no doubt, however, that many thinkers associated with liberation theology have struggled with the obvious "hierarchicalist" patterns of much of traditional Christian thought, a hierarchicalism that is most closely aligned with First Person emphases. This struggle is a very prominent feature of feminist theology's critique of patriarchalism. And since an ethics that features divine commands has often been embedded within these hierarchical-patriarchal teachings, it is important to offer some observations about that connection, especially since I have much sympathy for the feminists' critique of patriarchy.

PATRIARCHY AND HIERARCHY

In *A Theology of the Social Gospel* Walter Rauschenbusch presents Jesus as a champion of democracy. Indeed, Jesus' rejection of monarchical rule on earth as well as in heaven is, on Rauschenbusch's accounting, "one of the highest redemptive services of Jesus to the human race." This democratization project was, furthermore, intimately linked to the emphasis Jesus placed on God's Fatherhood, for when Jesus

took God by the hand and called him "our Father," he democratized the conception of God. He disconnected the idea from the coercive and predatory State, and transferred it to the realm of family life, the chief social embodiment of solidarity and love. He not only saved humanity; he saved God. He gave God his first chance of being loved and of escaping from the worst misunderstandings conceivable. The value of Christ's idea of the Fatherhood of God is realized only by contrast to the despotic ideas which it opposed and was meant to displace.[22]

While it is quite obvious that Rauschenbusch is deeply offended by the notion that God is a despot, it is not exactly clear what else it is from which he thinks Jesus "saved God." Was it hierarchy as such? Probably not, since Rauschenbusch hardly seems to think that God's will has become just one among many wills; God still possesses some sort of ineradicable *authority* over us in Rauschenbusch's scheme. Nor is it apparent that Rauschenbusch was a strong opponent of patriarchal authority. He may have preferred "the realm of family life" to the royal court as a model for understanding authority relationships but his favorite kind of family, as Janet Forsythe Fishburn has effectively demonstrated, was still the Victorian family in which the woman knew that her proper place of gentle influence was the domestic sphere.[23]

The conceptual links that connect hierarchy, patriarchy, and male imagery for the deity are in the process of being carefully analyzed these days. Some feminist thinkers are convinced that these three items comprise an interlocking system of thought and practice, a complex which must be rejected *in toto*; this is the argument of, for example, Naomi Goldenberg.[24] But there is by no means a consensus on this point among feminist theologians. Feminism obviously rejects patriarchy, the rule of adult males. But there is no clear agreement about whether opposition to patriarchy requires a rejection of all hierarchy as such, nor about whether the use of male imagery to depict the deity is intrinsically patriarchal. On this latter point Rosemary Ruether has argued that Jesus' references to God as a Heavenly Father were actually designed to undercut patriarchal assumptions.[25]

Feminist writers seldom use "hierarchy" as a positive term— and understandably so, given the ways in which hierarchical schemes have been used to oppress women. Nonetheless an affirmation of one very important form of hierarchy is implied by the insistence on the part of many feminist theologians that an emphasis on divine *transcendence* must be maintained.

The Creator-creature distinction is basic to biblical religion; there is no denying the fact that God is in a very crucial sense infinitely "higher" than we are. To be sure, a heaven-over-earth hierarchy has regularly been used to garner support for various forms of hierarchical arrangements *within* the human community. The appropriate response to this long-standing pattern of injustice, however, is the one made by Sallie McFague: she expresses serious doubts that "an immanental, exclusively feminist perspective [can] be absorbed into the Christian paradigm," while also insisting on the necessity of seeing "the genuine insights" that such a perspective "offers for needed revision in that paradigm."[26] Thus McFague is careful to note that the overall message of the Bible "contains a perspective undercutting patriarchy and all other *worldly* hierarchies" (emphasis mine).[27]

Nancy Van Wyk Phillips offers similarly qualified proposals in this regard:

> If mother imagery is used alone, God may disappear in nature, just as when father imagery is used alone, patriarchal oppression of women, of people of color, and of the earth are the result. To fear mother imagery, however, and to be convinced that it leads inevitably to pantheism and magic, is to indulge in fear of the woman and to reject what our mothers can teach us about what is holy. God is Mother and God is Father, and human life in its sexual concreteness points to the God who is all this and more.[28]

CALVINIST FEMINISM

These significant matters cannot be ignored by any ethicist who is concerned to explore the ways in which divine directives are designed to enable human persons to image the God who created both women and men in the divine likeness. Indeed McFague is right to see these issues as being so important that we must be open to the ways in which they might necessitate "needed revision" in the "Christian paradigm."

Strictly speaking, though, there are many Christian paradigms, since Christian thought has developed along pluralistic lines. The challenge to incorporate feminist concerns into our theological systems will take on different shapes in various confessional settings. In the present context, then, the question takes this form: what would a Calvinist feminism look like with reference to an understanding of ethical obedience to the divine will?

The project of formulating a coherent response to this question has been given a significant boost by Jane Dempsey Douglass's masterly study of Calvin's teachings regarding the role of women in church and society. Douglass is encouraged by Calvin's treatment of "women's silence" as a policy based on temporary expedience rather than eternal principle—an admittedly conservative posture which, while hardly satisfying to many of us today, was still more flexible than the views of other leaders of the Reformation.[29] The patriarchal assumptions that Calvin shared with his contemporaries stood in tension, Douglass argues, with his own understanding of the Christian freedom that has been made available to all persons whose lives have been touched by Christ's atoning ministry, a freedom that is nothing less than a

> liberation by Christ's work from the power of sin and evil and the anguished conscience in order to worship God, to devote oneself freely and energetically to making the kingdom of Christ manifest in the world, freedom to participate in history in the Holy Spirit's creation of the new society envisioned and empowered by God.[30]

The feminist movement has made it possible for us to gain a new awareness of the implications of this kind of perspective for contemporary patterns of human life and service. A Calvinist ethic that absorbs this awareness will still retain the classic themes of Reformed thought, many of which have appeared frequently in these pages: divine sovereignty, human surrender, an awareness of the need to turn from sinful idolatry to the service of God and neighbor. But a strong emphasis will also be placed on the ways in which women and men function together as mutually enabling partners under the divine rule. Such a view would avoid two opposing but equally erroneous patterns of understanding authority patterns within the human community: the long-standing oppressive teaching that a male-ruling-female hierarchy is the only appropriate way to mirror the God-ruling-humankind hierarchy, and the more recent heterodoxy that a healthy intrahuman egalitarianism can only be sustained by a kind of immanentistic God-human egalitarianism.

Many feminist thinkers would argue, of course, that the only way to rid ourselves of a male-ruling-female hierarchy is to abolish the very themes that I am insisting are essential to a Calvinist perspective, such as divine rule and human surrender. To give up these themes, though, would not only be to abandon Calvinism—it would be, I am convinced, to deny some crucial elements in the biblical picture as such. An alternative to oppressive patriarchy, then, must be found, not by rejecting these themes, but by exploring the ways in which they can function as a basis for a healthier intrahuman arrangement. My own sense is that an important resource in this regard can be found in the Reformed insistence that surrendering to the divine will means accepting the responsibility for sharing in the "dominion" that was assigned to the human pair at creation (Gen. 1:28).

The mandate to exercise dominion has been such a central theme in Calvinism that it has even been closely associated with *imago dei*: One very important way in which human beings "image" the divine nature is by performing a ruling function under the supreme authority of the divine rule.[31]

The positive implications of this dominion assignment for a proper understanding of the role of women have sometimes explicitly surfaced in Reformed discussions. Kuyper, for example, became almost rhapsodic on the subject in his Stone Lectures, in spite of the fact that he insisted on the same occasion that patriarchy was a pre-lapsarian norm.[32] He proclaimed to his Princeton audience in 1898:

> If Calvinism places our entire human life immediately before God, then it follows that all men or women, rich or poor, weak or strong, dull or talented, as creatures of God, and as lost sinners, have no claim whatsoever to Lord over one another, and that we stand as equals before God, and consequently equal as man to man. Hence we cannot recognize any distinction among men, save such as has been imposed by God Himself, in that He gave one authority over the other, or enriched one with more talents than the other, in order that the man of more talents should serve the man with less, and in him serve his God. Hence Calvinism condemns not merely all open slavery and systems of caste, but also all covert slavery of woman and of the poor . . . So Calvinism was bound to find its utterance in

the democratic interpretation of life; to proclaim the liberty of nations; and not to rest until both politically and socially every man, simply because he is man, should be recognized, respected and dealt with as a creature created after the Divine likeness.[33]

Kuyper provides us here with some hints in the right theological direction. But they are no more than hints. Mary Stewart Van Leeuwen has recently carried the creational case forward by spelling out the way in which the curse of Genesis 3:16 must be viewed against the background of the call to both women and men to share in the work of exercising dominion. Drawing on the work of Gilbert Bilezikian,[34] she notes that the divine predictions that the woman's "desire shall be for your husband" and that the man "shall rule over you" are brief formulations of the different ways in which men and women have—typically, at least—disobeyed the creational assignment to exercise "accountable dominion." In the patriarchal setting men have usually been guilty of abusing power by dominating others, while women have regularly looked for excuses (easily found in sexist societies) not to accept the dominion assignment.[35] Van Leeuwen puts the challenge to women succinctly: "To the woman who reduces all of womanhood to the nurturing of relationships and cries out to him [Christ], 'Blessed is the womb that bore you, and the breasts that nursed you,' Christ replies, 'No; blessed rather are those who hear the word of God and keep it' (Luke 11:27–28)."[36]

It would be wrong to suggest that there is nothing problematic about placing such a strong emphasis on dominion. There is a very real danger that the call for women to join men in the exercise of dominion will in its own way perpetuate long-standing patterns of male dominance—by fostering an attitude on the part of males, for example, whereby they "permit" women to join them in the kind of exercise of power that is shaped by patriarchal assumptions.

These problems must be given careful attention. But I doubt that they are best dealt with simply by rejecting the dominion theme altogether. The exercise of authority in human relationships is an important business, one that is crucial to the relationship between parents and children, government and citizens, as well as to the affairs of classrooms, basketball courts, and church assemblies.

To be sure, the use of authority has gone badly in all areas of human interaction, which means that the patterns whereby human beings exercise dominion together in God's world are desperately in need of transformation. A conscious effort to find better ways of sharing power together, as women and men who are created in the likeness of the divine Ruler, will not automatically solve those problems. But such an effort can be the occasion for thinking new thoughts about the proper place and role of authority in the human community.

"Bishop" Dinah

My attempts to promote a Calvinist absorption of feminist concerns are so far still very First Person oriented. How might they manifest a more trinitarian structure?

Consider the example of Dinah Hardenbergh, who was born in 1725 into the wealthy Van Bergh family of Amsterdam. After marrying clergyman John Frelinghuysen, she settled with him in the American colonies. He died soon after the birth of their second child, and she then married Jacob Hardenbergh, John's successor in their New Jersey parish. Dinah was deeply involved in the work of the pastorate, conducting Bible classes for women. She and Jacob were close friends of George and Martha Washington and strong supporters of the Revolutionary cause.

According to James Tanis, Dinah Hardenbergh was a person of some theological influence among the Calvinists of eighteenth-century America.[37] During the time when her second husband served as president of the Reformed theological college at New Brunswick, she came to be highly respected by the theological students. Tanis describes her ministry in these intriguing terms:

> Later in life her counsel was sought by domines young and old. She wrote to them humbly, yet as a bishop in her concern for the church—and for the College which was to her an extension of the church. She was a pastor to pastors. In the thought of Jufvrouw

Hardenbergh christological development became more and more pronounced and sacramental devotion played a larger part than in earlier American Reformed Pietism. The change was only one of emphasis, yet it marked a gradually changing thrust from the bolder doctrines of the Spirit to the sweeter doctrines of the Lord Jesus.[38]

Hardenbergh's Christology was grounded in an intentional trinitarianism, though, as is clear from her own description of her experience of a personal yielding to the divine promptings, as she recorded it in her diary:

> It was the beginning of the year 1747. Midnight had passed; and I continued earnest wrestlings, and drew near with a renewed dedication of myself to God, yielding myself unreservedly to Him and His ways and his service and His people. It was my inmost desire that I might receive larger measures of the renewing grace of the Holy Ghost—that my old and sinful nature might be more fully broken, the depravity of my heart subdued and the precious image of the Lord Jesus be more fully transferred to and impressed upon me, and all things become more and more new.[39]

In this testimony Dinah Hardenbergh's references to the Second and Third Persons can be read as being "softer" and more "internal" than her depiction of her relationship to the First Person. She yields to the Father's will, but longs also for "the precious image of the Lord Jesus" and "the renewing grace of the Holy Ghost." However, in suggesting that she pushed the theology of her day away from "the bolder doctrines of the Spirit to the sweeter doctrines of the Lord Jesus," Tanis gives the impression that it was her Christology in particular that did the primary "softening" or "sweetening." There is an important reminder embodied in this suggestion: any one of the members of the Trinity can be emphasized in a manner that results in a harshness that must then be softened—often by an intratrinitarian shift of emphasis.

There are no models of the deity that are safe from exploitative uses. When it is an aggressively angry human consciousness into which a conception of the Spirit is immanentized, the result may be "the bolder doctrines of the Spirit" to which a "sweeter" Jesus can serve as an appropriate antidote. But mean-spirited Christians can also see themselves as serving the cause of a mean-spirited Jesus. Indeed, not even maternal imagery is immune from being put to oppressive uses—the goddesses of pagan religions are quite capable of instilling terror in the hearts of those who worship them. A fatherly God, often assumed to be a source only of harshness and metaphysical distancing, might actually serve on occasion as a gentle corrective to distortions that have come to be associated with other ways of modelling our understanding of the deity.

What all of this suggests is that it is important to promote both a trinitarian breadth and a diversity of images, including mothering and other feminine imagery, in our depictions of divine authority and our relationship to that authority. In a tradition like that of Calvinism, it is especially necessary that these practices be directed toward the cultivation of a sense of God's "nearness," so that the tendencies toward a harsh distancing of divine authority that has sometimes been connected to a strong First Person orientation can be corrected by what Dinah Hardenbergh rightly saw as the renewing ministry of the Spirit and conquering of our depravity by "the precious image of the Lord Jesus."

Pentecostal "Newness"

Leon Hynson has argued that the ethical emphases of the Wesleyan-Holiness tradition, out of which the Pentecostal churches have emerged, can best be characterized in terms of the "creative, and sanctifying, liberating, dynamic, permeative."[40] These are not notions that one would quickly associate with First Person ethical traditions. Nor are they especially prominent in Second Person orientations. They do seem to comport well, though, with an emphasis on the work of the Holy Spirit. If they are important ethical ingredients and features, then, we would do well to look favorably on a stronger Third Person focus.

And they *are* important matters. Unfortunately little has been done within either the older Pentecostal or newer charismatic movements by way of exploring the implications of a strong emphasis on the Holy Spirit for ethical theory, although there have been some discussions of connections to social justice concerns.[41]

There are at least two areas where Pentecostal-charismatic thought does have implications for Christian ethics. One is a "macro" area and the other a "micro" one: the creating, liberating work of the Holy Spirit in the broad reaches of creation, and the application of that ministry to the life of the individual in the Christian community.

First, then, the "macro" area. The role of the Holy Spirit in creating new structures and patterns for human life in the world can clearly be seen in the ways in which Pentecostal Christians have dealt with questions regarding the roles of women. In both the Holiness and Pentecostal movements the initial impulse has been to treat women as equal to men in the exercise of authority in the Christian community.[42]

This Pentecostal impulse to depart from patriarchal patterns was due to a clear conviction that the Holy Spirit is creating "newness" in human affairs. This is in contrast to perspectives dominated by First and Second Person orientations. Where First Person emphases hold sway, as in Reformed thought, the tendency is to debate questions about women and authority in "creational" terms—here much attention is given to the curse of Genesis 3 and the Pauline appeal to the so-called "order of creation" (1 Cor. 11:7–10). In the Second Person scheme, attention will often be paid to the ways in which Jesus departed from patriarchal patterns in his relationships with women. While appeals to the creation and to the ministry of Jesus can provide some basis for non-patriarchal arrangements, they lack the clear proclamation of "newness" that an emphasis on the ministry of the Holy Spirit permits.

The theological underpinning for stressing this kind of novelty has actually been stated with some regularity by Reformed theologians; both Geerhardus Vos and Hendrikus Berkhof have argued at length that the future age, the new creation, is the proper "sphere" or arena for the Spirit's ministry.[43] As Abraham Kuyper put it, "the work of the Holy Spirit consists in leading all creation *to its destiny*, the final purpose of which is the glory of God."[44] Pentecostal Christians, on the other hand, have been less inclined—at least in the past—to state theological generalities. Instead, they have gone straight to the concretizations of the biblical text. Something new has happened in "the latter days," a newness that was promised in the ancient prophecy quoted by St. Peter at Pentecost: "I will pour out my Spirit upon all flesh, and your sons and daughters will prophesy, . . . yea, and on my menservants and my maidservants in those days I will pour out my Spirit; and they shall prosper" (Acts 2:17–18).

This ethical pattern, which stresses the "creative, sanctifying, liberating, dynamic, permeative," obviously has much in common with the basic emphases of liberation thought. This should not be surprising, since many liberation theologians have been much influenced by Hegelian and Marxist themes, which in turn draw upon a kind of secularized theology of the Holy Spirit, positing an inner dynamic in the historical process that breaks down structural barriers to the newness of an age of justice.

The commonalities between Pentecostal ethics and liberationism need not be seen as a liability. The fact that there are similarities suggests that the liberationist concern for justice might be made more available to those Christians who have resisted liberation theology because of what they view as its departures from Christian orthodoxy. Kenneth Hamilton's concerns are typical of many conservative critics. He sees in Gutierrez's espousal of a "'continuous creation, never ending, of a new way to be a man'" a tendency to identify salvation "with liberation from every oppressive structure" in such a way that what counts as "oppressive" and "liberating" will be decided by extrabiblical ideological norms.[45] John Yoder has argued along similar lines with reference to the use of the Exodus theme in liberation theology. He worries about the way in which that theme gets abstracted from its biblical setting so that the Exodus story of God leading a chosen people out of bondage to the separated obedience required by the Sinai charter becomes in the hands of liberationism a model for seizing power from an existing government.[46]

These are important issues to raise, even if they do not apply with equal force to all the writings which have been associated in one way or another with liberation theology. The more that contemporary Christians are forced to think about the patterns of ideological captivity the better, especially since the critics of liberationism often represent communities that have their own real problems with ideological distortions of the gospel. The Pentecostal and charismatic movements can play an important role in this much-needed dialogue about ideology, since they do place such a high premium on both the sanctifying of old realities and the creating of new possibilities for human interaction. The fact that they show an intense interest in these patterns while not carrying the kind of ideological baggage often associated with liberationist thought, along with their professed desire to establish continuities between the "older" and the "newer" manifestations of divine power, suggests that these movements can help the larger Christian community to think in healthier ways about the ways in which the Spirit is presently preparing the world for a transforming rule of peace and righteousness.

MORAL SUBJECTIVITY

In chapter seven, I offered some mediating observations about the points of dispute between narrativists and more "principle" oriented ethical theorists, as well as about the longer-standing arguments that Calvinists have carried on with their Anabaptist-Labadist opponents. In this chapter I have offered the further observation that these disputes can be viewed as arguments between First and Second Person ethical perspectives. And I have suggested that both perspectives can gain something from the kind of trinitarian focus that includes paying much attention to the ethical role of the Holy Spirit.

But what is it that a Third Person emphasis would actually add to the business of moral character-development and decision making? One very important contribution—the one that I want to concentrate upon briefly here—is the enrichment and expansion of our moral subjectivity. This contribution can be spelled out by looking at three key areas of our moral consciousness: the ways we function cognitively, volitionally, and affectively.

First the cognitive. As John Bolt points out, Calvin and Kuyper followed the same pattern in sorting out the general tasks associated with the trinitarian economy: the Father brings forth, the Son arranges—Jesus functions, in Calvin's words, as the "wisdom, counsel and the ordered disposition of all things"—and the Spirit provides the perfecting power.[47] While there are surely alternative schemes which the theological imagination might produce, this is not unhelpful as a way of organizing the Trinity's contribution to our moral cognition. The lawlike ordering of our moral experience stems from the Creator's will; Jesus provides us with a model of the ordered disposition of the moral life; and the Spirit grants us the power to move toward the eschatological goal of moral perfection.

A key element in this ongoing sanctifying work of the Spirit is the provision of the *charismata* for our moral lives. The gifts of the Spirit are, of course, more than moral in their intended scope and application. But they surely have a moral dimension. Thus the well-formed moral life will include, to follow the list given in 1 Corinthians 12, the utterance of moral wisdom and moral knowledge, the exercise of moral faith, the ability to bring about moral healing, the working of moral miracles, the ability to prophesy morally, the distinguishing among diverse moral spirits and the interpretation of moral tongues. "And all of these are inspired by the same Spirit."

Many of these gifts are clearly cognitive in nature, or at least they have strongly cognitive dimensions. An obvious thread running through several of them is the ability to *discern*. Discernment is crucial to the moral life, but it does not come automatically with the territory of any moral scheme. Laws and principles must be applied effectively. Moral examples cannot be properly imitated unless we know how and what to imitate. Character-formation requires the ability to place ourselves in those settings where the appropriate virtues can begin to "take" in our lives.

Lewis Smedes gives a nice account of the requisite giftedness associated with discernment:

> Discernment, not sheer intellect, not true grit, but simply being awake and having a nose for what is going on beneath the surfaces, and having a sense for the more fitting response to it—this is what makes for a class act on the moral stage. Discernment is the secret to living a creative and loving lifestyle with people we want to live with and have to work with; it is the key to making good choices when we are walking on paths where no one has posted signs to tell us where to go.[48]

Smedes goes on to observe that discernment "doesn't come easy. It is a gift, and like all personal gifts it comes only with exercise."[49] And for some of us, even then it comes only in small doses. For some people the largest measure they are able to achieve is to be able to discern which other people have received a larger portion of the gift—or at least to know enough to attach ourselves to that community to whom Jesus addressed this promise: "When the Spirit of truth comes, he will guide you into all truth" (John 16:13). Indeed, the fact that this promise *is* addressed to a community takes on a special significance when we think of the liberationists' appropriate insistence that we discern the more "macro" working of the Spirit in the world.

The second area of functioning is volitional. This is the dimension of moral consciousness that seems to be most readily identified with the ministry of the Spirit. This is not surprising; that much-used phrase "the power of the Spirit" seems to lend itself quite easily to a volitional emphasis. The lack of moral power is a common experience for most of us. *Akrasia* is a crucial topic for philosophical-theological exploration.[50]

The third area, the affective, has not always received the pneumatological attention that it deserves with references to moral subjectivity. Strictly speaking, one could acknowledge intellectually the proper norms or models for Christian morality and also have the volitional strength to do what is right and still lack the element requested in the biblical prayer, "Create in me a new heart, O Lord." It is the Holy Spirit who must instill the *longing* for justice within us, a *love* for the poor, a *compassion* for the needy, a heart that *desires* the good of the widow and orphan and prisoner and sojourner, a *felt* hope for the reign of peace and righteousness.

The sensitivity to the need for this kind of affective equipping of the moral consciousness has been most prominently displayed in various pietist traditions. To be sure, pietists have often advocated the importance of moral feelings in such a way that the work of justice has been given short shrift, substituting the platitude that "only changed hearts will change society" for the more profound insight that the long-range possibilities for achieving and maintaining a just order require that people operate with a felt disposition to do, and to love, justice. But the distortions ought not to distract us from an awareness of the significance of moral affections.

Gilbert Meilaender points to the crucial requirement in this regard by emphasizing the importance of cultivating "the *virtue* of justice, with its steady, habitual determination to make space in life for the needs and claims of others."[51] But more attention must be given in Christian ethics to the mechanism for creating this internal affective "space" in which the concerns of other persons can find their place in our moral consciousness. Father Henri Nouwen nudges us in the right theological direction here in reporting a discovery that he made during his stay at the Trappist Monastery of the Genessee:

> [P]rayer is the only real way to clean my heart and to create new space. I am discovering how important that inner space is. When it is there it seems that I can receive many concerns of others. . . . I can pray for many others and feel a very intimate relationship with them. There even seems to be room for the thousands of suffering people in prisons and in the deserts of North Africa. Sometimes I feel as if my heart expands from my parents traveling in Indonesia to my friends in Los Angeles and from the Chilean prisons to the parishes in Brooklyn.
>
> Now I know that it is not I who pray but the spirit of God who prays in me. . . . He himself prays in me and touches the whole world with his love right here and now. At those moments all questions about "the social relevance of prayer, etc." seem dull and very unintelligent. . . .[52]

And the same can be said, we must immediately add, about all questions concerning the moral relevance of the ministry of the Holy Spirit.

9

DIVINE AUTHORITY AND THE
QUEST FOR SOLIDARITY

Mᴏʀᴀʟ ᴀᴜᴛᴏɴᴏᴍʏ ʜᴀꜱ ʙᴇᴇɴ ᴍᴜᴄʜ emphasized in the
ethical theorizing of the past two centuries. And it has become a
matter of intense celebration in popular ethical thinking in this
century—a fact that I noted at the very beginning of this book. The
mood has not been one of unmitigated festivity, however. The
boastful "I did it my way" credo has not been the only ethical song
that has been sung.

Moral philosophers, even those who have seemed to endorse
with great enthusiasm the notion of the individual moral agent as a
self-legislator, have also demonstrated an interest in human soli-
darities. This is a matter on which, for example, consequentialists
and deontologists sometimes offer surprisingly similar formulations. Consider the cases of John Stuart Mill and Sir David Ross,
ethicists who loom large as representing radically opposed positions in many widely circulated taxonomies.

For Mill, the appeal to a community of decision-makers becomes very important when he discusses questions about qualita-
tive differences among pleasures in chapter 2 of *Utilitarianism*.
How do we decide matters of quality? And what reason do we even
have for thinking that the "higher" pleasures, the aesthetic and
intellectual enjoyments which Mill associates with our "nobler"
feelings, are to be preferred to those "lower" pleasures which are
so readily available to "the fool"?—a question which takes on a
special poignancy for Mill because of his conviction that our ca-
pacity for "nobler" experiences "is in most natures a very tender
plant."[1]

Our only recourse, Mill answers, is to draw upon the wisdom

of others, especially those persons who have experienced both the higher and the lower pleasures:

> From this verdict of the only competent judges, I apprehend there can be no appeal. On a question which is the best worth having of two pleasures, or which of two modes of existence is the most grateful to the feelings, apart from its moral attributes and from its consequences, the judgment of those who are qualified by knowledge of both, or, if they differ, that of the majority among them, must be admitted as final. And there needs to be the less hesitation to accept this judgment respecting the quality of pleasures, since there is no other tribunal to be referred to even on the question of quantity.[2]

The deontologist Ross highlights the importance of a community of decision-makers by arguing that collective wisdom is the only proper source of the "facts" to which we must direct our moral reflection. In the natural sciences we have ways of testing the judgments of "reasonably thoughtful and well-educated people" to see whether they are reliable; we can check them against sense-experience. But no such independent basis is available in moral investigation:

> We have no more direct way of access to the facts about rightness and goodness and about what things are right or good, than by thinking about them; the moral convictions of thoughtful and well-educated people are the data of ethics just as sense perceptions are the data of a natural science. . . . The existing body of moral convictions of the best people is the cumulative product of the moral reflection of many generations, which has developed an extremely delicate power of appreciation of moral distinctions; and this the theorist cannot afford to treat with anything other than the greatest respect. The verdicts of the moral consciousness of the best people are the foundation on which he must build; though he must first compare them with one another and eliminate any contradictions they may contain.[3]

It is not difficult to raise critical questions about these appeals. Many of us today will be less convinced than Mill was that the majority of people who have experienced both the "higher" and "lower" pleasures will naturally gravitate toward the sorts of experiences that he obviously preferred. Nor is it clear in these times of heightened cross-cultural awareness that "the moral convictions of thoughtful and well-educated people" form a body of data that possesses anything like the degree of coherence that Ross seemed to take for granted.

But we must not allow such questions to divert our attention from the significant fact that both Mill and Ross do find it necessary to stipulate the need for drawing upon "the moral consciousness of the best people."

Why this common desire, in two otherwise very different accounts of moral justification, to link one's moral deliberations to the deliverances of a "tribunal" of "competent judges"?

WHY A TRIBUNAL?

There are at least four factors at work in this kind of appeal to collective moral experience. Some of the matters relating to these factors have been touched upon in earlier parts of my discussion. But it is worth raising them again in this context, and looking also at a few themes not yet discussed, in order to ascertain what might be the implications of the communal impulses in recent ethical thought for a contemporary understanding of God's moral authority.

An obvious factor has to do with the need to have some basis for *commending* one's normative perspectives to an audience for its consideration. It is conceivable, of course, that an ethicist might subscribe to a doctrine without wanting to commend it to others. It is possible, for example, that someone might believe that there is only one obligation in the entire universe, namely, the obligation for him to pursue only his own self-interest. Brian Medlin has questioned whether such an outlook would deserve to be called an ethical doctrine—he doubts that it is either "ethical" or a "doctrine."[4] Medlin's doubts here seem to be grounded in his conviction that an ethical doctrine must be capable of being promulgated, which seems to include, in his view, the willingness to commend it to others for their consideration. And in the case of the perspective just mentioned, it is difficult to see how that promulgation might be spelled out.

Most philosophical ethicists, however, have clearly intended to commend their accounts of normative decision making to others for their consideration. Usually they have set forth their views as the best way of making sense of their audience's own convictions and inclinations. Or if they have presented their systems as correctives or alternatives to the ways in which people in their audience live out their moral lives they have typically done so by instructing the audience—MacIntyre's *After Virtue* is a good case in point here—about the ways in which their present moral experience is confused or misguided, pointing them to other times and places when moral convictions and impulses were in a healthier state of repair.

In any event, the attempt to show that a specific normative theory can make good sense of "the moral consciousness of the best people" seems always to be in order, even if the audience to which the argument is primarily addressed is not thought of by the presenter as a good sample of "the best people." Mill and Ross are obviously concerned with this matter of commending their theories to others as plausible accounts of the deliverances of collective ethical wisdom. The fund of common moral experiences serves, in their respective schemes, as the *explanandum* of moral theorizing.

But there is also a second factor at work in the appeal to collective moral experience: an obvious desire to rely on moral *expertise*. The respect for expertise is actually a strong current in twentieth-century moral philosophy, one that functions as a supplement—if not a counterbalance—to the celebration of autonomy. Autonomous decision making has seldom been proposed as a sufficient condition for healthy decision making. Perhaps some existentialist and "human potential" type proponents of "authenticity" come close to treating self-legislating action in this manner, but this is usually due to a sloppiness in spelling out their intended views.

In thinkers like Mill and Ross, healthy decision making requires that autonomy at least be conjoined to the possession of the right sort of normative perspective—a commitment to the principle of utility in Mill's case and a clarity about the nature of obligation in Ross's. But even the presence of these two elements—autonomy plus the right perspective—does not guarantee proper moral functioning. The making of wise moral decisions requires something more: the kind of expertise that comes from drawing on the insights of "the best people."

The recognition of the need for collective expertise seems to be linked to an uneasiness about our untutored moral sensitivities. This same uneasiness has sometimes been at work in the formulation of social contract perspectives, a fact that is often missed by people who insist that social contract theories are mere celebrations of the pre-social "isolated individual." Contractarian perspectives have often been informed by a motive that is decidedly *non-*"individualistic"—namely, a desire to transcend those psychological and social particularities that are associated with the isolation of our present situatedness, by specifying those conditions that guarantee that attention will be given to those sorts of concerns that the individual can be viewed as holding in common with others.

Whatever we make of the enthusiasm shown in recent moral philosophy for the autonomous individual, it is difficult to deny that philosophers have been rather nervous about the abilities, at least the cognitive abilities requisite for healthy decision making, of the very real moral agents whom they encounter in the world. The regular calls that ethicists issue for people to take advantage of collective expertise are evidence for the presence of some degree of cognitive insecurity.

A third factor is an interest in moral *vindication*. The desire to be vindicated is especially strong where there is an acute awareness of serious differences which are not presently resolvable, and there has been a strong interest in moral differences of this sort in recent ethical and meta-ethical discussion. To be sure, not all ethicists who have attended to the reality of such differences have been greatly disturbed by them. R. M. Hare is a good case in point in this regard; while conceding that the method of moral justification that he set forth in *Freedom and Reason* would not prohibit Afrikaner racists from consistently sticking to their positions, Hare nonetheless minimized the significance of this stalemate. Consistent fanatics, he argued, "are surely very few." Their influence lies in their ability to enlist the help of "a multitude of other people who . . . have not really thought through the argument."[5]

Other philosophers have been more troubled by the fact of ethical stalemates. I have already observed that William Frankena has built the desire for ultimate vindication against one's moral opponents into his analysis of what is going on in the very making of a moral judgment: to say that some course of action is right is, in his scheme, to claim that one's endorsement of that course of action would be vindicated by those persons—or by that ultimate Observer—who considered the issue under the optimal conditions for moral decision making.[6]

I have also noted that Frankena is fond of using biblical imagery in spelling out the nature of the tribunal whose vindication we (at least implicitly) claim in making moral judgments. A similar fondness for scriptural themes was displayed on occasion by Bertrand Russell, as in these comments about the influence of his grandmother on his moral development:

> She had the Protestant belief in private judgment and the supremacy of the individual conscience. On my twelfth birthday she gave me a Bible (which I still possess), and wrote her favorite texts on the flyleaf. One of them was "Thou shalt not follow a multitude to do evil;" another, "Be strong, and of a good courage; be not afraid, neither be Thou dismayed; for the Lord Thy God is with thee whithersoever thou goest." These texts have profoundly influenced my life, and still seemed to retain some meaning after I had ceased to believe in God.[7]

Russell's meaning here seems obvious and straightforward. He is pleased to have inherited a belief in the reliability of "private judgment and the supremacy of the individual conscience," and while he is quite willing to acknowledge the Protestant origins of this belief, he is confident that it can be sustained even when detached from its religious moorings. But Russell also recognizes that Christianity provided an important reinforcement for its insistence that people live in accordance with the dictates of their consciences: the conviction that conscientious living will ultimately be vindicated, even if under present conditions we are required to take a stand against a multitude of evil-doers. This is the "meaning" which Russell wanted to preserve, even if he could no longer accept the metaphysical undergirding which Protestantism provided for the sense that ultimate reality is on the side of those who do what is right.

Russell's comments also hint in the direction of our fourth factor: the desire to overcome moral *loneliness*. Autonomous decision making can be a very lonely business. If Anglo-American ethicists have said little about this fact it is because loneliness is a matter of mood, and they have not paid much attention in their writings to the moods of decision making. Moral moods have been more the stuff for existentialist reflection.

Nietzsche is often viewed as a lover of moral solitude, and in a sense this is an accurate description. But it is difficult to avoid the impression that he finds this love no easy thing to purchase. In *The Will to Power* he depicts the discontent that goes with the kind of solitude that he prescribes:

> Men who are destinies, who by bearing themselves bear destinies, the whole species of *heroic* bearers of burdens: oh how they would like to rest from themselves for once! how they thirst for strong hearts and necks, so as to be free from what oppresses them, at least for a few hours! And how vainly they thirst!—They wait; they look at everything that passes: no one approaches them with as much as a thousandth part of their suffering and passion, no one divines *in what way* they are waiting—At length, at length they learn their first piece of worldly prudence—not to wait any more; and soon another one: to be genial, to be modest, from now on to everything—in short, to endure even a little more than they have endured so far.[8]

Such are the burdens borne by those whom Nietzsche very candidly refers to as "these men of incomprehensible loneliness."[9]

FINDING CONCLUSIONS

It is easy for Christians to misuse the kind of discussion I am attempting here. There are genuine dangers involved when Christians attempt to probe the moods and motives and projects of secular thought. For one thing, we have had our own Christian moods and motives and projects so often analyzed and reanalyzed in the past century by representatives of modernity—Freudians, Marxists, existentialists, positivists—who take delight in probing what they think to be our deepest anxieties and insecurities, that there is something attractive about the idea of turning the tables as we examine their attempts to cope with reality.

And of course it is not all that difficult to find grist for this kind of mill. Russell and Nietzsche are two figures whose style of expression seems especially to lend itself to this kind of probing. But they are also people against whom there has been enough false-witness-bearing from Christian quarters that it is prudent to exercise some caution in this regard. The actual claims that they present for our consideration are interesting enough, without digging for meanings for which they themselves would not claim ownership.

My own purpose here in briefly exploring the differences between Christian and secular moral thinking draws some inspiration from Paul Tillich's formulation of what he termed "the method of correlation."[10] In advocating this approach Tillich was attempting to steer his way between two alternatives. One was the "kerygmatic theology" that he associated with Karl Barth, which treated non-Christian thought as so fundamentally misguided that all Christians could do was to "proclaim" in response to it. The other viewpoint was the kind of humanistic Christianity which treated one or another secular system as normative and attempted to accommodate the Christian message to its terms and standards.

Rejecting these alternatives, the method of correlation does not presume that commonalities and syntheses are easy to come by, or even that they are always within our reach. It functions more as what we might think of as a hermeneutic of encouragement: it embodies a commitment to explicating the questions of non-Christian thinkers in the hope of finding ways of "co-relating" their discussions with Christian concerns.

I am not altogether comfortable with Tillich's way of characterizing the method of correlation. His tendency is to say that Christians must look for the *questions* that people are asking and then try to find revealed *answers* to them: "The Christian message provides the answers to the questions implied in human existence."[11] It seems to me more satisfactory to think of the correlation as between, not secular questions and Christian answers, but between two agendas: secular thinkers pose both questions and answers and Christians, having immersed themselves empathetically in those conversations, turn to the questions and answers that are dealt with in revelation. There are times when God rejects the very questions that people ask, a pattern that occurs frequently in the ministry of Jesus.

But Tillich is right to insist on a dialogic co-relating in contrast to both kerygmaticism and accommodationism. My own sympathies for the formal approach set forth by Tillich are based on a mixture of predisposition and empirical evidence. Abraham Kuyper is reported to have said that he regularly had to adjust his Calvinist sensitivities to the surprising facts that the unbelieving world often acted much better than he expected and the church much worse. Others of us have had similar surprises.

It is important, though, to continue to treat them *as* surprises. My own theology tells me that if everyone were acting according to plan we would get much better things from the church and much worse from the world. But the surprises keep us from putting too much stock in what Christians actually produce, and they also keep us open to any lessons we might learn from the cultured despisers of religion. So we hold out the hope for dialogue, attempting to correlate wherever and whenever possible.

When the topic is moral authority the correlations are not uniformly easy to establish. Obviously there is much in recent secular moral thought that is simply antithetical to the views of those of us who accept biblical teaching. In chapter one we noted various ways in which non-Christian thinkers are offended by the very notion that human beings are required to bow before the will of a divine Creator. This offense is very real and we ought not to try to "correlate" it out of existence. There is no easy truce to be found between modern secularists and believers on the questions of moral authority and responsibility.

But neither must we settle for a relationship characterized by unrelieved hostility. As Christians explain the ways in which God's moral authority functions in their lives, it seems likely that many initial charges lodged against Christian morality can be shown to be in need of either retraction or revision. I think that I gave convincing reasons in chapter one, for example, that the claim that Christian morality is "infantile" cannot be plausibly maintained.

It is also necessary to be open to retraction and revision in the other direction. Christians have been all too eager to use labels like "Satanic" and "narcissistic" in characterizing secularist defenses of moral autonomy. A careful consideration of the actual cases developed in modern moral thought should lead us to make more nuanced assessments. Indeed it is possible to find themes associated with the advocacy of moral autonomy to which thoughtful

Christians can resonate. I have been trying to explicate a few of those themes in this chapter.

Not that I have been outlining these themes in preparation for an accommodationist settlement. It certainly would be misleading to suggest that even on some points we Christians and the secularists are saying "the same thing." I have no interest, for example, in populating the world of ethical investigation with "anonymous Christians."

QUEST AND FULFILLMENT

What Christians can say to secular moral theorists, it seems to me, is something of this sort: that at least some of the things that they are looking for in a moral perspective are fulfilled in a very significant way in the Christian scheme of things. Again, it is not my purpose here to give a detailed account of the agenda of recent moral theorizing; neither, then, will I attempt a carefully formulated account of how Christianity can be viewed as responding to this complex discussion. But a few programmatic comments along these lines are in order as I conclude the discussion that I have been pursuing in this book.

Alongside of the celebration of autonomy in the moral thought of the past one hundred years or so there has been a strong interest in moral community. I have mentioned four themes associated with this quest for community: ethicists have had an obvious concern to convince an audience of the correctness of their views; they have shown a deep respect for expertise; they have expressed a strong desire for moral vindication; and they have on occasion given poignant expression to a need to overcome moral loneliness.

Theological ethicists will sense an important opportunity here to explore ecclesiological themes as a way of establishing Christian links to these items on the secularist agenda. Indeed the mutual implications between ecclesiology and moral thought have been given much attention in recent Christian discussions; the emphasis on the church as a "community of moral discourse" has figured prominently in writings representing various points of view in the Christian ethical dialogue of the past few decades.[12]

There are other points of departure, though, for exploring the connections between the two agendas. One is a discussion of God's own nature as it is depicted in the Scriptures. Karl Barth was right to make much of the fact that the very first chapter of the Bible gives a glimpse of a God who is very much immersed in a dialogue with an audience: "Let *us* make humankind in *our* own image" is the resolution of a deity, as Barth puts it, "who is not . . . solitary, but includes in Himself the differentiation of I and Thou."[13]

No Christian group has run more of a risk of viewing the deity as a solitary monarch than Calvinism. Yet as we have seen, Calvinists have attempted to avoid this depiction by viewing the omnipotent Sovereign as immersed in lawlike consistency and covenantal fidelity. If this awareness of the divine commitment to loving communion with human beings can also be conjoined with a conscious emphasis on God's trinitarian nature, the result would be the kind of picture laid out so clearly by the Cistercian theologian, Roch Kereszty:

> God is not, as it were, an isolated kingly hermit, but an infinitely powerful and intense communication of life between the Father and the Son in the Spirit. . . . The Triune God is the model of perfect community that makes us understand why a human person becomes truly himself only if he is integrated into a community. . . . [T]he central Christian mystery, if presented in the "language" of our times, is perhaps more "relevant" today than ever before. The total self-giving of God to man in Christ that constitutes the infinite value of the human person, the Trinitarian communion as the archetype, source, and ultimate assurance of every human communion, corresponds to the most pressing needs and the secret hopes of modern man.[14]

Kereszty is suggesting in a rather straightforward manner the kind of correlation I have been pointing to. At least some people in recent times—I have been focusing specifically on philosophers—have shown a strong interest in the possibilities for moral community. The Bible presents us, Kereszty says, with a vision of community, human community grounded in divine community, that "corresponds" to these "most pressing needs and hopes" of modernity.

This seems to me to be a most helpful and important way of stating the correspondence. Modern moral philosophers have been searching for a point of view that will satisfy deep human needs for consensus, certainty, vindication, and solidarity. The Christian religion respects that quest. But it also teaches, as Augustine stated it so clearly, that our restlessness, in whatever form it manifests itself, can only be quieted when we find a blessedness that we cannot manufacture for ourselves. Like all of the other expressions of our human restlessness, our moral quest can only find a satisfying resting-place when we arrive at the divine Source.

The correlation here was seen clearly by, of all people, Rousseau, when he described the proper task of the legislator in *The Social Contract*:

> The task of discovering the best laws, i.e., those that are most salutary for each nation, calls for a mind of the highest order. This mind would have insight into each and every human passion, and *yet* be affected by none. It would be superhuman, and *yet* understand human nature through and through. It would be willing to concern itself with our happiness, but would seek its own outside us. It would content itself with fame far off in the future; i.e., it would be capable of laboring in one century and reaping its reward in the next.[15]

Rousseau seems quite attuned to the concerns that have motivated the quest for a proper grasp of the moral point of view in recent ethical thought. But Rousseau is also very aware of what it would take to instantiate these characteristics. He immediately adds this observation: "Law-giving is a task for gods not men."

The fact that someone like Rousseau could establish this correlation so unambiguously tells us something about what a method of correlation both is and is not capable of producing. There are various ways in which one can proceed from the acknowledgment that it would require a divine nature fully to realize and occupy the moral point of view. One could argue that since there is no deity we are left with no option but despair. Or one could insist that the picture of a deity, while not corresponding to anything that is the case, nonetheless provides us with an ideal that we can attempt to approximate as best we can, given our finitude.

Or one can testify to the conviction that the god-like perspective sketched out by the philosophers is indeed instantiated in the One who calls us to obedience in the context of a community of worshippers.

Of course, the testimonies presented by those of us who embrace this last option will not be compelling to those who are convinced that human authority, while not exactly divine in the fullest sense of the term, is the best thing we will ever come up with in our explorations of the farthest reaches of the moral universe. But this does not mean that the dialogue must necessarily stop at the point where some of us say that there is a God and others deny the truth of our testimonies. We can agree, perhaps, to continue to talk together about the moral quest that got us to thinking about the ultimate nature of moral reality. Then we can tell our stories about why we have come to see things in the way that we do, expanding those narratives to include accounts about why and how our respective pilgrimages make sense to each of us.

And in all of this we Christians can hope that our moral stories will echo something of that Word about the human drama that so deserves to be called good news that it could never have been invented by the likes of us.

NOTES

INTRODUCTION

1. Jean-Pierre de Caussade, *The Sacrament of the Present Moment*, trans. Kitty Muggeridge (New York: Harper & Row, 1982), 49.

2. Ibid., 58.

3. Marilyn McCord Adams, "Problems of Evil: More Advice to Christian Philosophers," *Faith and Philosophy* 5 (April 1988): 139.

1. COMMANDS FOR GROWNUPS

1. Thomas à Kempis, *The Imitation of Christ*, ed. with an Introduction by Harold C. Gardiner (Garden City, N.Y.: Doubleday & Co., Image Books, 1955), 143.

2. Peter Geach, *God and the Soul*, Studies in Ethics and the Philosophy of Religion (New York: Schocken Books, 1969), 117.

3. John Courtney Murray, *The Problem of God: Yesterday and Today*, St. Thomas More Lectures (New Haven: Yale University Press, 1964), 105–106.

4. Graeme de Graff, "God and Morality," in *Christian Ethics and Contemporary Philosophy*, ed. Ian T. Ramsey (New York: Macmillan, 1966), 34.

5. Joseph Fletcher, *Situation Ethics: The New Morality* (Philadelphia: Westminster Press, 1966), 26.

6. Lewis B. Smedes, *Mere Morality: What God Expects from Ordinary People* (Grand Rapids, Mich.: Eerdmans, 1983), 5.

7. Patrick H. Nowell-Smith, "Morality: Religious and Secular," reprinted in *Christian Ethics and Contemporary Philosophy*, ed. Ramsey, 103.

8. Jean Piaget, *The Moral Judgment of the Child*, trans. Marjorie Gabain (New York: Free Press, 1965), 106.

9. Ibid.

10. Ibid., 107.

11. For a concise account of Kohlberg's scheme, see Lawrence Kohlberg, "Stages of Moral Development as a Basis for Moral Education," in *Moral Education: Interdisciplinary Approaches*, eds. Beck, Crittenden, and Sullivan (Toronto: University of Toronto Press, 1971).

12. Erich Fromm, *Escape from Freedom* (New York: Avon Books, Discus Edition, 1941), 50.

13. Ibid., 45–46.

14. Ibid., 46.

15. Karl Marx, *Economic and Philosophic Manuscripts of 1844*, ed. with an Introduction by Dirk J. Struik, trans. Martin Milligan (New York: International Publishers, 1964), 111.

16. Geach, *God and Soul*, 127.

17. See my *Politics and the Biblical Drama* (Grand Rapids, Mich.: Eerdmans, 1976), 39–41.

18. Paul Tillich, *Systematic Theology*, 3 vols. (Chicago: University of Chicago Press, 1951–63), 1 (1951): 92–96; see also 3 (1963): 264–282.

19. Herman Bavinck, *The Philosophy of Revelation* (Longman, Green & Co., 1909; repr., Grand Rapids, Mich.: Baker Book House, 1979), 262–263.

2. ETHICS AND WORLDVIEW

1. See, for example, Henry Stob, *Theological Reflections: Essays on Related Themes* (Grand Rapids, Mich.: Eerdmans, 1981), 130.

2. Brian J. Walsh and J. Richard Middleton, *The Transforming Vision: Shaping a Christian World View* (Downers Grove, Ill.: InterVarsity Press, 1984), 35.

3. Leslie Stevenson, *Seven Theories of Human Nature* (New York: Oxford University Press, 1974), 4–5.

4. In this regard see Alvin Plantinga's much discussed essay, "Advice to Christian Philosophers," *Faith and Philosophy* 1 (July 1984): 253–271.

5. For a good collection of Robert Merrihew Adams's essays see his *The Virtue of Faith and Other Essays in Philosophical Theology* (New York: Oxford University Press, 1987). Some of Adams's essays are included also in the useful anthology *Divine Commands and Morality*, Oxford Readings in Philosophy, ed. Paul Helm (Oxford: Oxford University Press, 1981).

6. James G. Hanink and Gary R. Mar, "What Euthyphro Couldn't Have Said," *Faith and Philosophy* 4 (July 1987): 241.

7. Robert M. Adams, "Divine Commands and the Social Nature of Obligation," *Faith and Philosophy* 4 (July 1987): 272.

8. Hanink and Mar, "Euthyphro," 249.

9. John Piper, *Desiring God: Meditations of a Christian Hedonist* (Portland, Ore.: Multnomah Press, 1986), 262.

10. Jeremy Bentham, *An Introduction to the Principles of Morals and Legislation* (London: W. Pickering, 1823), 1:53.

11. Ibid., 1:59.

12. John Stuart Mill, *Utilitarianism, Liberty, and Representative Government*, with an Introduction by A. D. Lindsay, Everyman's Library (New York: E. P. Dutton & Co., 1951), 26.

13. Piper, *Desiring God*, 19.

14. Diogenes Laertius, *Lives of Eminent Philosophers*, trans. R. D. Hicks, rev. ed., The Loeb Classical Library (Cambridge: Harvard University Press, 1950), 2:657.

15. Mill himself alternates between the use of "pleasure" and "happiness," explicitly equating the two in his account of "What Utilitarianism Is"; see chapter 2 of *Utilitarianism*.

16. See C. S. Lewis's letter of 5 November 1959 in *Letters of C. S. Lewis*, ed. with a Memoir by W. H. Lewis (London: Geoffrey Bles, 1966), 289.

17. Hanink and Mar, "Euthyphro," 249.

18. Ibid.

19. A well-known recent discussion of the stages of maturation in the Christian faith is James W. Fowler, *Stages of Faith: The Psychology of Human Development and the Quest for Meaning* (San Francisco: Harper & Row, 1981). See also the critical evaluations of Fowler's approach in Craig Dykstra and Sharon Parks, eds., *Faith and Development and Fowler* (Birmingham, Ala.: Religious Education Press, 1986).

20. Hanink and Mar, "Euthyphro," 248.

21. Ibid., 248–249.

22. Paul Arthur Schilpp and Maurice Friedman, eds., *The Philosophy of Martin Buber*, The Library of Living Philosophers, vol. 12 (La Salle, Ill.: Open Court, 1967), 10.

3. ON BEING FAIR TO "INDIVIDUALISM"

1. H. H. Rowley, *The Faith of Israel: Aspects of Old Testament Thought* (London: SCM Press, 1956), 100.

2. Steven Lukes, *Individualism*, Key Concepts in the Social Sciences (Oxford: Basil Blackwell, 1973), 69–70.

3. In regard to Roman Catholic ecclesiology see Avery Dulles's ex-

cellent discussion in his chapter entitled "The Church as Mystical Communion" in *Models of the Church* (Garden City, N.Y.: Doubleday & Co., 1974), especially pp. 44–49, 51–54. See also F. W. Dillistone, *The Structure of the Divine Society* (Philadelphia: Westminster Press, 1951), 101, 106–107, 159–160, 176–177. For a discussion of this motif in Eastern Orthodoxy see Stefan Zankov, *The Eastern Orthodox Church*, trans. and ed. Donald A. Lowrie (Milwaukee, Wisc.: Morehouse Publishing Co., 1929), 69–71; and Nicolas Zernov, *Eastern Christendom: A Study of the Origin and Development of the Eastern Orthodox Church* (London: Weidenfeld & Nicolson, 1961), 227–229. For a perspective on society and the state as "organisms" see Thomas J. Higgins's *Man as Man: the Science and Art of Ethics*, rev. ed. (Milwaukee, Wisc.: Bruce Publishing Co., 1958), 348, 426–430; also Jacques Maritain, *Man and the State* (Chicago: University of Chicago Press, Phoenix Books, 1951), 9–10, 12–13.

4. See the discussion of Afrikaner "organicism" in T. Dunbar Moodie, *The Rise of Afrikanerdom: Power, Apartheid, and the Afrikaner Civil Religion* (Berkeley: University of California Press, 1975), 154–160.

5. In acknowledging the relevance of the marriage analogy Sir Ernest Barker notes that the agreement between spouses "is necessary to the existence of marriage. But it does not explain, or create, the institution of marriage. The institution is an inherent part of the divine scheme; and the agreement of the parties is simply an agreement to fit themselves into that scheme, which exists per se apart from their agreement." See the note to Otto Gierke, *Natural Law and the Theory of Society: 1500 to 1800*, trans. with an Introduction by Ernest Barker (London: Cambridge University Press, 1934), 241–242. This assessment is endorsed by J. W. Gough, *The Social Contract: A Critical Study of Its Development* (Oxford: Clarendon Press, 1936), 67; Gough sees the marriage analogy as illustrating "the half-truth of the social contract theory" (p. 67).

6. Ronald Nash, "Three Kinds of Individualism," *Intercollegiate Review* 12 (Fall 1976): 40.

7. James H. Cone, *The Spirituals and the Blues: An Interpretation* (New York: Seabury Press, 1972), 67–68.

8. Frederick S. Perls, *Gestalt Therapy Verbatim*, ed. John O. Stevens (New York: Bantam Books, 1969), 4.

9. Frederick Douglass, *My Bondage and My Freedom*, with an Introduction by James M'Cune Smith (New York: Miller, Orton & Mulligan, 1855; repr., New York: Arno Press and the New York Times, 1968), 423.

10. Helmut Gollwitzer, *The Christian Faith and the Marxist Criticism of Religion*, trans. David Cairns (New York: Charles Scribner's Sons, 1970), 112.

11. See Dietrich Bonhoeffer, *Life Together*, trans. John W. Dober-stein (London: SCM Press, 1954).

12. F. W. Dillistone, *Divine Society*, 181.

4. THE REFORMATION'S "NAKED SELF"

1. Jacques Maritain, *Three Reformers: Luther–Descartes–Rous-seau* (New York: Charles Scribner's Sons, 1955), 18, 35.

2. Ibid., 4.

3. Ibid., 19.

4. Alasdair MacIntyre, *After Virtue: A Study in Moral Theory*, 2d ed. (Notre Dame, Ind.: University of Notre Dame Press, 1984), 260.

5. Alasdair MacIntyre, *A Short History of Ethics: A History of Moral Philosophy from the Homeric Age to the Twentieth Century*, Fields of Philosophy (New York: Macmillan, 1966), 121.

6. Ibid., 122.

7. Ibid., 122–123.

8. Ibid., 121.

9. Ibid., 123–124.

10. Ibid., 124.

11. Ibid., 126.

12. MacIntyre, *After Virtue*, 52–53.

13. Ibid., 53.

14. Ibid., 53–54.

15. MacIntyre, *Short History*, 124.

16. MacIntyre, *After Virtue*, 172.

17. Ibid., 113–114.

18. MacIntyre, *Short History*, 126–127.

19. John Calvin, *Institutes of the Christian Religion*, 2 vols., trans. Ford Lewis Battles, ed. John T. McNeill, Library of Christian Classics, vols. 20–21 (Philadelphia: Westminster Press, 1960), II, VIII, 8.

20. Ibid., II, VIII, 51.

21. Ibid., II, VIII, 1.

22. MacIntyre, *After Virtue*, 173.

23. For studies of the scope and nature of Calvin's political and economic interests, see Andre Bieler, *The Social Humanism of Calvin*, trans. Paul T. Fuhrmann, with a Foreword by W. A. Visser't Hooft (Richmond, Va.: John Knox Press, 1964); W. Fred Graham, *The Constructive Revolutionary: John Calvin and His Socio-Economic Impact* (Richmond, Va.: John Knox Press, 1971); and Harro Hopfl, *The Christian Polity of John Calvin*, Cambridge Studies in the History and Theory of Politics

(New York: Cambridge University Press, 1982; Cambridge Paperback Library, 1985).

24. Calvin, quoted in Graham, *Constructive Revolutionary*, 158–159.

25. Calvin, *Institutes*, I, III, 2.

26. One attempt to tell this story in detail is found in chapters 5 and 6 of Herman Dooyeweerd, *Roots of Western Culture: Pagan, Secular, and Christian Options*, ed. Mark Vander Vennen and Bernard Zylstra, trans. John Kraay (Toronto: Wedge Publishing Foundation, 1979).

27. MacIntyre, *After Virtue*, 53–54.

28. Calvin, *Institutes*, II, II, 17.

29. Ibid., II, II, 18.

30. Ibid.

31. David Cairns, *The Image of God in Man*, with an Introduction by David E. Jenkins, rev. ed., The Fontana Library of Theology and Philosophy (London: Collins, 1973), 137.

32. Abraham Kuyper, *Lectures on Calvinism*, L. P. Stone Foundation Lectures, 1898 (Grand Rapids, Mich.: Eerdmans, 1931), 49.

33. Peter Berger, "On the Obsolescence of the Concept of Honor," in *Revisions: Changing Perspectives in Moral Philosophy*, ed. Stanley Hauerwas and Alasdair MacIntyre, A Series of Books on Ethics, vol. 3 (Notre Dame, Ind.: University of Notre Dame Press, 1983), 177.

34. Ibid., 176.

35. William J. Bouwsma, "Calvin and the Dilemma of Hypocrisy," in *Calvin and Christian Ethics*, ed. Peter De Klerk, Fifth Colloquium on Calvin and Calvin Studies (Grand Rapids, Mich.: Calvin Studies Society, 1987), 3.

36. Ibid., 6.

37. Ibid., 7–8.

38. Ibid., 8.

39. Charles Haddon Spurgeon, *Spurgeon's Sermons*, Memorial Library (Grand Rapids, Mich.: Zondervan Publishing House, n.d.), 6:349.

40. Calvin, *Institutes*, I, I, 1.

41. Ibid., IV, VII, 21.

42. Ibid., II, II, 10.

5. EMOTIVISM AS PLAGIARISM

1. S. U. Zuidema, *Sartre*, trans. Dirk Jellema, Modern Thinkers Series, ed. David H. Freeman, International Library of Philosophy and Theology (Philadelphia: Presbyterian and Reformed Publishing Co., 1960), 56.

2. Eric Russell Bentley, *A Century of Hero-Worship: A Study of the Idea of Heroism in Carlyle and Nietzsche with Notes on Other Hero-Worshippers of Modern Times* (New York: Lippincott, 1944), 115.

3. Jean-Paul Sartre, *Existentialism and Humanism*, trans. with an Introduction by Philip Mairet (London: Methuen & Co., 1968), 29–30.

4. Ibid., 23.

5. Iris Murdoch, *The Sovereignty of Good*, Studies in Ethics and the Philosophy of Religion (New York: Schocken Books, 1971), 80.

6. Sartre, *Existentialism*, 34.

7. Arthur F. Holmes, *Contours of a World View*, Studies in a Christian World View (Grand Rapids, Mich.: Eerdmans, 1983), 16–27.

8. Friedrich Nietzsche, *Twilight of the Idols and the Anti-Christ*, trans. with an Introduction and Commentary by R. J. Hollingdale, Penguin Classics (Middlesex, England: Penguin Books, 1968), 53.

9. Patrick Riley, *Will and Political Legitimacy: A Critical Exposition of Social Contract Theory in Hobbes, Locke, Rousseau, Kant and Hegel* (Cambridge, Mass.: Harvard University Press, 1982), 19.

10. Ibid.

11. Sartre, *Existentialism*, 34.

12. MacIntyre, *After Virtue*, 113.

13. Ibid., 214.

14. See Paul Ricouer, *Freud and Philosophy: An Essay on Interpretation*, trans. Denis Savage, The Terry Lectures (New Haven, Conn.: Yale University Press, 1970), 32; and Merold Westphal, "Taking Suspicion Seriously: The Religious Uses of Modern Atheism," *Faith and Philosophy* 4 (January 1987): 26–42.

15. Nietzsche, *Twilight*, 66.

16. MacIntyre, *After Virtue*, 74–75.

17. Ibid., 75–77.

18. Ibid., 263.

19. Ludwig Feuerbach, *The Essence of Christianity*, trans. George Eliot, with an Introduction by Karl Barth, and Foreword by H. Richard Niebuhr, The Library of Religion and Culture, vol. 11 (New York: Harper & Row, Harper Torchbooks, 1957), 12.

20. Calvin, *Institutes*, I, I, 1.

21. Westphal, "Taking Suspicion," 30.

22. José Miguez Bonino, *Christians and Marxists: The Mutual Challenge to Revolution* (Grand Rapids, Mich.: Eerdmans, 1976), 70.

23. Martin E. Marty, *Varieties of Unbelief* (New York: Holt Rinehart and Winston, 1964), 192.

24. It is developed, for example, by Herman Dooyeweerd in *In the Twilight of Western Thought: Studies in the Pretended Autonomy of Philosophical Thought*, University Series, Philosophical Studies (Nutley,

N.J.: Craig Press, 1965); and Bob Goudzwaard, *Idols of Our Time*, trans. Mark Vander Vennen, with a Foreword by Howard A. Snyder (Downers Grove, Ill.: Inter-Varsity Press, 1984).

25. Friedrich Nietzsche, *Thus Spoke Zarathustra: A Book for Everyone and No One*, trans, with an Introduction by R. J. Hollingdale, Penguin Classics (Middlesex, England: Penguin Books, 1961), 216.

26. Nietzsche, *Twilight*, 54.

27. Letter #168 to Jacob Burckhardt, in *Nietzsche: A Self-Portrait from His Letters*, ed. Peter Fuss and Henry Shapiro (Cambridge, Mass.: Harvard University Press, 1971), 142, quoted by Carl A. Raschke, *The Interruption of Eternity: Modern Gnosticism and the Origins of the New Religious Consciousness* (Chicago: Nelson-Hall, 1980), 103.

28. Calvin, *Institutes*, II, IV, 1.

29. Murray, *The Problem of God*, 8–9.

30. Ibid., 10.

31. Ibid., 119.

32. Ibid.

33. Ibid., 120.

6. GOD THE POLITICIAN

1. J. N. Figgis, "Political Thought in the Sixteenth Century," *The Cambridge Modern History*, vol. 3 (Cambridge: Cambridge University Press, 1904), 747, 767.

2. Quentin Skinner, *The Foundations of Modern Political Thought*, vol. 2, *The Age of Reformation* (Cambridge: Cambridge University Press, 1978).

3. For an excellent account of Calvin's own address to the concrete issues of Genevan life see Graham, *The Constructive Revolutionary*.

4. See, for example, Calvin, *Institutes*, II, II, 12–17.

5. David Little, *Religion, Order, and Law: A Study in Pre-Revolutionary England* with a Foreword by Robert N. Bellah (New York: Harper & Row, 1969; repr., Chicago: University of Chicago Press, 1984), 37.

6. Ibid., 35.

7. Francis Oakley, *Omnipotence, Covenant and Order: An Excursion in the History of Ideas from Abelard to Leibniz* (Ithaca, N.Y.: Cornell University Press, 1984), 82.

8. Little, *Religion*, 41.

9. Skinner, *Foundations*, 2, 148.

10. Calvin, *Institutes*, IV, XX, 32.

11. Skinner, *Foundations*, 2:319–320.

12. Ibid., 2:192.

13. Little, *Religion*, 41. Little borrows this characterization from Gisbert Beyerhaus.

14. Frederick Carney, "Associational Thought in Early Calvinism," in *Voluntary Associations: A Study of Groups in Free Societies*, ed. D. B. Robertson (Richmond, Va.: John Knox Press, 1966), 51.

15. Perry Miller, *Errand into the Wilderness* (Cambridge, Mass.: Harvard University Press, Belknap Press, 1956), 63.

16. John Preston, *The New Covenant, or the Saints Portion* (London, 1629), 330–331, quoted in Miller, *Errand*, 64.

17. See H. Algra, *Het Wonder van de Negentiende Eeuw: van vrije Kerken en kleine luyden* (Franeker: Uitgeverij T. Wever B. V., 1966), 19–37, 233–240; for a brief account in English of this strain of Dutch Calvinism see J. R. Beeke, ed., *Sovereign Grace in Life and Ministry: Memorials of Four Pastors who Served Netherlands Reformed Congregations in North America*, (Sioux Center, Iowa: Netherlands Reformed Book and Pub. Committee, 1984), 253–258.

18. Carney, "Associational Thought," 52.

19. Calvin, *Institutes*, IV, XX, 16.

20. Little has rightly complained, in the Preface to the 1984 edition of his book, about the "reductionistic" tendencies in a number of recent accounts of early Calvinist political thought; see Little, *Religion*, viii.

21. See J. N. Figgis, *Studies of Political Thought from Gerson to Grotius, 1414–1625*, 2d ed. (Cambridge: Cambridge University Press, 1931); and Francis Oakley, "On the Road from Constance to 1688: The Political Thought of John Major and George Buchanan," *Journal of British Studies*, 1, no. 2 (May 1962): 1–31.

22. J. D. Douglas, *Light in the North: The Story of the Scottish Covenanters*, The Advance of Christianity through the Centuries, vol. 6 (Grand Rapids, Mich.: Eerdmans, 1964), 13.

23. Ibid., 87–88.

24. Skinner, *Foundations*, II, 2:192–194.

25. Ibid., 2:343–344.

26. Calvin, *Institutes*, IV, XX, 8.

27. Skinner, *Foundations*, 2:193.

28. Calvin, *Institutes*, IV, XX, 8.

29. Skinner, *Foundations*, 2:233.

30. Ibid., 2:192.

31. Ibid., 2:343–344.

32. Samuel Rutherford, *Lex, Rex: The Law and the Prince; A Dispute for the Just Prerogative of King and People* (London: John Field, 1644), 127–128.

33. Ibid., 265.

34. B. Katherine Brown, "A Note on the Puritan Concept of Aristocracy," *The Mississippi Valley Historical Review* 41 (June 1954): 112.

35. Rutherford, *Lex*, 139.

36. Kenneth D. McRae, "The Plural Society and the Western Political Tradition," *Canadian Journal of Political Science* 12 (December 1979): 682.

37. Ibid., 686.

38. Gough, *The Social Contract*, 6.

39. Sheldon Wolin, *Politics and Vision: Continuity and Innovation in Western Political Thought* (Boston: Little, Brown and Co., 1960), 166–168.

40. Ibid., 171.

41. Ibid., 192.

42. See John Howard Yoder, *The Politics of Jesus: Vicit Agnus Noster* (Grand Rapids, Mich.: Eerdmans, 1972), 23, 39, 46–47, 50n.

43. See Hopfl, *The Christian Polity of John Calvin*, especially chapters 7–9.

44. Wolin, *Politics*, 168.

45. George Gillespie, *Aarons Rod Blossoming; Or, The Divine Ordinance of Church-Government Vindicated* (London: Riebard Whitaker, 1646), "To the Candid Reader" (preface), n.p.

46. Ibid., 187–188.

47. Theodore Beza, "Right of Magistrates," in *Constitutionalism and Resistance in the Sixteenth Century: Three Treatises by Hotman, Beza and Mornay*, trans. and ed. Julian H. Franklin (New York: Pegasus, 1969), 129.

48. Gillespie, *Aarons Rod* (preface), 174–183.

49. Rutherford, *Lex*, 138.

50. Gillespie, *Aarons Rod* (preface), n.p.

51. Preston King, *The Ideology of Order: A Comparative Analysis of Jean Bodin and Thomas Hobbes* (New York: Harper & Row, 1974), 186.

52. Thomas Hobbes, *Leviathan: On the Matter, and Power of a Commonwealth Ecclesiastical and Civil*, ed. Michael Oakeshott, with an Introduction by Richard S. Peters, Collier Classics in the History of Thought (New York: Collier Books, 1962), 132.

7. NARRATIVE, CHARACTER, AND COMMANDS

1. William K. Frankena, *Ethics*, 2d ed., Foundations of Philosophy Series (Englewood Cliffs, N.J.: Prentice-Hall, 1973), 43–52.

2. Robert L. Holmes, "Violence and Nonviolence," in *Violence: Award-Winning Essays in the Council for Philosophical Studies Competition*, ed. with an Introduction by Jerome A. Shaffer (New York: David McKay Co., 1971), 128.

3. An important instance in this regard is William Frankena's essay "Prichard and the Ethics of Virtue," *The Monist* 54 (1971): 1–17, in which Frankena develops themes that were incorporated into the second edition of his *Ethics*; see *Ethics*, 62–70.

4. Several of these essays are collected in Alasdair MacIntyre's *Against the Self-Images of the Age: Essays on Ideology and Philosophy* (London: Duckworth & Co., 1971; repr., Notre Dame, Ind.: University of Notre Dame Press, 1978); see especially the articles in Part 2.

5. Stanley Hauerwas acknowledges his debt to MacIntyre in his *Peaceable Kingdom: A Primer in Christian Ethics* (Notre Dame. Ind.: University of Notre Dame Press, 1983), xxiv–xxv; see also the essays Hauerwas and MacIntyre wrote for their co-edited collection, *Revisions: Changing Perspectives in Moral Philosophy*, A Series of Books on Ethics, vol. 3 (Notre Dame, Ind.: University of Notre Dame Press, 1983), 1–42.

6. Gilbert C. Meilaender, *The Theory and Practice of Virtue* (Notre Dame, Ind.: University of Notre Dame Press, 1984).

7. James W. McClendon, *Ethics: Systematic Theology*, vol. 1 (Nashville: Abingdon Press, 1986); see also his article "Narrative Ethics and Christian Ethics," *Faith and Philosophy* 3 (October 1986): 383–396.

8. For a lengthy critical exploration of narrativism see Paul Nelson's helpful *Narrative and Morality: A Theological Inquiry* (University Park, Pa.: Pennsylvania State University Press, 1987). Nelson rightly worries, for example, whether narrativism can provide a legitimate basis for engaging in the critical evaluation of specific narratives. I have no doubt that the narrativists whom I discuss here want to avoid relativism. Whether they can only do so by allowing for narrative-independent moral criteria, as Nelson argues, is an important question; I would be inclined to explore the possibility of formulating a kind of "meta-narrative." I am not as convinced as both the narrativists and their critics sometimes seem to be that narrativism generates inevitable problems with "public discourse."

9. Hauerwas, *Peaceable*, 23.

10. McClendon, *Ethics*, 1:52.

11. Hauerwas, *Peaceable*, 123.

12. Meilaender, *Theory of Virtue*, 17.

13. McClendon, "Narrative Ethics," 384.

14. For critical studies of the therapeutic culture see Christopher

Lasch, *The Culture of Narcissism: American Life in an Age of Diminishing Expectations* (New York: Warner Books, 1979); and Edwin Schur, *The Awareness Trap: Self Absorption Instead of Social Change* (New York: Quadrangle/The New York Times Book Co., 1976).

15. This is the picture given by, for example, Gerard Egan, *You and Me: The Skills of Communicating and Relating to Others* (Monterey, Calif.: Brooks/Cole Publishing Co., Wadsworth Publishing Co., 1977), 74–75; and David W. Johnson, *Reaching Out: Interpersonal Effectiveness and Self-Actualization*, 2d ed. (Englewood Cliffs, N.J.: Prentice-Hall, 1981), chapter 2.

16. Eric Berne, who popularized "script-analyses," treated acting according to "script" as an unhealthy pattern. But his description of the "cure" for scripted behavior is equally dependent on dramatic categories: "At a certain point, with the help of the therapist and his own Adult, he is capable of breaking out of his script entirely and putting his own show on the road, with new characters, new roles, and a new plot and payoff." *What Do You Say After You Say Hello?: The Psychology of Human Destiny* (New York: Grove Press, 1972), 363.

17. McClendon, *Ethics*, 356.

18. Ibid.

19. Ibid.

20. Hauerwas, *Peaceable*, 16.

21. Alasdair MacIntyre, "Epistemological Crises, Dramatic Narrative and the Philosophy of Science," *The Monist* 60 (October 1977): 468.

22. Ibid., 467.

23. Cornelius Van Til, *The Defense of the Faith* (Philadelphia: Presbyterian and Reformed Publishing Co., 1955), 396.

24. Ibid., 159.

25. Ibid., 94.

26. Ibid., 28.

27. Dooyeweerd, *In the Twilight of Western Thought*, 1–7.

28. Nicholas Wolterstorff, *Reason Within the Bounds of Religion*, 2d ed. (Grand Rapids, Mich.: Eerdmans, 1984), 22.

29. Ibid., 67–68.

30. Ibid., 74.

31. Ibid., 73.

32. Ibid., 72–73.

33. Ibid., 74–75.

34. Van Til, *Defense*, 28.

35. Ibid., 94.

36. Meilaender, *Theory of Virtue*, 5.

37. James M. Gustafson, *The Contributions of Theology to Medi-*

cal Ethics, 1975 Père Marquette Theology Lecture (Milwaukee, Wisc.: Marquette University, 1975), 84.

38. Ibid.

39. Calvin, *Institutes*, II, VIII, 51.

40. For a more extensive discussion of my observations here about Just War doctrine see my essay "Can War Bring Peace? A Re-examination of the Just-War Theory in the Nuclear Age," in *Perspectives on Peacemaking: Biblical Options in the Nuclear Age*, ed. John A. Bernbaum (Ventura, Calif.: GL Publications, Regal Books, 1984); and also my essay "Biblical Justice and Peace: Toward an Evangelical-Roman Catholic Rapprochement," in *Evangelicals and the Bishops' Pastoral Letter*, ed. Dean C. Curry (Grand Rapids, Mich.: Eerdmans for the Christian College Coalition, 1984).

41. A good example of this is George R. Bach and Peter Wyden, *The Intimate Enemy: How to Fight Fair in Love and Marriage* (New York: Morrow, 1969).

42. My comments here are discussed in more detail in my essay "The Spiritual Thrust of Just War Doctrine," *New Oxford Review* 55 (March 1988): 11–14.

43. Calvin, *Institutes*, IV, XX, 12.

44. St. Augustine, *Letters*, vol. 3, trans. Sister Wilfred Parsons (New York: Fathers of the Church, Inc., 1953), Letter 138.

45. E. Brooks Holifield, *The Gentlemen Theologians: American Theology in Southern Culture, 1795–1860* (Durham, N.C.: Duke University Press, 1978), 138.

46. Sydney E. Ahlstrom, "From Puritanism to Evangelicalism: A Critical Perspective," in *The Evangelicals: What They Believe, Who They Are, Where They Are Changing*, ed. David F. Wells and John D. Woodbridge (Nashville: Abingdon Press, 1975), 272.

47. Canons of Dort, I, 12, in *Ecumenical Creeds and Reformed Confessions* (Grand Rapids, Mich.: Board of Publications of the Christian Reformed Church, 1979), 87.

48. See Klaas Runia, "Experience in the Reformed Tradition (and Its Relation to Spiritual Life)," *RES Theological Forum* 15, nos. 2 and 3 (April 1987): 10–12. See also the editor's "Who are the Netherlands Reformed Congregations?" in J. R. Beeke, ed., *Sovereign Grace in Life and Ministry: Memorials of Four Pastors Who Served Netherlands Reformed Congregations in North America* (Sioux Center, Iowa: Netherlands Reformed Book & Pub. Committee, 1984), 253–258.

49. See, for example, F. Ernest Stoeffler, *The Rise of Evangelical Pietism*, Studies in the History of Religions, vol. 9 (Leiden: E. J. Brill, 1965); and Dale W. Brown, *Understanding Pietism* (Grand Rapids,

Mich.: Eerdmans, 1978). For the influence of Pietism in North America see the excellent collection, F. Ernest Stoeffler, ed., *Continental Pietism and Early American Christianity* (Grand Rapids, Mich.: Eerdmans, 1976).

50. McClendon, *Ethics*, 1:58.

51. Krister Stendahl, "The Apostle Paul and the Introspective Conscience of the West," in *Paul Among Jews and Gentiles and Other Essays* (Philadelphia: Westminster Press, 1976), cited in McClendon, *Ethics*, 1:58.

52. McClendon, *Ethics*, 1:58.

53. Ibid.

54. Hauerwas, *Peaceable*, 35.

55. Ibid., 39–41.

56. Ibid., 26.

57. Ibid., 28.

58. R. L. Adams and R. J. Fox, "Mainlining Jesus: The New Trip," *Society* 9, no. 4 (February 1972): 53.

59. MacIntyre, *After Virtue*, 173.

60. Andrew A. Bonar, *Diary and Life*, ed. Marjory Bonar (London: Banner of Truth Trust, 1960), 9–10.

61. Ibid., 370.

62. Stoeffler, *Rise of Pietism*, 162–169.

63. For examples of accusations of Labadism among the Dutch Reformed in North America see James Tanis, *Dutch Calvinistic Pietism in the Middle Colonies: A Study in the Life and Theology of Theodorus Jacobus Frelinghuysen* (The Hague: Martinus Nijhoff, 1967), 143–145, 151, 159; and William O. Van Eyck, *Landmarks of the Reformed Fathers, or What Dr. Van Raalte's People Believed* (Grand Rapids, Mich.: Reformed Press, 1922), 189, 196.

64. Stoeffler calls her "that highly gifted and controversial lady" on page 142 of his *Rise of Pietism*; see also pp. 168–169.

65. "Anabaptism" has also been used, on occasion, as a term of criticizing fellow Calvinists; see, for example, the incident cited by James D. Bratt in *Dutch Calvinism in Modern America: A History of a Conservative Subculture* (Grand Rapids, Mich.: Eerdmans, 1984), 97, 108, 113.

66. See Hauerwas, *Peaceable*, xx; and McClendon, *Ethics*, 1:27–35.

67. Meilaender, *Theory of Virtue*, 125.

68. For an extensive discussion of the issues see John Howard Yoder, "Reformed Versus Anabaptist Social Strategies: An Inadequate Typology," *TSF Bulletin* 8, no. 5 (May-June 1985): 2–7; and my "Aban-

doning the Typology: A Reformed Assist," *TSF Bulletin* 8, no. 5 (May-June 1985): 7–10.

69. Willem Balke sees Calvin as acknowledging the legitimacy of the basic impulse of the Anabaptists: "It is not always clear whether Calvin was attacking Anabaptist perfectionism or Libertine perfectionism. For the most part, Calvin used a more moderate tone when he opposed Anabaptist concepts. In principle he was somewhat in agreement with them, but according to Calvin, they carried their inclinations much too far, and this led to great confusion." Willem Balke, *Calvin and the Anabaptist Radicals*, trans. William Heynen (Grand Rapids, Mich.: Eerdmans, 1981), 251.

70. For an elaboration of this point see Balke, *Calvin*, 265–267.

71. Holifield, *Gentlemen Theologians*, 142.

72. William K. Frankena, "Concluding More or Less Philosophical Postscript," in *Perspectives on Morality: Essays by William K. Frankena*, ed. Kenneth Goodpaster (Notre Dame, Ind.: University of Notre Dame Press, 1976), 209.

73. Frankena, *Ethics*, 112.

74. William K. Frankena, "On Saying the Ethical Thing," in *Perspectives*, ed. Goodpaster, 123.

8. THE TRIUNE COMMANDER

1. One of the best treatments of the ways in which various christological themes interact with ethical programs is James M. Gustafson, *Christ and the Moral Life* (New York: Harper & Row, 1968).

2. See G. K. Chesterton, *St. Francis of Assisi* (Garden City, N.Y.: Doubleday & Co., 1924; Image Books, 1957), especially chapter 8, "The Mirror of Christ."

3. An obvious case in point is Yoder's *The Politics of Jesus*; see also Alan Kreider, *Journey Towards Holiness: A Way of Living for God's Nation*, with a Foreword by Howard A. Snyder (Scottdale, Pa.: Herald Press, 1987).

4. For a sampling of popular treatments in this regard see D. W. Faunce, *The Christian in the World* (Boston: Roberts Brothers, 1875); G. Campbell Morgan, *Discipleship* (Westwood, N.J.: Fleming H. Revell, 1961); W. E. Sangster, *The Secret of the Radiant Life* (Nashville: Abingdon Press, 1957); and Charles M. Sheldon, *In His Steps: What Would Jesus Do?* (New York: Permabooks, 1949).

5. Marjorie Reeves gives a good account of Joachim's trinitarian

scheme in her *Joachim of Fiore and the Prophetic Future* (London: SPCK, 1976), 1–28.

6. See Max L. Stackhouse, *Ethics and the Urban Ethos: An Essay in Social Theory and Theological Reconstruction* (Boston: Beacon Press, 1972), chapter 6.

7. See Lyle E. Schaller, *Looking in the Mirror: Self-Appraisal in the Local Church* (Nashville: Abingdon Press, 1984), 73–88.

8. H. Richard Niebuhr, "The Doctrine of the Trinity and the Unity of the Church," *Theology Today* 3 (October 1946): 371–384.

9. Ibid., 373, 381.

10. Ibid., 374–376.

11. Ibid., 376–377.

12. Ibid., 383–384.

13. See Edgar Sheffield Brightman, *A Philosophy of Religion*, Prentice-Hall Philosophy Series (New York: Prentice-Hall, 1940).

14. Kuyper, *Lectures*, 71–72.

15. John Bolt, *Christian and Reformed Today* (Jordan Station, Ontario: Paideia Press, 1984), 143.

16. Ibid., 135–147.

17. Kuyper, *Lectures*, 72.

18. John Howard Yoder develops this narrative-framework in *The Priestly Kingdom: Social Ethics as Gospel* (Notre Dame, Ind.: University of Notre Dame Press, 1984); see also his *The Christian Witness to the State*, Institute of Mennonite Studies Series, no. 3 (Newton, Kans.: Faith and Life Press, 1964), especially chapters 7 and 8.

19. Herman Bavinck, "Wat Zou Jezus Doen?" *De Bazuin*, 48 (1900), no. 8, trans. and quoted in Bolt, *Christian and Reformed*, 142.

20. Kenneth Hamilton, "Liberation Theology: An Overview," in *Evangelicals and Liberation*, ed. Carl E. Armerding, Studies in the World Church and Missions (Phillipsburg, N.J.: Presbyterian and Reformed Publishing Co., 1977), 6.

21. Allan Boesak, in *Black and Reformed: Apartheid, Liberation, and the Calvinist Tradition*, ed. Leonard Sweetman (Maryknoll, N.Y.: Orbis Books, 1984), is very clear about the call to respect the ordering purposes of the Creator in dealing with the structures of political life; see especially chapters 3 and 10.

22. Walter Rauschenbusch, *A Theology for the Social Gospel* (Nashville: Abingdon Press, 1945), 174–175.

23. See Janet Forsythe Fishburn, *The Fatherhood of God and the Victorian Family: The Social Gospel in America* (Philadelphia: Fortress Press, 1981), especially pp. 120–127.

24. See Naomi R. Goldenberg, *Changing of the Gods: Feminism and the End of Traditional Religions* (Boston: Beacon Press, 1979).

25. Rosemary Radford Ruether, *New Woman, New Earth: Sexist Ideologies and Human Liberation* (New York: Seabury Press, 1975), 66.

26. Sallie McFague, *Metaphorical Theology: Models of God in Religious Language* (Philadelphia: Fortress Press, 1982), 155–156.

27. Ibid., 166.

28. Nancy Van Wyk Phillips, "Imaging God as Mother," *Reformed Review* 40 (Autumn 1986): 50.

29. Jane Dempsy Douglass, *Women, Freedom, and Calvin*, The 1983 Annie Kinkead Warfield Lectures (Philadelphia: Westminster Press, 1985), 7, 88–107.

30. Ibid., 121.

31. For a discussion of this theme in Reformed anthropology, see G. C. Berkouwer, *Man: The Image of God*, trans. Dirk W. Jellema, Studies in Dogmatics (Grand Rapids, Mich.: Eerdmans, 1962), 70–71. An impressive exegetical case is made for the image-as-dominion view by D. J. A. Clines in his 1967 Tyndale Old Testament Lecture, "The Image of God in Man," *Tyndale Bulletin* 19 (1968):53–103.

32. Kuyper, *Lectures*, 80.

33. Ibid., 27.

34. Mary Stewart Van Leeuwen, "Sex Education at the Christian College," *The Reformed Journal* 37, no. 9 (September 1987): 20, citing Gilbert G. Bilezikian, *Beyond Sex Roles: A Guide for the Study of Female Roles in the Bible* (Grand Rapids, Mich.: Baker Book House, 1985), 55, 229.

35. Van Leeuwen, "Sex Education," 20–21.

36. Ibid., 22.

37. James Tanis, "Reformed Pietism in Colonial America," in *Continental Pietism and Early American Christianity*, ed. F. Ernest Stoeffler (Grand Rapids, Mich.: Eerdmans, 1976), 57–59; see also his *Dutch Calvinistic Pietism*.

38. Tanis, "Reformed Pietism," 59.

39. *Sketch, and a Translation from the Dutch, of the Diary of Dinah van Bergh* (1869), 63; quoted in Tanis, "Reformed Pietism," 59.

40. Leon O. Hynson, *To Reform the Nation: Theological Foundations of Wesley's Ethics*, with a Foreword by Albert C. Outler (Grand Rapids, Mich.: Zondervan, Francis Asbury Press, 1984), 123.

41. See, for example, *Pneuma: The Journal of the Society for Pentecostal Studies*, vol. 9, no. 2 (Fall 1987). See also Cardinal Leon Joseph Suenens and Dom Helder Camara, *Charismatic Renewal and Social Ac-*

tion: A Dialogue (Ann Arbor, Mich.: Servant Books, 1979); and Sheila MacManus Fahey, *Charismatic Social Action: Reflection/Resource Manual* (New York: Paulist Press, 1977).

42. Charles H. Barfoot and Gerald T. Sheppard, "Prophetic Vs. Priestly Religion: The Changing Role of Women Clergy in Classical Pentecostal Churches," *Review of Religious Research* 22, no. 1 (September 1980): 2–17.

43. See Geerhardus Vos, "The Eschatological Aspect of the Pauline Conception of the Spirit," in *Biblical and Theological Studies*, by the members of the Faculty of Princeton Theological Seminary (New York: Charles Scribner's Sons, 1912), 209–259. See also Hendrikus Berkhof, *The Doctrine of the Holy Spirit*, The Annie Kinkead Warfield Lectures, 1963–1964 (Richmond, Va.: John Knox Press, 1964); and H. Berkhof, *Christian Faith: An Introduction to the Study of the Faith*, trans. Sierd Woudstra (Grand Rapids, Mich.: Eerdmans, 1979), especially chapter 36.

44. Abraham Kuyper, *The Work of the Holy Spirit*, trans. Henri de Vries, with an Introduction by Benjamin B. Warfield (New York: Funk and Wagnalls, 1900), 22.

45. Hamilton, "Liberation Theology," 6–7.

46. John Howard Yoder, "Exodus and Exile: The Two Faces of Liberation," *Cross Currents* 23 (Fall 1973): 297–309.

47. Bolt, *Christian and Reformed*, 80.

48. Lewis B. Smedes, *Choices: Making Right Decisions in a Complex World* (San Francisco: Harper & Row, 1986), 97.

49. Ibid.

50. For an illuminating treatment of this topic, see A. van den Beld, "Romans 7:14–25 and the Problem of *Akrasia*," *Religious Studies* 21:495–515.

51. Meilaender, *Theory and Practice*, 5.

52. Henri J. M. Nouwen, *The Genesee Dairy: Report from a Trappist Monastery* (Garden City, N.Y.: Doubleday & Co., Image Books, 1981), 74–75.

9. DIVINE AUTHORITY AND THE QUEST FOR SOLIDARITY

1. Mill, *Utilitarianism*, 11–13.

2. Ibid., 13

3. W. D. Ross, *The Right and the Good* (Oxford: Clarendon Press, 1930), 40–41.

4. Brian Medlin, "Ultimate Principles and Ethical Egoism," in

Problems of Moral Philosophy: An Introduction to Ethics, ed. Paul W. Taylor, 2d ed. (Encino, Calif.: Dickenson Publishing Co., 1972), 121.

5. R. M. Hare, *Freedom and Reason* (New York: Oxford University Press, 1963; Galaxy Books, 1965), 220–221.

6. Frankena, *Ethics*, 110–113.

7. Bertrand Russell, "My Mental Development," in *The Philosophy of Bertrand Russell*, ed. Paul Arthur Schilpp (The Library of Living Philosophers, 1944; repr., New York: Harper & Row, Harper Torchbooks, 1963), 1:5.

8. Friedrich Nietzsche, *The Will to Power*, trans. Walter Kaufmann and R. J. Hollingdale, ed. Walter Kaufmann (London: Weidenfeld and Nicolson, 1967), 509.

9. Ibid., 515.

10. Tillich, *Systematic Theology*, 1:3–7, 67–73.

11. Ibid., 1:72.

12. See, for example, Bruce C. Birch and Larry L. Rasmussen, *Bible and Ethics in the Christian Life* (Minneapolis, Minn.: Augsburg Publishing House, 1976); James M. Gustafson, *The Church as Moral Decision-Maker* (Philadelphia: Pilgrim Press, 1970); Stanley Hauerwas, *A Community of Character: Toward a Constructive Christian Social Ethic* (Notre Dame, Ind.: University of Notre Dame Press, 1981); Thomas W. Ogletree, *The Use of the Bible in Christian Ethics* (Philadelphia: Fortress Press, 1983); and Allen Verhey, *The Great Reversal: Ethics and the New Testament* (Grand Rapids, Mich.: Eerdmans, 1984).

13. Karl Barth, *Church Dogmatics*, vol. 3, bk. 1, *The Doctrine of Creation*, ed. G. W. Bromiley and T. F. Torrance, trans. J. W. Edwards, O. Bussey, and Harold Knight (Edinburgh: T & T Clark, 1958), 192.

14. Roch A. Kereszty, *God-Seekers for a New Age: From Crisis Theology to "Christian Atheism,"* Themes for Today (Dayton, Ohio: Pflaum Press, 1970), 135–136.

15. Jean Jacques Rousseau, *The Social Contract*, trans. and with an Introduction by Willmore Kendall (Chicago: Henry Regnery Co., 1954), 41.

INDEX